Making Dinosaurs Dance

AMERICAN ALLIANCE OF MUSEUMS

The American Alliance of Museums has been bringing museums together since 1906, helping to develop standards and best practices, gathering and sharing knowledge, and providing advocacy on issues of concern to the entire museum community. Representing more than 35,000 individual museum professionals and volunteers, institutions, and corporate partners serving the museum field, the Alliance stands for the broad scope of the museum community.

The American Alliance of Museums' mission is to champion museums and nurture excellence in partnership with its members and allies.

Books published by AAM further the Alliance's mission to make standards and best practices for the broad museum community widely available.

Making Dinosaurs Dance

A Toolkit for Digital Design in Museums

Barry Joseph

ROWMAN & LITTLEFIELD
Lanham • Boulder • New York • London

Published by Rowman & Littlefield
An imprint of The Rowman & Littlefield Publishing Group, Inc.
4501 Forbes Boulevard, Suite 200, Lanham, Maryland 20706
www.rowman.com

86-90 Paul Street, London EC2A 4NE

Cover image credits:
Artifacts from visitor observations within the Hall of Human Origins. Courtesy of the author

DNA investigation storyboard. Courtesy of the author

Example of data analysis from public pilots. Courtesy of the author

Mapping out the entire game. Courtesy of the author

Museum staff playtesting Playing With Dinos. Courtesy of the author

Teens in *Minecraft*. Courtesy of the author

The production workflow. Courtesy of the American Museum of Natural History

The AR video shoot. Courtesy of the American Museum of Natural History

Holding the AR card target to the camera (left). Feeding the augmented buffalo (right). Courtesy of the author

The Virtual Reality Lounge at Mead Festival in the Hall of Northwest Coast Indians. Courtesy of the author

AR bat you can hold in your hand. Courtesy of the author

British Library Cataloguing in Publication Information Available

Library of Congress Cataloging-in-Publication Data Available

ISBN 978-1-5381-5973-6 (cloth)
ISBN 978-1-5381-5974-3 (paper)
ISBN 978-1-5381-5975-0 (electronic)

♾™ The paper used in this publication meets the minimum requirements of American National Standard for Information Sciences—Permanence of Paper for Printed Library Materials, ANSI/NISO Z39.48-1992.

Dedication

One cloudy Brooklyn day, my wife and I told my son, Akiva, we were going to spend the day at the American Museum of Natural History. This was years before I could even imagine I might work for that venerable institution.

Akiva, at around a year and a half, took up a chant that continued all the way from home through the subway ride into Manhattan. It sounded something like "Moosha Moosha Mooshme. Moosha Moosha Mooshme," a child's cry of anticipation. When we exited the subway, however, and went straight to lunch in the cafeteria, his face fell. Akiva became nearly inconsolable, convinced (we surmised) that we had not actually gone to the museum. The chanting continued, now forlorn, "Moosha Moosha Mooshme," as if he were searching for a lost friend.

After lunch, as we entered the planetarium, the light returned to his eyes. The excitement returned to his chant, as he realized we had finally arrived at the place he had been attempting to summon all day (and as we finally put two and two together): The Moosha Moosha Mooshme, or, as adults like to call it, The Museum of Natural History. This book is dedicated to Akiva, for creating a mantra that expresses the intense passion a museum can generate among its visitors, and for all those who want a reminder to never lose focus on that core relationship between a museum and its patrons.

Years later, on a family vacation, my daughter and I perused books in the store of the Shelburne Museum in Vermont. Miri was five years old and by then I worked full time at the American Museum of Natural History. A picture book caught our attention that detailed all the staff required to bring a dinosaur bone from a dig site in Montana into an exhibit at the Smithsonian. At the end of the book my daughter looked stricken. She had just connected the dots, realizing that if we were on vacation my work must be on hold. "Daddy, if you are here," she asked me, in all sincerity, "who is cleaning the dinosaurs?" I gently took her face in my hands and inquired, with bemused interest, "Sweetheart, what is it you think I do for a living?" She could not say. And so this book is dedicated as well to Miri, in response, and to all those equally in the dark about what it means to design museum-based digital engagement.

"Change is the process by which the future invades our lives."

– Alvin Toffler, Writer and Futurist

Contents

Acknowledgments

As with digital engagement, it takes a team to pull off a book.

First, I want to thank all without whom the projects within this book could not have been achieved.

Starting with the Education Department: Ruth Cohen (for having the vision and fighting the good fight), Preeti Gupta, Brian Levine, Danny Zeiger, Hannah Jaris (special shout out!), Julia Zichello, Leah Golubchick, Mark Weckel, Nathan Bellomy, Nick Martinez, Ravi Rampatsingh, Joshua Sosa, Ro Kinzler, Karen Taber, Eric Hamilton, Mikael Colboc, and course instructors Christina Chavez, Abbey Novia, Brittany Klimowicz, Christina Newkirk, Christine Marsh, Fariha Wasti, Marissa Gamliel, Rebecca Saunders, Alejandro Laserna, and many unnamed teacher assistants and colleagues within the department.

Next, the SciViz Team: Vivian Trakinski, Laura Moustakerski, Natalia Rodriguez Nunez, Eozin Che, Lauren Kushner, Jason Morfoot, Shay Krasinski, Brian Foo, and Nick Bartzokas.

Next, the scientists, the staff within their departments, and postdocs: Abbie Curtis, Alex de Voogt, Ana Ragni, Bushra Hussaini, Daniel Barta, Felicity Arango, John Denton, John Maisey, Mark Norell, Mary Blair, Morgan Hill, Susan Perkins, Nancy Simmons, Nathan Leigh, Ruth O'Leary, and William Harcourt-Smith.

Elsewhere in the Museum, my deep appreciation to Martin Schwabacher, Tom Baione, Andrew Epstein, Sacheen Sawney, Pierce Lydon, and other colleagues around the Museum within Exhibitions, Communications, other Education divisions, and more. You know who you are (and I hope you liked your postcard).

From outside the Museum, I need to start with all of the graduate students from Columbia University's Instructional Technology and Media program, and from New York University's Digital Media Design For Learning, Games For Learning, and Educational Communication and Technology programs. Specifically, I want to thank Andreina Yulis, Carl Farra, Chris Wallace, Cooper Wright, Elliot Hu-Au, Eric Teo, Erin Okabe-Jawdat, Hani Zandi, J. Shepard Ramsay, Jullie Harten, Keren Perry-Shamir, Matthew Sinclair McGowan, Nicky Chase, Noca Wu, Pimnipa Kangsanan, Ruth Sherman, Sang Nong, Tianjiao Zhang, Todd Taylor, Tom Sarachan, Wang Xi, Yael Ezer, and all others who worked with me on related projects.

In addition, these projects were only possible through the deep involvement of outside experts: Chris Vicari, Nick Fortugno, Jeremy Kenisky, David Ng, Joel Levin, Shane Asselstine, and Marisa Jahn.

Finally, it was an honor to get to share here the words of all who let me interview them about their work within other museums.

Phew! Now to thank all those without whom this book would not exist: Alice Walker (who helped me view my work in a new way), Madlyn Larson (who suggested I write this book), Elizabeth Merritt (who suggested I reach out to the American Alliance of Museums), Dean Phelus (who accepted the proposal for this book), and Charles Harmon (who patiently worked with me and oversaw the editing of the book from proposal to production).

I want to thank all of the readers who took the time to read some or all of the text, first many of those named previously but especially those who arrived fresh to the material: Neal Stimler, France Therrien, Madlyn Larson, and Stephanie Mehta.

Finally, to my peer mentor group, Rik and Eve, who were here for it all—work, book, and everything in-between—and whom I could never thank enough.

Introduction

DESIGNING A BOOK

I was so proud to work at the Girl Scouts of the United States of America, the national headquarters of the century-old movement. As the Vice President of Digital Experience, we used the tools of user-centric design to innovate new mobile platforms to directly support the growth and dreams of 1.4 million girls and the eight hundred thousand volunteer leaders in Troops around the country. And yes, there was a jar at the reception desk, refilled each day with a box of Girl School Cookies.

When the pandemic hit, and Troops canceled all in-person meetings, right in the middle of cookie-selling season, everyone knew their job was at risk. Six months later, when the organization rolled out its COVID-related workforce reduction, I learned I was right to be concerned. It turned out even someone with twenty-five years of experience leading digital design could be let go at a time requiring an all-hands-on-deck pivot from in-person to digital engagement.

As they often say, when one door closes another opens. In my case, one open door led back to my past. Before the Girl Scouts I had worked as the Associate Director of Digital Learning at the American Museum of Natural History. My six years there were part of a fifteen-year run collaborating with a wide range of museums to bring digital engagement into their programming. My time at Girl Scouts had prevented me from continuing my involvement with museums. But now that I was launching my own digital engagement consultancy, I was free to reconnect with any industry I chose.

When I reconnected with the museum sector, I was heartbroken by the devastation I was seeing. One-third of museums were still closed due to pandemic-related shutdowns. Experienced professionals with years of service had been let go. Those who remained who were not furloughed were working reduced hours, with reduced pay, often forced to take accrued vacation days. Former colleagues I spoke with were demoralized. What could I possibly contribute to help the sector both in its recovery and in the years to come?

While I built my consultancy, I often heard from people familiar with my projects, whether from my blog, social media feed, or conference presentations. They shared how digital projects at the American Museum of Natural History still inspired them in their own work. They encouraged me to write a book to share best practices. How did we manage to bring so much innovation in digital design into the Museum? How did we create the space to allow us to iterate in such a public way? How did we meaningfully include youth as co-designers?

Luckily, our work was well-documented. Even though some projects featured in this book are case studies begun nearly a decade ago, I still have records detailing what happened at every step. I wrote a blog with over 350 posts when I was at the Museum, sharing our efforts in great detail. Private Google Docs hold all of the meeting notes, design documents, curricular plans, and more. Presentations in Keynotes, video documentation, and data from evaluations and research fill in the gaps. Taken together, I felt like I had all the research needed to spin the tales that needed to be told.

As I reconnected with long-lost colleagues, I mentioned the book to one of my favorites, Elizabeth Merritt, the Founding Director of the Center for the Future of Museums. The Center is within the American Alliance of Museums which, she informed me, had just put out its own call for book proposals, published through Rowman & Littlefield.

"How many times in your professional conversations have you joked, 'I'll save that for when I write my book?'" the American Alliance of Museums website asked. "Well, maybe that day has finally come!" This might come as no surprise, but I applied. All that was needed was a short description. If their editorial team felt it had promise, I would be invited to submit a full proposal. Before long I heard back and was invited to make a submission, which I did.

I waited anxiously for their response. Each day I watched my inbox until, a few weeks later, the email arrived. To my great disappointment, I learned all the ways the proposal failed to meet their needs. "It read more like a collection of blog posts," they said, and "could have benefited from greater analysis." I was disappointed because I knew they were right.

After re-reading the email, however, I found a glimmer of hope. While they never said they had accepted the proposal, they had also never said it was rejected. At that point, I had to make a decision. I could thank them, hang my head low, and move on. Or . . . I could boldly act as if the email had included what I wished it might say. I replied with the following: "So would the review committee like me to revise my proposal? Their concerns are fair, and I think given the opportunity my book would sufficiently address them."

They replied right away that, yes, they would be open to a revised proposal. Hurrah! I immediately took their critiques to heart. I revisited my dozens of projects at the American Museum of Natural History, as well as my interviews with remarkable colleagues around the world, to identify key themes and best practices. It was not until then that the idea of the Toolkit began to emerge, a set of five practices we consistently sought to apply regardless of the project (after workshopping the book at the Muse-Web conference in 2021, I added a sixth). The book began to come into focus—it would be a resource to help digital designers, specifically those in museums but of use within a wide range of settings.

I submitted the revised proposal. A few weeks later I received an email similar to the first. It thanked me for my submission, but said neither that it was accepted nor rejected. However, what it did say was that my contract was in the mail! We were off and running. Two years later, readers like you could hold their own copy.

I share this behind-the-scenes tale to make it the first example of what this book is all about. This book did not magically come together in a flash of insight because I had a great idea and then everything fell into place. I developed the book in part by workshopping it at museum conferences (user research, public piloting), writing a sample chapter for the proposal to validate if the idea had any merit (rapid prototyping), and eventually rewrote that chapter and the entire proposal (iterative design). Writing this book required me to believe in the value of my ideas and my ability to express them, act boldly, respond to setbacks, and be open to receiving critical feedback throughout.

This way of approaching a project is exactly what this book is all about.

BOOK ORGANIZATION

Looking back, I like to think that my work has been a robust exploration of how design practices, youth development, and digital pedagogy can advance a museum's capacity to engage learners—in the Halls, in classrooms, and online—in exciting and innovative ways. Nothing motivates me more than being told something can't be done. Not everyone, however, responds the same. People often resist trying something new when discouraged by others or if trapped in a system that fails to reward risk. I treasure those times at work when I can be a source of hope for people in those situations, to help them respond to such nay-sayers and pave a path forward. My intention is for this book to serve a similar purpose for you, to be a tool of resistance against the negativity and doubters, to open up possibilities for your design practices.

While this book is a guide for professional designers, it is also the behind-the-scenes book I always wished I had. Books about the American Museum of Natural History tend to run in two streams: children's books full of awe and wonder and adult-oriented non-fiction full of dry facts and figures. Why can't books for adults also generate awe and wonder? Why can't they be infused by the electric passion so many hold for the Museum and its collections? I hope this book can convey some of the excitement and humility that came from walking daily through its esteemed Halls.

A few words of warning about what this book is not, just to set the right expectations. It is not a history of the Museum; it has a more narrow focus on just my half dozen years working on staff.

This book is not a tell-all to air grievances; I strive to treat all with respect and always presume best intentions.

This book is not a comprehensive overview of all digital design at the Museum nor of my own work; rather, I carefully selected projects as case studies with which I was intimately involved and which highlight the Toolkit. The case studies are a tiny shard of digital design that happened within the Museum, alongside the work performed by talented staff in Exhibitions, Communications, Education, and more.

Finally, this book is not *just* about the American Museum of Natural History. Each chapter tackles one topic through one or more case studies. The case studies are followed by an interview addressing similar themes at another museum somewhere else in the world, to compare and contrast, then Tips and Strategies Exercises, for use in a classroom, a book club, a work discussion, or for your own personal reflection.

The book can be read in any order. Treat it like a refreshing river you can dip into when seeking inspiration or the mood strikes. If, however, you read from front to back, you will encounter the following structure.

The first chapter of the book provides background on the professional journey that led me to the Museum, in part to provide context for the case studies that follow, addressing questions like: How does someone like me (with no prior history studying about nor working at museums) end up working at a place like the American Museum of Natural History? Why was a new position created for me to fill, and how did that pave the way for a half dozen years of innovations in digital design?

This chapter then introduces and describes the Six Tools for Digital Design:

- User research
- Rapid prototyping
- Public piloting
- Iterative design
- Youth collaboration
- Teaming up

The main body of the book then explores five areas with rich potential for digital experience design in museums:

- The second chapter focuses on combining digital experience design with **physical museum assets in a guided format**. The case study looks at *Crime Scene Neanderthal*, in which student interns invited family visitors to become Neanderthal Detectives and, armed with a paper guide and a mobile app, explored both virtual and cast Neanderthal fossils to solve a science-based mystery in the Hall of Human Origins. It includes an interview on designing persona-based storytelling in Greece and France.
- The third chapter focuses on **game-based learning**, looking specifically at *Pterosaurs: The Card Game* (a youth co-developed, exhibit-inspired product with an augmented reality component), *Playing with Dinos* (a mobile app that delivered quick social games in the dinosaur halls), and how

a youth program created an exhibit-related set of *Minecraft* assets for the Museum's website. It includes an interview on designing for narrative and movement in Washington, DC.

- The fourth chapter focuses on developing **mobile augmented reality games**, digging deep into *MicroRangers*, a multiyear, quarter-million-dollar project that invited visitors to enter Museum exhibits through an augmented reality mobile app and tackle science-based problems in collaboration with both scientists and microscopic organisms. It includes an interview on designing for locations in Minnesota.

- The fifth chapter focuses on developing **extended reality** experiences, specifically how we leveraged existing 360 videos at the Margaret Mead Film Festival, rapid prototyped our own paleontology behind-the-scenes 360 videos, then A:B tested marine virtual reality experiences in the Hall of Ocean Life. It includes an interview on designing for offsite experiences in Chicago.

- The sixth chapter focuses on developing **science visualizations** through three projects: an astro-visualization that addressed the topics of mass and gravity through a round of mixed reality Martian golf, interactive science visualizations leveraging computed tomography scans of bat skulls that visitors could hold in their hands, and the multitouch table in Finding Flamingos, a youth program focused on how Conservation Biologists protect endangered flamingos through geographic information system mapping and predictions software. It includes an interview on designing spaces for learning in Washington, DC.

A set of tools requires the right frame of mind if they are to be put to good use. So, before we jump in, I leave you with two inspiring quotes for approaching the future.

The first comes from Sebastian Chan. Seb is the Director and CEO of the Australian Centre for the Moving Image, spreading human-centered design across the museum. At the end of 2020, he reflected on his blog that

> reading . . . oral histories [of old video game designers] reminded me of how little the museum sector tells, or records, its own stories. And how, with the pandemic, this has heightened the stakes. Museum technology used to be optional. For a medium- or large-sized museum it no longer is. It is as essential as plumbing.[1]

Seb is reminding us that we need to tell our stories about digital design in museums—both the highs and lows—so we can learn from the past as we design the future. As you engage in your own work, I hope you will draw from these stories as you learn to tell your own.

Finally, Mo Willems, the children's book author, was interviewed about his creative processes in the *New York Times*.[2] He said that so much is prescribed these days, with people saying things like "Creativity opens you up to brand-new worlds." He thinks this is ridiculous. "It doesn't open anything up to brand-new worlds," he complained. "You don't *know* what it opens you up to." Creativity is not a process for following a pre-set line from A to B. Instead, Willems said, creativity is "a line from A to strawberry pizza."

Now, maybe you won't be happy with strawberry pizza, but that doesn't mean your creativity tool is broken. To Willems, creativity is a process for discovering the unknown, for being open to wherever it leads. If you get strawberry pizza and still don't like it, that's fine. Take from it what you can, then try again, holding an inviting attitude toward whatever comes next.

I hope with this book in hand you can grow whatever might become your own version of a strawberry pizza, paving a digital path to a future that increases for all meaningful engagement with our civic and cultural treasures.

NOTES

1. Seb Chan, "Looking Backwards to Go Forward—Words from Talks in Late 2020," *Medium*, December 16, 2020, https://sebchan.medium.com/looking-backwards-to-go-forward-words-from-talks-in-late-2020-b20f90ce6375.
2. "Mo Willems Has a Message for Parents: He's Not on Your Side," *New York Times*, November 13, 2020, Magazine Section.

1

Six Tools for Digital Design

ENTER THE MUSEUM

As young children growing up in the suburbs of New York City, my sister and I loved nothing more than to roll around the floors of the mysterious, cave-like Hall of Gems and Minerals at the American Museum of Natural History.

Later, as teenagers, my friends and I would arrive after dark at the Museum on a Saturday night to catch Laser Floyd or Laser Zeppelin in the planetarium.

In my twenties, I would gather friends within the Museum's cafeteria to organize massive, user-generated, site-wide scavenger hunts, then spend hours dashing through the Halls in our epic quest.

In my thirties, I would bring my children to the Museum to search for dinosaurs in the Discovery Room or explore the hands-on interactives in the latest special exhibit.

Never once, in all of those years, did I ever remotely consider that I could say, in my forties, I would start working full time in the Education Department of the American Museum of Natural History.

My professional life began two decades earlier, during the heady new media explosion of the mid-1990s. After hopping from one web start-up to another, I landed at RadicalMedia, an advertising agency looking to spin up a new media division. I learned many valuable things from my years there as part of their inaugural class of "web producers," not the least of which was that for-profit work was not in my DNA.

My pivot to non-profit began at Web Lab, founded by Marc Weiss. When I read an article about his new efforts to fund independent voices on the web, I immediately recognized their team lacked anyone with any significant online expertise. I wrote Marc a letter informing him of this discrepancy and suggested that, to correct it, he hire me right away. To his great credit, and my endless appreciation, he did.

During this period, as I began to teach on the side, I realized I was ready for a deeper dive into the world of informal learning. I was no longer comfortable with the securities of working with primarily all white, middle-class men like myself. I wanted to collaborate with people from a wider range of backgrounds, in a setting that didn't necessarily view being white or male or middle class as normative.

I soon found my home for the next dozen years at Global Kids, a New York City–based afterschool organization that supports youth in underserved communities to take action on critical issues facing our world. I built up a program developing digital literacy among youth around New York City. I was excited that my work was supporting underserved youth of color to have access to some of the same skills and resources I found so valuable when I was their age (and around which I was now building my career). Over time, Global Kids taught me what it meant to be a youth development specialist, applying a hands-on, strengths-based model to informal learning spaces, while supporting me to develop digital youth media programming in which youth developed digital leadership skills by designing media that put their voice out into the world.

We worked with many partners—the Newshour on PBS, Microsoft, the New York Public Library—and soon expanded to museums as well—the Field Museum in Chicago, the US Holocaust Memorial Museum in Washington, DC, and, yes, the American Museum of Natural History in good old New York City.

Through these projects I learned two things. First, museums lagged far behind other learning institutions when it came to digital innovations in their learning programs. One could always point to exceptions, but they were still exceptions.

Second, there was tremendous interest at many museums to turn these exceptions into the rule, to build a stronger digital learning footprint. Impressed as I was by the recent work with the American Museum of Natural History, when I saw they were looking for a new Director of Youth Learning, even though I had no formal training in museums and even less experience with science learning, I threw my hat into the ring.

When I applied for the position, I noticed something about my work history—every position I ever had was either created for me or even with me. When I joined RadicalMedia the position of Web Producer was new, and I worked with both Web Lab and Global Kids to design those new positions. Now, after nearly twenty years, I was applying for the first time to a position previously held by another. What this meant I could not say, but I figured it must have meant something about my professional identity and roles someone like me might play within organizations.

I was invited in for an interview but, in the end, was not offered the position. Instead, I got something better. During my interview, Ruth Cohen (Senior Director, Center for Lifelong Learning) asked me if I would be open to considering a different position, something new, something that would be created with my skills in mind, to lead the development of a new digital learning strategy within the Education Department.

I was floored, then I laughed to myself, in disbelief. There I was, again, being asked to design a new position. And, of all places, at the American Museum of Natural History! I could hardly believe my luck. In that moment, all of my years leading digital production and digital innovation, developing youth curriculum and youth digital media production, and advancing digital programming within the museum sector were coming together like the voices in a choir singing, in harmony, the same phrase: "Say yes!"

A year later I began working as the Museum's first Associate Director of Digital Learning. I reported to the indomitable Preeti Gupta (their new Director of Youth Learning, and much more suited to the position than myself), who oversaw the afterschool programming for middle and high school students. That would become an excellent location from which I could work with both Preeti and Ruth to frame a strategy for building the internal capacity of the department to offer cutting-edge science learning designed for the digital age.

We developed two tracks of learning. One focused on providing youth access to the digital tools of science being deployed throughout the Museum's research efforts, like three-dimensional printers, online tools for collaborative research, and coding languages. The second focused on leveraging popular or cutting-edge digital media or technology for informal science learning, like *Minecraft*, telepresence robots, and augmented reality.

Now, in retrospect, I can see they were all developed through the application of key practices I am sharing through this frame of a toolkit, Six Tools for Digital Design: user research, rapid prototyping, public piloting, iterative design, youth collaboration, and teaming up.

Before digging into each tool, we need a shared point of reference, a context within which we can apply the tools. Throughout this book, we will be applying these tools to both case studies from the American Museum of Natural History and interviews for comparison with colleagues at institutions around the world.

Let us start then with our first interview, traveling to San Francisco to visit the California Academy of Sciences, after which we will use it to explore each of the six tools.

Designing Games for Exhibits at the California Academy of Sciences

In 2013, Rik Panganiban became the Senior Manager of Digital Learning at the California Academy of Sciences, the oldest scientific research institution of its kind in the western United States. He was responsible for leading the Academy's efforts to engage young people in authentic scientific inquiry and science storytelling using digital tools, from mobile games to three-dimensional printing to digital dome shows. Rik is also a great friend and old colleague of mine from Global Kids, so I was delighted when he agreed to let me chat with him about how he worked with Bay Area teens to create digital engagement for museum visitors.

"It's a super cool place to work," Rik told me, in part because the Academy is both very old and brand new. On the historical side, the Academy was founded in 1893. They had a beautiful six-story facility in downtown San Francisco that saw eighty thousand visitors a year. Everything changed in 1906 when the Great Quake destroyed most of San Francisco, including the museum and nearly all of its research collections. The museum was rebuilt in Golden Gate Park, including a world-class aquarium and planetarium. In 1989, a second quake caused structural damage to the facility, leading to an even bolder plan to re-vision everything they do. Completely rebuilt in 2008, their new headquarters combines a natural history museum, aquarium, planetarium, living rainforest, and scientific research institution all under one roof.

Rik's work combines three things he is passionate about: science exploration, digital media creation, and youth civic engagement. "Seriously, each of those things are amazing on their own," he told me, "but together they are ridiculously awesome!"

Rik's path from Global Kids to a museum was similar to mine. We both designed and led digital learning programs for underserved teens in New York City, focusing on youth leadership, civic engagement, and twenty-first-century citizenship. "During my time at Global Kids," Rik shared, "I was profoundly moved by the potential for digital media to open up young people to new ideas, new possibilities, and new visions of themselves and their place in the world."

When he joined the Academy, Rik hoped that he had found another place that was ready to walk what he termed "the risky path of digital learning." He asked himself: How would a venerable, 160-year-old institution deal with the sometimes messy, kludgey, and uncharted nature of digital learning?

It did not take long for him to find out.

On his first day on the job, he was tasked with working with a group of teens to create a digital game on earthquake preparedness to be included within an upcoming exhibit, *Earthquake: Life on A Dynamic Planet*. On one hand, it was hard. The teens struggled to use a just-out-of-beta software package to create the game. Rik was their "guide on the side" with very little science background and completely new to the Academy. Meanwhile, the exhibits team was scrambling to complete their work on the rest of the exhibit.

On the other hand, the young people were excited and committed to creating a science game for the public. They enjoyed making cardboard versions of their game while Rik provided access to an entire museum full of visitors who could play-test their prototypes. Playing with visitors, watching their reactions, and asking for their feedback all helped the youth feel confident they were on the right track and should keep going. Rik was aware the youth needed more than his support in order to pull this off. The lead exhibit project manager provided the teens detailed insight into what it took to create a professional museum exhibit, from conception to execution. Using Skype, an expert in Los Angeles on earthquake science and preparedness helped them understand how to survive a quake. Finally, to give them insight into the game development process, Rik brought in a game developer who helped them see the possibilities for what they might achieve, and the harsh realities of what was too ambitious to complete in time before the end of the program. The game developer then helped them finish the final 15 percent of the game code and design, acting as a consultant for them. "Giving our teenagers the opportunity to assign and vet the work of a professional game developer was definitely a big first for them."

This new digital game had many hurdles to overcome. Would the teens finish their game before the course concluded? If so, would their game pass muster with the academy's research, legal, marketing, and exhibit departments? If so, would the exhibits team be able to incorporate the game into the exhibit in time for its launch? If so, would the public be interested in playing a computer game created by a bunch of teenagers in an afterschool program?

"As it turned out," Rik shared with pride, "the answers to all of those questions was 'Yes!'" The whole initiative was a big test, for the teens, the Academy, and, of course, Rik himself. And they all passed. The game was approved and incorporated into the Academy's earthquake exhibit, with more than a million people visiting the exhibit and the game being played thousands of times.

After the successful launch of the game, Rik knew he was in the right place. "It was tremendously gratifying knowing that I was at an institution that was ready to take calculated risks in piloting untested digital learning programs with youth, and disseminating to the public the work created by those teens."

When I asked Rik what he learned from the process, he responded that "the youth media creation process is typically much, much faster than how a professional museum operates." He attributed to naivete his initial presumption that a month from game completion to exhibit opening would give the designers enough time to incorporate it. "But exhibits at the Academy are typically planned down to the tiniest detail months and months in advance," he soon learned, "so we probably caused our exhibit designers some unnecessary stress that could have been avoided with better planning and communication on our part."

Figure 1.1. Tech Teens look at *Earthquake Academy* game. *Rik Panganiban*

On the other hand, the process taught the Exhibits Department the value of working more nimbly in their design process, which they later applied through conceiving and launching their next exhibit in just a few months, rather than over several years. "So our youth are teaching us."

The experience also forced the Academy to explore where to find the balance between the needs for a high-quality user experience and the educational goals of a youth-led development process. As the game was in development, Rik held conversations with exhibits and marketing that focused on balancing Academy standards with authentic youth expression. "On the one hand, anything that reaches the public has to meet the Academy's standards for scientific accuracy and quality," Rik explained. "On the other hand, we don't want to hold our youth to a high standard they cannot hope to reach in the limited time they have in our programs, and with the limited experience that they have."

That taught Rik, as he moved on from the earthquake game to other youth-led digital design projects, to "incorporate more user research, prototyping, evaluation and iterating on their designs before the final project is due." He learned not to have the young people pin all their hopes and dreams on one massive keystone project. Instead, he told me, "I would like them to create smaller, lower-stakes products that they can see all the way through the design process, but that all build toward a larger uber-project."

This might be more time consuming, but it is all necessary in the end. "As a facilitator, I can get caught up in the impatience of my youth, instead of holding the line on the need to follow a more methodical, data-driven process," he shared. "It's something I'm still working on."

For Rik, youth programs like these help youth see themselves as science storytellers to the public, using the digital media and tools he and his colleagues exposed them to. "For some, science may be on their career path," he reflected. "For others, it's one interest among others. But we want all of our youth to get to do their own science explorations and investigations, connect with working scientists, create their own science stories, and use some form of digital media to tell that story to the public."

This kind of journey, Rik is well aware, does not always follow a straight line forward. "There will certainly be 'failures' and challenges along the way," he said, "which is all part of what makes this road such an interesting one to walk."

The Six Tools for Digital Design

Let us now revisit the Six Tools for Digital Design: user research, rapid prototyping, public piloting, iterative design, youth collaboration, and teaming up.

None of these tools are digitally native—all six can be used on non-digital projects using analog methods—but combined they are a powerful way to develop digital engagement. Ignoring them, meanwhile, increases the chance of failure.

In addition, if you would like to learn more about any of the six tools, turn to **Appendix: Design Reading List** at the end of this book to discover other amazing resources you can explore.

1. User Research

The Academy's earthquake game had four hurdles to overcome, the final being if the public would be interested in playing a computer game created by youth. What a risk to take without first knowing the answer to that question! The three earlier hurdles might be cleared with no problem—the youth could have successfully completed the game, the green light given by the required museum departments, and the exhibits team incorporated it into the exhibit—but none of that would matter if visitors did not want to interact with it or found it unengaging.

Could Rik have put something in place to increase the chance of achieving what, in the business world, is often termed a product/market fit? In other words, before he started development, what could he have done to make sure the market for the game is large enough to be worth the investment of resources and that the game is designed to meet the needs of that market?

Rik suggested an answer when he listed lessons learned to incorporate in the future: user research.

When a new project is being developed, creative energies might focus on the new shiny thing that has everyone excited. User research, however, can be a bit humbling. It challenges us with questions like, "I'm glad to see you so excited about your new thing and all, but what makes you so confident anyone else will feel the same?"

It might be a good idea to market test ideas for new exhibits or interactives with visitors. "From 1 to 5, how interested would you be in an exhibit on dogs, on artificial intelligence, on the future of cities?" However, that is not the place to start.

The place to start is to put those new ideas aside and learn first who your users are, what they need, and how they connect with you. It would be quite different instead to ask, "What would you like to learn more about, how do you like to learn, and when do you look to a museum to provide that experience?"

User research challenges our assumptions by looking at people's needs as well as their pain points. Pain points are those moments that create friction between what people want and what's required to get it. When you learn people's needs you can identify opportunities for designing products that meet them. When you learn their pain points, you can design solutions that "reduce friction" and smooth their path, creating opportunities for them to look to you to make things easier. By the time a product jumps past all of its hurdles, and finally arrives in the market, you have now increased the chance that users will experience what you made with delight, or relief, recognizing immediately how it brings value to their lives.

End users should experience on first encounter a sense that someone understands them, which is what at the end of the day user research is all about: building empathy.

To build empathy between a designer and an imagined user, there are many techniques one can use.

Focus groups: Identify the types of users you have in mind. A parent with young children, young professionals, people passionate about a particular topic, etc. Gather people together who fall into your category, around six to a dozen, then meet for thirty to fifty minutes. Prepare questions in advance, like "What's hard about being a parent today?" and "How did you first get interested in toxic snails?" Then just listen. Pay attention to where they express emotions, and note whether the emotions are positive or negative. Watch for their needs and those pain points. Capture anything specific—words, images, references—that are key to how they identify.

Interviews: Sometimes one-on-one interviews are best, whether in person, on a phone, or via a remote videoconference system. They can be formalized, with scheduled appointments, or you can walk up to someone alone at an exhibit or in the cafe and simply ask if you can take a few minutes of their time.

Surveys: While focus groups and interviews provide qualitative data, in-person and web-based surveys are an excellent way to gather quantitative data. Open-ended questions can be harder to process, but they will help you to avoid prescribing the answers you receive. Combining surveys with focus groups can be quite effective, using the surveys to identify interesting areas to explore, or for sharing survey results to engage potential users in interpreting the key lessons you might take away.

Observations: In my early days at the Museum, whenever I passed a visitor engrossed in their mobile phone, I would surreptitiously sneak a peek at their screen. I wanted not to presume that their screen time was disconnecting them from the museum experience. I also knew it was possible they were booking a dinner reservation for later in the week or reading a news headline. I also knew they might be editing a photo they just took before sharing it on social media, checking the time for the IMAX ticket they purchased, or coordinating with a family member in a different Hall. Observing without permission can be creepy, and even unethical, so it's good to ask when you can. Sometimes incentives can be involved, like helping visitors skip a long entry line into the museum or even providing free tickets. Having a clipboard can make one look official, setting others at ease, and is a perfect place to hold your observation form, remind you of the questions you are collecting data to answer, structure your notes, and keep you on track.

Heat maps: If you are interested in how bodies move through a particular space, heat mapping can be helpful. Get out a map of the space, then watch a few individuals or groups move through it. Draw their route as they navigate the space, adding additional information of interest (e.g., locations stopped, time spent, objects touched, overheard comments, etc.). In one project described later in this book, we found that most visitors in one Hall tended to walk toward the right. Multiple trips can be mapped into one visualization to depict the relationship between visitors and the space, highlighting both popular and overlooked locations.

Artifacts: Finally, you can learn a lot about someone based on the things they leave behind. Sometimes they are public, like postings on social media. Other times they can be upon request, like written responses to prompts left at an exhibit or in a comment book.

Activities like these can be used to produce different types of documentation and visualizations that highlight the key lessons to be applied. Two of the most common these days are personas and journey maps. There is no one way to do either of these, but there are lots of great examples out there to inspire and guide your efforts.

Personas: Personas are a way to visualize a data-based yet fictionalized character who represents your intended user. It is one thing to use a marketing tool like segmentation to say you are designing for twenty-five- to thirty-five-year-old moms with two children under the age of five. It is another to look at a single sheet that introduces me to Siobhan, a twenty-nine-year-old from an Irish American family who has a two-year-old boy, a five-year-old girl, a job in advertising, and a passion for poetry. Having a qualitative way to connect with quantitative data can make our end users more real as we design for their needs. It also allows us to share within a team a common vision of who they are designing for while reducing opportunities for incorrect presumptions to fill that gap. The persona, of course, is not a real person, but if it is designed based on real information learned by looking at many potential users, identifying and communicating what they have in common, a persona can be a powerful first step toward identifying both your end users and opportunities to serve them.

Journey mapping: A touchpoint describes a moment when an end user interacts with your organization or product. Seeing an ad for a new exhibit is a touchpoint, as is going online to buy the ticket, having their bag checked when entering the museum, and asking a security guard for directions to the bathroom. A journey map begins by taking a persona and walking it through every stage of their interactions with the product or experience, identifying all of the touchpoints along the way.

If a persona tells the story about the user, a journey map tells the story of your relationship with that user. The map can highlight where the product is bringing delight and where it brings nothing but frustration. More can be included, such as thoughts and feelings, and before long your journey map has turned into an experience map, visualizing on one page the key things you have learned about how your ideal user is experiencing what you offer.

If these practices are new to you, try not to be overwhelmed. As one c-suite executive once told me (not to my benefit, now that I think about it), "It's not rocket science."

There is an art to all this, but by looking at inexpensive and easily accessible resources and practices, these are skills anyone can develop.

2. Rapid Prototyping

Returning to our interview, Rik told us that while the youth were designing a digital game they first explored their ideas through an analog version in cardboard. This allowed them to make their ideas manifest, in a quick and cheap way.

When you make a prototype, a decision has to be made; you can debate endlessly about whether you should color a knob red or blue, but when you build the prototype you have to make a decision. Once a decision has been made, you can respond to a real thing in the world, not just what you might imagine in your head. It moves things forward by rapidly generating insight.

I take a lot of inspiration from the Hasso Plattner Institute of Design at Stanford, commonly known as the d.school. They tell students, "Prototype as if you know you're right, but test as if you know you're wrong." I love that. Make a decision with confidence, then bring it into the world so you can hammer on it to reveal its flaws.

A key modifier in their quote is "as if." You do not need to know the right thing in order to build a prototype; you just have to act as if you do when designing it, to avoid including any ambiguity. This recognizes that one of the main reasons we build a prototype is because we have no idea what the right thing actually is. Instead, we have questions. Will people prefer red or blue, or will color make no difference at all? When I prototype, the first thing I do is come up with key questions we want answered, and then build something to help us learn the answer. Interacting with the prototype (or watching others do so) should lead us to respond, "Ah, now I see."

From that perspective, prototypes are questions in search of an answer. The success of a prototype should not be measured by whether it works, but by whether it resolved the question that birthed it.

Some people view a prototype as a proof-of-concept. A proof-of-concept *can* be a type of question, such as "Is this a good idea?" and "Can it actually work?" If the prototype works, the concept has been validated. That prototype can then become the foundation of the project, leveraging all of the invested resources.

However, what if the prototype was *not* a proof-of-concept and included assets that should not end up in a final project? For example, Rik's students did not intend for the Exhibits Department to install a cardboard version of their game. What if, as in this case, the prototype was just designed to answer one particular set of questions, not to represent a smaller version of a final project?

More importantly, and more commonly, what if senior staff insist on treating every prototype as a proof-of-concept, regardless of why it was developed? Then you get into situations where prototypes are kept siloed, hidden from outside eyes, as they can become threats to the status of the project for fear of confusing high-level decision makers. If that happens, it can become extremely difficult to fully utilize the other tools for digital design explored in this book.

The good news is prototyping digital engagement is a powerful way to save time and money by learning as fast as possible if assumptions about your project actually hold up. In addition, it can be surprising how far you can take analog materials to represent a digital experience, as we will explore throughout this book.

3. Public Piloting

Once the Academy's young designers had built their game prototype, they could physically interact with ideas that had previously lived solely in their heads. Once they could touch it, I am confident they noticed things that needed to change.

However, to make the most of a prototype, it needs to be moved beyond its designers and get into the hands of the potential end users. That means creating a pilot to evaluate how visitors experience the prototype.

A pilot is a test project that engages users to validate an idea, tactic, or strategy. In the Academy example, the youth used a cardboard prototype to validate if the game was engaging and educational.

A pilot can be big or small. It can last an hour or a year. It can include five people or five thousand. There are many excellent organizations that can be hired to manage this process for a museum. In this book, however, I am more interested in inspiring you to see what you can do on your own, with minimal resources, as fast as possible, with information you can put to use immediately.

I break piloting down into four phases:

- **Pre-pilot phase:** This phase begins the moment the possibility for a pilot emerges until the moment it is approved to move forward.
- **Pilot planning phase:** This phase covers everything from the moment a pilot is approved until the moment before it launches.
- **Pilot phase:** This phase covers what occurs from the moment everyone is ready for that first user to experience the prototype until everything is taken down after the last user has concluded.
- **Post-pilot phase:** Finally, this phase covers everything that happens after the pilot has stopped interacting with users.

Within these four phases, I recommend tracking two streams of activities: product development (building the prototype and designing how users will engage with it) and evaluation and assessment (determining what you want to learn from the pilot, how data will be collected, collecting the data, and then analyzing it against success measures). The following are activities you might want to consider (and includes many of the other tools in the Toolkit):

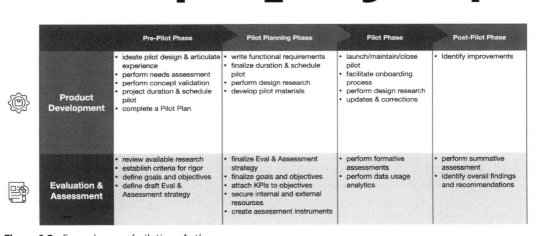

	Pre-Pilot Phase	Pilot Planning Phase	Pilot Phase	Post-Pilot Phase
Product Development	• ideate pilot design & articulate experience • perform needs assessment • perform concept validation • project duration & schedule pilot • complete a Pilot Plan	• write functional requirements • finalize duration & schedule pilot • perform design research • develop pilot materials	• launch/maintain/close pilot • facilitate onboarding process • perform design research • updates & corrections	• Identify improvements
Evaluation & Assessment	• review available research • establish criteria for rigor • define goals and objectives • define draft Eval & Assessment strategy	• finalize Eval & Assessment strategy • finalize goals and objectives • attach KPIs to objectives • secure internal and external resources • create assessment instruments	• perform formative assessments • perform data usage analytics	• perform summative assessment • identify overall findings and recommendations

Figure 1.2. Four phases of piloting. *Author*

1. Pre-Pilot Phase

For Product Development:

Ideate pilot design and articulate experience. Don't just settle on the first good idea. Develop at least three before settling into a pilot design. Then write it down, create an elevator pitch, or do whatever it takes to get the idea out of your head and into an external format.

Perform needs assessment. Define your users. Perform user research. Determine if the experience being piloted will meet their needs.

Perform concept validation. Share your ideas with potential users to validate any baked-in assumptions from the needs assessment.

Project duration and schedule pilot. Determine how long each piloting session will last, how many there will be, and map them to a calendar.

Complete a Pilot Plan. Combine everything above into one document. Call this your Pilot Plan. Ensure the plan addresses the following questions:

- How was the idea for the pilot developed, and who was involved?
- What is being developed and by whom?
- Who is it for and what will they experience?
- How will the pilot be designed to meet the needs of the pilot users (and was the idea validated with a sample user group)?
- What is the pilot duration and schedule?
- In addition, you might also want to explore both value and viability. Pilots deliver value by answering key questions, and there are different reasons one might seek these answers:
  - to validate assumptions and/or solutions about customer needs and pain points
  - to iteratively improve existing products/services
  - to reality check effectiveness before committing full resources
  - to surface key lessons through user research
  - to drive innovation

Depending on the reason, there are questions you can address in the Pilot Plan to ensure the answers to be delivered will return the value on your invested efforts. However, even a pilot promising strong value may lack the resources or planning required to make it viable. Consider if the appropriate levels of resources are available to support the pilot in the areas of human, technology, and fiscal resources.

This Pilot Plan can be used with key stakeholders to get resources approved to move to the Pilot Planning phase.

For Evaluation and Assessment:

Meanwhile, parallel to the product development activities, consider the following:

Review available research. Have others before you considered the same or a similar question or idea? Try not to rebuild the wheel.

Establish criteria for rigor. How rigorous does this entire process need to be? There is *no* right answer here. Do you have a large team with a big budget and a funder waiting for your results, or is it just you with no budget and no pressure to deliver? What's the minimum effort you need to put in to learn something reliable and valid?

Define goals and objectives. Goals refer to your outcomes (increase visitors' earthquake preparedness) while objectives are actions taken to achieve that goal (create a fun and educational game; install it within the earthquake exhibit). What are your goals for the prototype, if it achieved everything one might hope? (Note: In the next phase you will add measurements to evaluate how well the objectives achieved the goals.)

Define draft Evaluation and Assessment strategy. As with the Pilot Plan, draft a document that both gathers all of the previously mentioned materials and describes the methods that will be used to conduct evaluation and assessment of the prototype. Will there be user interviews? Pre- and post-surveys? Videos to be observed? Usage data to be analyzed? Assessment activities document what occurred; evaluation activities compare what occurred against your success measures.

2. *Pilot Planning Phase*

For Product Development:

Write functional requirements. If you are new to the term, this is essentially a reminder to define in as much detail as you can all the features the prototype will provide to the end user.

Finalize duration and schedule pilot. Reconfirm and lock in the duration and scheduling of your pilot sessions.

Perform design research. Continue user research. Now that the project is moving forward, it might be time to create a larger body of documentation of what has been learned to date, such as completing personas for the intended audiences.

Develop pilot materials. Whatever your end users will be interacting with, build it!

For Evaluation and Assessment:

Finalize the Evaluation and Assessment strategy. The last version was just a draft, as you were not yet sure if you would be approved to implement it. Since it has now been approved, revisit and finalize it, including the following elements.

Finalize goals and objectives. Revisit and finalize the goals and objectives.

Attach key performance indicators (KPIs) to objectives. Now that you have finalized the goals and objectives, it is time to build your KPIs, metrics, and, if you want to go all in, your benchmarks.

KPIs are, simply, the things you measure. For example, how long did visitors play with the earthquake game prototype? The metrics are how you will get data related to that indicator, such as timing people as they play the game, or analyzing user data recorded on the device.

The benchmarks are how you define what success looks like. In other words, visitors will spend at least two minutes playing the game, more than 90 percent will report they would recommend the game, and the majority will report learning at least one thing from playing the game.

So you will need to define the benchmarks for your project—the key indicators of what success will look like—and then determine your metrics—the data point you will collect to quantifiably measure your progress.

Secure internal and external resources. What and who do you need to pull this off? It's time to ensure it all will be available.

Create assessment instruments. Finally, write those interview questions, create those surveys, and prepare any other methods being used to collect data.

3. Pilot Phase

For Product Development:

Launch, maintain, then close the pilot. This is the moment you have been waiting for, when potential end users start interacting with your prototype. Launch and close each piloting session (maybe there is only one; maybe there are dozens). After the last session, close out the entire pilot (at which point you are done collecting data). Of course, until you are ready to close the pilot, make sure to do the following:

Facilitate the onboarding process. Within museums, a pilot session is often short and self-contained. However, some pilots might require users to engage over multiple sessions (e.g., such as logging into a website across multiple days). In pilots like that, you might want to think about how to bring the users into the pilot for their first time, to ensure it goes smoothly.

Perform design research. Given what you are learning, do the personas need to be updated? Have you learned enough to create a journey map of the visitors' experiences with your prototype?

Updates and corrections. Whoops! Something did not work as expected. Better update that prototype in time for that next piloting session.

For Evaluation and Assessment:

Perform formative assessments. Implement your study. Collect that data.

Perform data usage analytics. If the digital engagement produces user data, analyze that data.

4. Post-Pilot Phase

For Product Development:

Identify improvements. Now that the pilot has concluded, identify improvements to the user experience that should be made if the prototype or any aspects of it are ever used again.

For Evaluation and Assessment:

Perform summative assessment. Now that the data collection has concluded, assessment can be made across the scope of the entire piloting process. Include data usage analytics.

Identify overall findings and recommendations. Evaluate the pilot by comparing your assessment findings with the earlier defined success measures (KPIs). Determine the key findings and recommendations, then write them up in a report.

That's it! Now, if this ever feels like too much effort, that you do not have the time, that there are too many steps, or that you lack the required resources, treat this all not as a dictate but as an ideal, a goal to shoot for. Just do what you can manage, as any pilot done with thought and intention—no matter how rough or small—can increase your knowledge and your product's chance of success.

Your goal when piloting is to bring something out to museum visitors to create actionable information, fast, with the least resources. It means being flexible, and creative, and being open both to interrogating and listening to what you learned.

4. Iterative Design

What did the Academy teens do after they ran their pilot? They took what they learned and implemented it in the next design of their game. Everything that is made is designed and everything that is designed goes through multiple iterations or refinements before it is released.

An iterative design process can be defined in many ways, and with different terms, but the overall process is fairly consistent across them all. Ideas are generated, goals and/or requirements are defined, something is created, something is tested, data is collected and then compared against the earlier goals and/or requirements, revisions are made, and new iterations move back through the process, repeating until resources like time, money, and/or patience run out.

The key thing in an iterative design process is not how one defines these steps but the overall approach to design. Designing through a "building, testing, refining" cycle recognizes that success emerges not through a brilliantly conceived idea but through on-the-ground learning, from expecting that something needs to be broken before it can be fixed, through the humility to recognize design is a collaboration with end users.

Iterative design relies on what author Mo Willems was alluding to when he said that creativity is "a line from A to strawberry pizza." When you iterate, you have to be open to the direction you are led. Expect the unexpected. You might learn that great idea you had is really two, and one needs to be removed (and perhaps relaunched in a new project). You might find that core feature, essential in the first iteration, is just a distraction by the tenth time around from everything else working together in such harmony.

Often in museums we lack the resources to iterate as fully as we might like. But, as with these other tools for digital design, a richly iterated product is the ideal. See how many cycles you can fit in.

5. Youth Collaboration

Rik led a design process that intentionally valued placing youth in the driver's seat (even if many might think them too young to drive). He recognized their lack of skills when compared, for example, to the exhibit team, the expert on earthquakes, or the game designer, but he solved for it by bringing the adults in as mentors and educators. Rik set reasonable goals for the youth to achieve but validated their output across the Academy to ensure it met organizational expectations. He supported them to take charge of every step of the process and appreciated that their lack of polish could be presented as a feature, not a bug.

While Rik privileged the educational impact digital design had on the program, this book is more interested in how youth, as co-designers, bring value to their museums. Rik highlighted how the museum learned from the youth, about how to design in a faster way to create engagement for their visitors. He also recognized they brought a unique voice into the exhibit halls, not only through their age but also from the diversity of backgrounds and perspectives they carried into the design process.

It is crucial to highlight that Rik worked hard to ensure the youth were not set up to fail, that expectations were not placed too high, and that they were not left to their own devices. The teens did not make decisions in a vacuum; instead, Rik scaffolded the process so by the time the teens made decisions they were informed decisions. They were not left on their own to build something and learn later if it worked; experts were involved to guide them while validation was sought through interactions with the public.

Rik's model—supporting a group of youth to lead—is only one model of digital design in museums with youth. On the flip end, we have youth providing advice or participating in focus groups, playing a smaller but important role. In between, as we will see often in this book, youth can participate as co-designers alongside professionals, not in charge but as equals.

The goal at the end of the day here, the tool to be deployed for advancing digital design in museums, is to look for mutually beneficial collaborations from diverse perspectives that can meet the needs of the museum, visitors, and youth in learning programs.

6. Teaming Up

As I have already referenced, Rik was able to develop the exhibit game on earthquakes only by teaming up with others, both within the museum (exhibits, marketing, research, legal) and externally (scientist, game designer). Remove any of these partners and the project might have failed.

My son was in first grade when I started my new position at the Museum. At first, he understood this to mean I would be developing mobile apps, and he wanted to know if that meant he would now get a discount. Then he said, with a hint of concern for his dad, "If you do that on your own that will be a lot of work."

Often it is hard to remember the village it takes to raise up digital design in a museum.

Consider first all the people you need within your museum, whose time needs to be scheduled, whose permission is required. Then remember they are all already working on something else, on more than their fair share, and probably severely time-crunched and under-resourced. Are you sure you can't manage without them? If not, how can you make sure every minute of their time is essential, well spent, and that you appreciate their efforts? How can you better understand their needs to make the collaboration mutually beneficial for all? How can you make the ask to them in the clearest, most direct way?

Next, consider all the people you need from outside the museum. If you have little to no funds, at least provide a stipend, or find ways to make the engagement meaningful for them as well.

Ultimately, you want to ensure that any new project, right from the start, has the team in place required to achieve all of your goals.

With that we have reviewed the Six Tools for Digital Design. The rest of the book will now explore different ways one can use these tools by exploring examples at both the American Museum of Natural History and other museums from around the world, beginning with a project with one of my favorite names: *Crime Scene Neanderthal*.

2

Designing Guided Adventures

In Summary | tl;dr

    Subject: This chapter focuses on using the Six Tools of Digital Design to combine digital experience design with physical museum assets in a guided format.

    Case study: The case study in this chapter focuses on *Crime Scene Neanderthal*, a youth co-designed and facilitated in-Hall experience that invited museum visitors to use a mobile app and other tools to investigate a science-based mystery. It was designed to address the question: Can a youth program produce a prototype of a mobile app that can inform the Museum's overall mobile app strategy?

    User research: Throughout the development and testing of *Crime Scene Neanderthal*, the needs and interests of museum visitors within the Hall of Human Origins and its associated Learning Lab were identified in four different ways. First, through the questions frequently encountered by the staff of the Learning Lab. Second, through sessions tracking visitors moving through the Hall. Third, user interactions with *Crime Scene Neanderthal* were collected and analyzed. Finally, observations and interviews were designed to better understand the infrastructure developed to deliver the experience.

    Rapid prototyping: Each element of *Crime Scene Neanderthal* was developed, tested, and frequently iterated through paper prototypes and digital prototypes, first within the classroom and then in context within the Hall and the Lab. Each was driven by a series of questions that tested the impact of specific design decisions.

    Public piloting: Formal piloting sessions were held on weekends over three months, led by teen facilitators/evaluators who recruited visitors as they entered the Hall.

    Iterative design: All elements of *Crime Scene Neanderthal*, from large to small, were iterated over the course of the design process, such as modified signage, improvements to the app user experience, writing and rewriting the facilitator scripts, and changing the flow of the user journey.

    Youth collaboration: *Crime Scene Neanderthal* was co-developed, facilitated, and co-evaluated by teenagers in an afterschool youth program. We constrained their process by defining in advance the location (the Lab and the Hall), the mode of visitor engagement (a facilitated experience combining physical objects, tools of science, print materials, and a mobile app), and the focus of the content (Neanderthals). We empowered the youth by supporting them to take the lead on the overarching narrative, develop the questions driving each step of the mystery, write the facilitator script, and shape the overall visitor experience.

Teaming up: *Crime Scene Neanderthal* brought together a team internal to the Museum—such as those focused on educational product design, afterschool programming, and Learning Labs—with companies and individuals external to the Museum—such as local graduate school interns and a mobile app developer.

Comparison: The chapter concludes by offering, for comparison with *Crime Scene Neanderthal*, a project that also combined digital experience design with physical museum assets and facilitation (not live, but delivered through a mobile device), developed with both the Acropolis Museum in Athens, Greece, and the Cité de l'Espace in Toulouse, France.

CONTEXT AND GUIDING QUESTIONS

When I enter the white-walled Sackler Educational Laboratory for Comparative Genomics and Human Origins at the American Museum of Natural History (AMNH), my gaze usually turns to the wall of skulls: *Sahelanthropus tchadensis*, and Lucy, and a Neanderthal, and dozens more. Not real skulls, of course, but fossil cast specimens—scientifically accurate replicas—that can be picked up and observed by students or visitors in order to, say, classify species and build an evolutionary tree.

Adjacent to the skulls is scientific equipment, like microscopes, for extracting and examining DNA from strawberries. Classes come in during the week, and visitors on the weekend, to do forensic anthropology, learn how skeletal form relates to locomotor function, and engage in other hands-on learning with real tools of science.

The back of the room is filled with additional equipment to support these activities, a lab-sized sink, and next to that a refrigerator running so cold it can often be hard to hear the instructor over its deafening hum. The front of the room has a whiteboard—marking the room as a space for learning, in case there was any question—and the middle of the lab is filled like a mushroom-crowded field with blue-topped tables, each seating six.

For a visitor to the Museum, the Lab can be hard to find, only accessible right in the middle of the Hall of Human Origins. The new-ish Hall is one of the youngest in the Museum. Opened in 2007, it replaced a series of Halls on the topic that date back to the 1920's Hall of the Age of Man, one of the country's earliest in-depth exhibits on human evolution. With so much new research in this area, the Hall drew upon a significant amount of untapped knowledge. It also integrated into its design a new conceptual approach to the topic, combining both genetic and fossil evidence to trace the history of human origins. Soon after it opened, however, new research made some details already out of date. And therein lay the brilliance of pairing the Hall with a dedicated Learning Lab—while the Hall could introduce visitors to the broader narrative of human evolution, the Lab could leverage the latest educational techniques to communicate the most up-to-date research, hands-on and through live facilitation.

When I first began at the Museum I sat in the Lab, at one of those blue tables, to meet with its manager, Samara Rubinstein, to understand her needs for the Lab and explore how digital tools might address them. I was also exploring where those needs might intersect with my own—to find existing spaces in the Museum that could be turned into innovation centers that enabled rapid prototyping of new tools and practices that could drive impact throughout the Museum. I suspected the Lab might fit the bill.

Our meeting was one of a series in which I sat with education managers around the Museum to introduce my new role, perform an audit of digital tools used for learning, and identify potential areas of collaboration. I started my meeting with Samara by explaining that we were meeting so I could learn more about her and so she could learn how I could be a resource in her use of digital media. I asked her about herself, how she got to the Museum, and how the Lab functioned.

I then explained that my goal was to build everyone's capacity to tease apart tools from their affordances, and ensure their use was aligned with educational and program goals. We meticulously reviewed every single digital tool used in the program to identify how each was used, what educational objectives were addressed, and to what extent they aligned with teaching specific scientific practices, scientific concepts, digital literacies, and youth development practices. All of this would be combined across my audit to produce a baseline to establish how effectively the youth-facing arm of the Education Department was deploying digital tools for learning and to identify areas of growth.

With the audit complete, we concluded with my favorite topic: exploring the edge points, for herself and the Lab. The idea of "edge points" is a concept we developed within my former team at Global Kids. It played a key role in how I found myself actually working in a museum. For many years we received funding from the MacArthur Foundation to support civic and cultural institutions to bring cutting-edge digital media into their youth educational programs. Our goal, however, was more than just developing a new slate of courses; we aimed to inspire new practices that could adapt and grow over time. We focused on where digitally engaged programming could be a disruptive force challenging the educators and/or the institutional culture to work on the edge of their comfort level, at the point where digital media met learning to reveal new vistas ripe for exploration. At the end of the day, we wanted to better understand the following question: How do institutions find their balance working on this edge?

What I sought from the manager of the Sackler Lab was not a list of new technologies she might want to incorporate into her space, but rather what new work would challenge her, challenge the Lab, challenge the Museum, in such a way that, should it succeed, it would open the possibility space for more digital innovations in the future. And even should it fail to meet all of its objectives, what projects could they take on, what initiatives could they launch, in which every step along the way would generate learning that could become the foundation for future digitally engaged initiatives.

As Samara began to describe her edge points, she often backed away from them, not trusting this was something that could ever be approved. This is what I find thinking on the edge often helps us to do, creating an opportunity to push back against the voices in our head that say something isn't possible, isn't worth considering, better left alone.

In many ways, that is how I saw my new role at the Museum, as a voice of hope to counter any internalized work culture that expects to hear "no," to encourage colleagues instead to approach the horizon and peek, ever so carefully, over the edge.

"Almost half of our weekend visitors are from overseas," Samara explained. "What if we had an app that could help non-English speakers engage with the activities." And what if that mobile app could augment the skulls with layers of information? And . . . before long we had identified her edge point: leveraging a mobile app to augment the visitor experience to the Lab.

The "Sackler App" was soon added to my list of strategic projects. It was initially defined as "a mobile app for use by visitors to the Sackler Lab and the Hall of Human Origins to increase opportunities and methods for engaging with their content, such as with augmented reality (AR) features, and provide new ways to reflect upon and revisit the material once they leave the museum." Note that AR was included to be illustrative, not prescriptive, and there was an equal focus on in-Museum and at-home engagement (something which would change before the project came to a close). And not one word about Neanderthals; that would come much later.

The first gatekeeper, the head of Education, saw value in it, or at least in our putting resources into exploring it. First hurdle cleared.

The next gatekeeper was within the Communications Department. Coms was nominally responsible for all things digital: the Museum's website, social media presence, mobile apps. And yet . . . Education drove the youth-facing section of the website, and Exhibitions made their own exhibit-related apps, and in fact digital media was in production all over. So in practice digital production was often a balancing act between not stepping on toes and getting things done.

From the Coms perspective, the mobile app stores were full of AMNH products, confusing visitors and distracting from the primary Museum offering, our *Explorer* app. The idea of adding even one more option was pushing against the grain. On the other hand, Coms could recognize how the use case for the Sackler Lab was fairly unique.

In the end, the opportunity to learn something new won the day.

All we needed now was to identify a funder. If no one had space in their budget for it (and no one did) then we needed an outside supporter whose interests aligned with our own. And a year after our initial conversation, we found them. Or rather, they found us. An existing funder of educational programming wanted to double their contribution. It was up to us to decide where the funding would go. I was delighted to hear our ask would focus on digital learning (my area at the time). It would need to involve a youth program, with a typical classroom structure, but also include an in-hall, youth-led visitor engagement component. It could incorporate a videogame, like *Minecraft*, if I wanted, or focus on mobile AR. So what did I think?

We had less than twenty-four hours to submit our plans for the new "Sackler Youth AR Program," which, as we were prepared, we delivered in due time.

Within a few months the funding was secure, as was the approach: a youth-driven program where high school students would be invited to co-develop a "digitally enabled learning experience" exploring the topic of human evolution. Twenty youth would "work together with scientists, educators and digital learning partners to develop a prototype for a mobile augmented reality app" that was promised to provide a bridge between the Sackler Lab and related exhibit content in the surrounding Hall of Human Origins.

Let's pause for a moment. Each of these AMNH case studies will begin with an introduction to the context that gave birth to a visitor-facing digital project; in this case, the context was my new role at the Museum seeking an innovation space, the desire by the Lab for a visitor-facing app, and a funder looking to support a new youth program. Each introduction will then conclude, as you will see momentarily, with the initial guiding questions. Mark these questions (in your mind or with a bookmark) as we will return to them in the end of each chapter to measure the success of each initiative. Don't let me off the hook!

There were many guiding questions embedded within this new educational program's learning objectives, but those are outside the scope of this book (which is focused on developing visitor-facing digital engagement, not youth programming). But one outcome spoke to the broader topic: *Can a youth program produce a prototype of a mobile app that can inform the Museum's overall mobile app strategy?* In other words, whether or not this new program produced something that would live on in the Lab, could the prototype itself, and the process of employing youth in the development process, support Coms in its work strategizing the mobile experience of our visitors?

CRIME SCENE NEANDERTHAL

What follows is an account of the evolution of *Crime Scene Neanderthal* (*CSN*), a project designed to answer the guiding question outlined earlier: Can a youth program produce a prototype of a mobile app that can inform the Museum's overall mobile app strategy?

We began with a few design constraints. We knew who some of the designers would be (youth in an afterschool program, a museum scientist-educator). We knew at least one medium that would be involved (a mobile app). We knew where it would be used (in both the Lab and Hall). And we had a process for developing a design document (a youth program).

The knowns, however, were far outweighed by the unknowns: what exactly were we asking the visitors to do? What was the scientific subject matter? How would the experience utilize both the Lab and the Hall? What materials would be required (both digital and analog)? Would it be a self-guided or a facilitated experience?

What is most important here is what we did not do next. We did not hunker down for a few days in a conference room in an effort to answer all of these unresolved questions, and then send out our requirements to a tech developer. Nor did we meet with a talented design firm, give them access to our hopes and fears, and then wait to see what they might deliver. Instead, we put our questions through a process using the Six Tools for Digital Design:

- User research
- Rapid prototyping
- Public piloting
- Iterative design
- Youth collaboration
- Teaming up

To ensure the freedom and flexibility required to support an iterative design process, we needed a solid curriculum in place for the youth. That meant our first task was to determine the scientific content and the design skills they would need to learn, and the structure of the program itself.

In the year and half that passed from the first time I sat with Samara, she had since moved on from the Museum and a new Lab manager had joined, Julia Zichello. Julia had a background in both art (a bachelor of fine arts from Pratt and time working for Milton Glaser) and science (a doctorate in Biological Anthropology). This was a powerful and unique combination. While working in the Lab with school groups on the weekdays and general visitors on the weekend, she could easily geek out on science—fluent in phrases like "gel electrophoresis"—yet never lose sight of how confusing it could all be for a learner.

Julia was excited to help drive what the final product might help her to solve. Specifically, she was well aware of the questions (and confusions) people brought into the Lab and how much time she and her staff spent trying to resolve them. Meeting with myself and Marissa Gamliel, the dedicated and animated Museum educator who would develop and lead the curriculum, we listed all of these questions on a board. We evaluated which ones the Hall was best equipped to address (through its exhibits) as well as the Lab (through hands-on science activities). And we took into consideration which questions were most common.

As our subject matter expert, Julia recommended we go with the topic of Neanderthals: the most frequent questions from visitors pertained to Neanderthals, common misunderstandings about them are easy to clarify, and there was material on the subject located all around the Hall. From that moment on the "Sackler Youth AR Program" was re-branded "The Neanderthal Next Door." The new name referred to the fact that evolution is not linear; us *Homo sapiens* lived at the same time as the Neanderthal (for a time, as neighbors) and, at least in some cases, got cozy enough that we now carry a percentage of Neanderthal DNA within us all.

With the subject matter identified, we could now start building learning objectives for the youth program (e.g., evolutionary theory, comparative skeletal anatomy, fossil discoveries, and cultural artifacts). We also knew they needed to learn some pedagogical skills as well, such as facilitating engagement with visitors and understanding how activity guides function within a museum. Finally, we knew they had to develop certain digital literacy skills, such as with augmented learning design, mobile literacy, and data visualization.

All of those skills would then be deployed through the design skills we needed to cultivate: thinking critically about what inspired curiosity among visitors to the Hall, developing design principles, user-testing prototypes, and incorporating results into revised iterations.

This was a lot to teach high school students. We rose to the challenge and built a curriculum that could support it. Eventually, nineteen high school seniors were selected for The Neanderthal Next Door, committing to come twice a week, over fourteen weeks, in this intensive program focused on producing a design document for the final experience. We called this Phase 1, engaging high school students in a process to work the known constraints through a design process that could flesh out the full experience.

Phase 1: Iterating Toward a Design Document

We utilized the Museum's collections. We used the halls. We used our youth development expertise. And we combined all three to engage the youth, build a learning community, and develop their knowledge base around Neanderthals and their place within the history of human evolution. Let's explore how next, with that as a foundation, they deployed the Six Tools for Digital Design.

Marissa, the lead facilitator, with support from Matt McGowan, a thoughtful graduate student skilled in design practices from New York University's Digital Media Design for Learning program, prepared the teens. Their goal was to direct them to perform end user observations within the Hall while mapping visitor pathways. They reminded the teens we wanted to understand as much as we could about the visitors we imagined would experience our new mobile app. Who is this person? What do they need that our product should try to address?

The facilitators instructed the youth to get out their design notebooks, rotate one page to a landscape orientation, divide it into three columns, and then label each one.

The first column was labeled "What." Here they would record concrete observations of visitors within the Hall, using adjectives and other descriptive language.

The second column was labeled "How." Here they would record how the visitors were doing what they were doing. Was it hard or easy for them? What adjectives could be used to describe their emotional state?

The final column was labeled "Why." Here they would record their guesses for why the visitor was doing what they were doing.

Meanwhile, the teens were encouraged to record in their notebooks any snippets of Hall-related conversations that could be discreetly overheard (emphasis on "discreet").

Students were then put into pairs and instructed to follow and observe visitors from the moment they first entered the Hall. While Partner 1 would capture the What/Why/How, partner 2 would be doing something else. Armed with their notebook and a timing device, this youth would record the route taken by the visitors as they passed through the Hall, capturing how long they spent pausing at each location.

After a few weeks, as their collection of data grew, it was time to process their observations within their pairs. We gave them printed maps of the Hall and instructed them to trace each visitor's route, annotating their paths with key observations they had made along the way.

These pairs were then combined into groups of four, reviewing each other's work and then translating their observations into news headlines, which we described as noteworthy quotes, surprises, or other interesting bits.

An observation like this—"They transition to the back of the exhibit, stand there, and discuss something"—was turned into headlines like this: "Conversations happen in back of hall!"

Here are a few more examples:

This observation—"They seemed to just be passing through and not actually interested in this exhibition"—became this headline: "For many, Hall of Human Origins a road, not a destination!"

This observation—"Reading description of the Neanderthal diagram, skeletal model; discussing it with other members of the group. Spends a lot of time on just one model, moving slowly just to look and view one diagram. Huge interest in the glass case with skeleton"—became this headline: "Interested visitors love skeletons!"

And this observation—"'That's crazy! That's where we come from,' said one mom while looking at one diorama. People spend most of their time at a few dioramas then quickly look over the rest"—became this headline: "Mom struck by human origins! Dioramas start strong, end weak!"

Headlines were written on post-it notes and then stuck on the wall. The teens were invited to explore them, group them if they like, and watch for themes.

Marissa and Matt created three columns on the whiteboard: Users, User Needs, and Surprising Insights. The teens were tasked with filling in the columns using their headlines as a starting point, while including any observations or insights which led them there.

Under *Users* they identified "old people," "people younger than thirty who like taking photos," "tourists," "college students," "teenagers," and "parents with children." Given what we knew about the Hall and general museum visitors, that seemed about right (even if we might have used different terminology).

Under *User Needs* they identified observations that might have been less obvious. Visitors needed:

- A guide in a different language
- Deeper methods to create comprehension
- A change in lighting

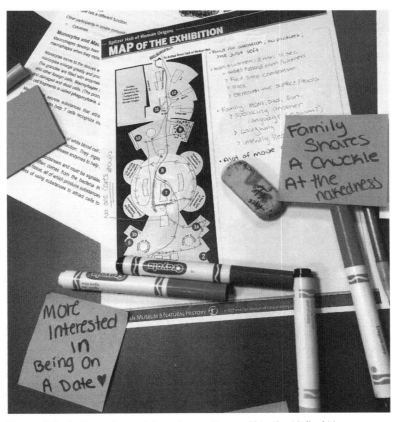

Figure 2.1. Artifacts from visitor observations within the Hall of Human Origins. *Author*

- Higher-level engagement strategies
- Things they can relate to themselves
- Interactives
- Info to relay to their kids
- The left side needs to be more interesting than the right

The final column, *Surprising Insights*, is where the teens really got to show their unique observational abilities:

- Most visitors tend to walk toward the right
- They like taking selfies
- People are very interested in the brain panel
- They only look at pictures
- They like dioramas
- People like being on their phones!
- Children often come with facilitators
- Self-absorbed
- Parents often relay inaccurate information
- The DNA panel is romantic

DNA is romantic? That was certainly news to us.

Each step of this user empathy process was scaffolded, leading them toward a set of informed design principles. But we still had one more step.

There are many design programs and studios that put their techniques out for others to use, often for some reason as decks of cards. One of my favorites is from the design program at Stanford, called the d.school. I use it so often I can barely close the box anymore. Sometimes I read them in order. Sometimes I scatter them around and pick one to review at random. Their black cardboard box is designed to look like an old cassette tape and is labeled the *Bootcamp Bootleg* (it was originally designed for graduates of their *Bootcamp: Adventures in Design Thinking* course). In any case, the design-thinking card we brought into The Neanderthal Next Door at this point was "Point-of-View Madlibs." The idea is to help our young designers put themselves deeper into the shoes of our visitors and shock them, so to speak, out of their own perspective through encountering something unexpected. Sometimes a new perspective can reframe a design challenge into an actionable problem, one that can inspire a new round of ideation. And few things are more unexpected and random than the surrealistic associations generated through a good round of Madlibs.

Using the raw data just generated on the board, we asked our teen developers to come up with the craziest combinations across the three columns. They turned "[USER] needs to [USER'S NEED] because [SURPRISING INSIGHT]" into Madlibs like these:

"Old people need a change in lighting or guide because the DNA panel is romantic."
"Most people need a change in lighting or guide because they walk to the right."
"Parents need interactives to relay info to their kids."
"Young couples need something to direct their attraction to the scientific concepts presented because they are self-absorbed."
"People younger than thirty who like taking photos need something to direct their attraction to the scientific concepts presented because they only look at pictures."

At long last, with the data collection and user empathy work in place, we could turn to developing design principles.

Marissa and Matt introduced design principles from both Google and Facebook. Using them for inspiration, together we developed the following dozen principles that could constrain and inspire the work ahead. (As you review, try to imagine what decisions were made along the way and what sort of visitor observations could have informed each one.)

1. **Consistency**—everything is consistent throughout the design, both print and user experience.
2. **Do one thing really, really well**—for example, focus on Neanderthals.
3. **Informative**—make sure information is up to date and can effectively convey the information to the user.
4. **There's always more information out there**—where? In the Hall? in the world?
5. **Repeatable**—there should be always more to learn about Neanderthals, and the guide, the Hall, and the Museum. It also should make people *want* to return.
6. **Strong production value**—it should look and feel great, work, and show we cared.
7. **More autonomy for users**—a choice over what you can do, not just a linear path.
8. **Engaging**—it has to be interesting enough for people to want to do it. Comic relief—it should be entertaining. People should want to do the activity.
9. **Take home friendly**—everyone wants something to take home. It should have value once taken home.
10. **Relevant to all ages**—from pre-kindergarten to seniors.
11. **Enhance content in the Halls and Sackler Lab**—a good experience should make the Hall experience more accurate, up to date, detailed, etc. Get people from the Hall into the Sackler Lab, and make a connection between the two.
12. **Facilitated**—the guide encourages dialogue among visitors and with AMNH staff.

These design principles allowed us, for the first time, to describe a user experience, but only in the most general terms: a facilitator would use the tools provided to guide a visitor through a high-quality experience that engaged them in Neanderthal-related content while supporting them to make meaningful decisions. And at the end, participants would have something of value (if only to them) to take back home.

What we needed now was one concept that held it all together. While a design principle can easily be revisited and modified in the future, once a concept is locked in there is no turning back.

We explored a number of ideas. Would visitors be led through the Hall and into the Lab to use real information to explore a day in the life of a fictionalized Neanderthal? Would visitors be invited to collect and interpret evidence as if they were in a police procedural, investigating a murdered Neanderthal, using real scientific processes but within a fictionalized narrative? Or would visitors enter a narrative as close to realistic as possible, taking on the role of a museum scientist tasked with doing research on extinct Neanderthals?

The youth developed and debated ideas like these. I worked with Matt and Marissa to guide the discussion, referring to the design principles if ever they got stuck and to ensure they were in alignment, and helping them move past weaker ideas while digging deeper into the stronger ones. Julia was on hand, as the formal voice of both Hall and Lab, to provide feedback and confer final approval, which she did. Together we landed on a new name for the project which, itself, telegraphed which of the ideas we had selected: in a nod to a popular television series, it would now be called *CSN*, or *Crime Scene Neanderthal*.

We still needed to clarify who the experience was for. Yes, they said it might be for all ages, but something designed for "everyone" is often designed for no one. We needed them to get more specific.

Visitors were broken out across two different axes, distinguishing the more museum literate from the less, and the more Neanderthal-literate from the less. That gave us a grid like this:

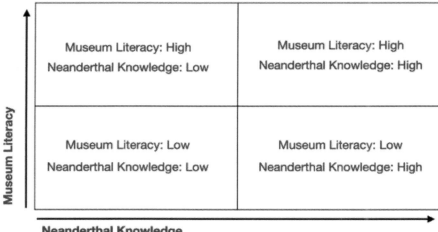

Figure 2.2. Segmenting visitors by museum literacy and Neantherthal knowledge. *Author*

We discussed what we had learned from our observations. We debated which of the four quadrants would be most interested in something like *CSN*. We decided to focus on the visitors most aligned with the lower-left quadrant, which is to say those less familiar with both museums and Neanderthals.

Now that we knew who the visitors were in real life, we needed to decide who they were within *CSN*. We had already decided they were in a police procedural. Did that mean they were stepping into the shoes of a character we had created for them? How much detail did we need for this roleplay to be effective? The more we tried to figure out this detective character the more it felt we were getting off track. The visitor would be told they were a detective solving a mystery, and that was that; they could be trusted to fill in the blanks.

What was the mystery to be solved by the visitor? Our co-designers had been challenged to brainstorm scientific questions that could be framed as a mystery. We tasked them with framing a good question, proposing the related educational content, and suggesting the activity to be performed by the visitor. They returned examples like:

Question: Could a N. have made a tool which could cause damage?
Educational content: How experimental archeologists reconstruct the past to better understand it.
Activity: Rebuild a virtual tool and make virtual marks to compare

Question: Was a human the perpetrator?
Educational content: Teach basic evolution concepts.
Activity: Sequence N. DNA and compare against sequenced human DNA.

Question: Could tooth decay have caused the death?
Educational content: How N. teeth work, and what they ate.
Activity: Look at the real physical fossil evidence in the Lab.

To help us decide we went back to the Design Principles. Marissa and Matt suggested that "Do one thing and do it well" might lead us to one central mystery. We landed on: "Who do these bones belong to and what happened to him (or her)?" We could have gone broader, asking a question like "What made the Neanderthals go extinct?" but instead we narrowed the focus. This helped us to control the narrative while still incorporating important scientific information and questions.

For the narrative, we determined that bones had been found during excavation for a new building. Before construction could continue, the mystery of the bones' origins would have to be solved through collaboration between a representative of the Museum (the facilitator) and the hired Neanderthal Detective (the visitor). The Detectives would decide what type of evidence they would like to pursue in order to solve the mystery: physical evidence (like bones), genetic evidence (like DNA), or cultural evidence (like making weapons).

With the concept in place, the end user defined, and the central mystery framed, we needed to break the project down into bite-sized units that could be fleshed out by small groups of youth developers. And each unit had to be tied to a physical location, in the Hall or Lab.

Returning to their earlier ideas for mysteries, we realized those could be repurposed as steps along the way toward solving the central mystery. They revisited and revised the list of question/content/activity and added in their locations, the exact evidence visitors would engage with, what roles would be played at this point by both facilitator and Detective, and whether it all aligned with the design principles.

The teens were stepped through an iterative design process in which they developed their activity, received feedback and critiques (first from the instructors, later their peers, and eventually from Julia, whose sign-off was required), and returned for revisions. At first, for example, they could sit down with an instructor and just talk through the experience, but eventually they had to walk their peers through the Hall itself, running it with a paper prototype. Throughout, they were challenged to clarify what was required from print materials, physical objects, and the app, as well as developing a script for the facilitators. At each step we directed the youth with clear prompts and materials to help them clearly communicate and develop their ideas.

For example, Marissa and Matt passed out worksheets, explaining the storyboarding process. Each team was required to create a storyboard to sketch out each part of the user experience. They were required to focus on the facilitators' interactions with the visitors at different parts of the hall, the visitors' interface with the physical guide (if any), and how the AR would appear in the app. The storyboard was matched with a script, detailing what the facilitator might say and more detailed illustrations of print or digital content.

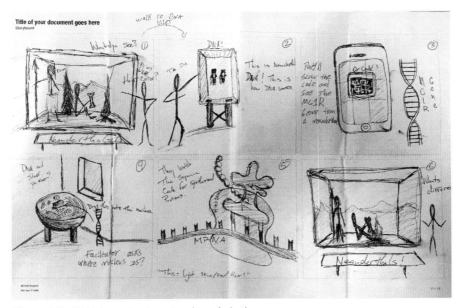

Figure 2.3. DNA investigation storyboard. *Author*

In all they created storyboards for eight visitor activities, including the Museum/visitors' inter-action, and the visitors' interactions with the exhibits, the laboratory instruments, and the mobile games and activities. All of which was written up in a final one-hundred-page design document for our outside app developer and internal print design team.

The design document described an introductory activity, in which the visitor agrees to participate and accept a "dossier" which detailed the narrative, the mystery, and how they might solve it. The visitors would then make their first choice. Would they move over to the DNA display and play a mobile game to genetically identify the bones? Or would they move over to the skeletal display and use AR to locate the found bones on the in-Hall model? Completing an activity would earn them an evidence sticker, to be placed on a printed sheet alongside their answers to the written prompts (e.g., Did the bones come from a chimpanzee, a human, or a Neanderthal?); these sheets would be collected over the course of *CSN* to be turned in as evidence to support their final conclusion.

Figure 2.4. The three types of *Crime Scene Neanderthal* evidence stickers. *Author*

After this set of stations, the facilitator presented new options to choose from. Would they head to the Neanderthal diorama to speculate about the color of the victim's hair? Or would they head to the music display and practice performing an augmented Neanderthal flute, then head into the Lab to train a microscope on funeral flowers?

Finally, the third activities each explored a different cause of death. Death by disease was explored in the Lab, using pipettes and a mobile app simulation of a process called gel electrophoresis. Death by weapon was explored through creating a virtual weapon using a Neanderthal technique, virtually using it on a virtual object, then comparing its markings against the marks on the found bone (a scientifically accurate reproduction of a Neanderthal bone, marked up by Julia). Death by wild animals was explored at the Hominid versus Hyena display, using the app to compare marks that could be made by different animals.

After this third activity the visitor returned to the first document they received at the start. It read: "After detailed research in collaboration with Museum personnel, *I found/did not find* evidence that the fossils *were/were not* of Neanderthal origin. I based my findings on the following evidence." After making their decision, the facilitator would thank the visitor for their time and reward them with a physical object, like a three-dimensional-printed Neanderthal bone or a toy replica of a Neanderthal flute.

To conclude the youth program, and this first phase, the youth invited family and friends to our auditorium (we invited the funders), and after a presentation the co-designers led the guests into both the Hall of Human Origins and the Sackler Educational Laboratory to give their first walk-through to potential future Neanderthal Detectives.

Figure 2.5. Teen co-designers lead Crime Scene Neanderthal walk-through. *American Museum of Natural History*

Phase 2: Spring Public Prototyping

Rotunda is the membership magazine for the AMNH. Three months after the *CSN* design document was presented to our external team of developers, the spring issue of *Rotunda* led with the following headline: "Solve a Science-Based Mystery Designed by Teens." The article opened with the tease: "The Museum's Sackler Educational Laboratory is looking for a few good Neanderthal detectives—and you just might fit the bill."

Even alongside articles on a deceptive octopus, the lifecycle of a parasite, and the nearly indestructible tardigrade, the article on *CSN* was unique. Everything else in this *Rotunda*—in fact, in most all issues of the magazine—promoted finished products to be experienced by members, such as new exhibits, science talks, bird walks, space shows, and Imax films. *CSN*, however, stood apart in two ways. First, it was co-designed by teens from the educational programs. This fact could have been pushed to the background; most of the incredible staff behind the other Museum programming featured that issue and the processes they used to develop them were left undiscussed. Instead, the article on *CSN* informed members that

> family visitors who participate in *CSN* will be led by student interns, armed with a paper guide and a mobile app, to explore both virtual and cast Neanderthal fossils to solve a science-based mystery. It's part of an experimental approach to engaging youth in science learning by challenging students to co-design a unique Museum experience for families.

Second, the article did not shy away from the fact that *CSN* was still a product in development. In fact, we were explicitly inviting our members to come work with us to not just experience something wondrous but to collaborate with us in creating something new.

> In April and May, Members will have a chance to experience the program firsthand when the student developers return to the Museum to test the prototype with the public, guiding groups of families and youth to dioramas and microscopes to unravel such puzzles as: how do we know a Neanderthal's hair color? What can clues tell us about Neanderthal culture? What killed off this recent human relative?

Our goal during this phase was to collect as much data as we could to determine whether *CSN* was working, what improvements it might need, and how best to integrate it into both the visitor journey and the logistics of running the Lab and the Hall. This required a more agile group of teens, dedicated to interacting with the public, facilitating their *CSN* experience, and collecting and analyzing data.

Teens from The Neanderthal Next Door program were invited to apply, but this time there would only be spots for eight. Over fourteen weeks, they would come in for afterschool sessions but also commit to four all-day weekend public prototyping sessions. That is, every Saturday or Sunday visitors might encounter two to four interns, who would return during the week to share what they learned with their peers. We told the teens they would be learning about facilitating activities within the Sackler Lab, prototyping a beta version of the Activity Guide while facilitating its use among visitors, and learning more about the content they would be supporting. The results of our collaboration might produce a new design document and a proposal referred back to the original funder for finalizing this project.

In addition, as an intern, they would receive a stipend of four hundred dollars.

To be considered they had to include a one- to two-page essay, addressing the following:

- Why are you interested in the internship?
- What have you learned so far in the program that you are interested in teaching others about?
- What effect do you hope the final guide will have on visitors?
- How will this experience at the Museum help you further your academic and/or career goals?

The submitted essays spoke to their awareness that this opportunity might bolster their college and career resume, speak to their interests in science, improve the visitor experience, and leverage their unique perspective as teenagers. This was summed up nicely in the following successful application:

> I'm applying to the internship because it will help me get experience to make decisions about my future career, as well as be a fun way to apply my current skills. I would like to enter either the sciences or the humanities, and this is a blend of both. It allows me to apply my writing skills to develop an interactive experience for museum guests while learning about paleontology and early hominids. In addition, being an avid video game player, I have an idea of what is fun and what isn't, and so I can help make this interactive museum guide into something that succeeds at being both fun and informative. . . . As for the final guide's effect on visitors, I hope that it will fill in the human evolution-related gaps in science education.

Once the teens were selected, we could move them from observing visitors from a distance to engaging directly with the public. Luckily, the Museum has extensive experience with training both high school and college students to offer tours and work science carts that provide visitors with hands-on learning around the campus. And those programs were led by the incomparable Nickcoles Martinez.

Nick was a staff member who had also been a participant in the Museum's education programming when he was in college. That helped him to balance the educational needs of the Museum with the developmental needs of today's teens. His ability to combine the two created deep learning experiences for New York City youth and engaging experiences for Museum visitors from all around the world. A competitive chess player back in high school and now as an adult an active gamer, Nick always seemed in touch with youth culture, something his interns seemed to respect.

Nick not only helped us to ensure the training was in place for the *CSN* teens, but he was also watching closely, as there was a good chance, if the project succeeded, that one of his youth intern programs could take over *CSN* in a future phase.

Once the teens were trained on the new print materials (designed in-house), the app (designed by an outside firm), and the hands-on tools Julia prepared in the Lab, they were ready to fulfill the promise made by *Rotunda*: to invite visitors to become Neanderthal Detectives and solve a good science-based mystery.

Dressed in blue vests and armed with iPads, the pairs of teens took turns facilitating and taking notes. They introduced the mystery to visitors in the form of a letter from the Metropolis Central Department of Public Works. Addressed to Neanderthal Detectives Inc. from a Ms. Ima Fossel (say it out loud), the letter explained that the city recently uncovered a collection of bones when exploring a site for a new stadium. "We must discover the precise origin of these mystery items," it read. "We need you to tell us whether this can be labeled a 'Crime Scene Neanderthal.'" To do so, the letter explained, the visitor/detective must work with Museum scientists (the teen facilitators) to make predictions, gather and analyze data, draw conclusions, and then submit their final report.

The letter was contained in a printed dossier along with "evidence sheets" for each activity. The facilitators also kept close at hand physical objects they might need to pull out, like the scientifically accurate yet curiously damaged Neanderthal bone. The mobile app on their iPad offered supporting material for each station.

At the DNA exhibit, *Whose DNA is it?* challenged museum visitors to playfully re-sort genetic combinations to match the DNA found on the victim against known DNA patterns of chimpanzees, humans, and Neanderthals.

At the skeletons display (of a chimpanzee, human, and Neanderthal), *An Unknown Bone* guided visitors through an AR activity to identify the species of the victim by matching the victim's remains (four virtual bones) onto the skeletal structure within the Hall.

By the Neanderthal diorama, visitors used *Hairs to Neanderthals* to "capture" the MC1R gene, walk to the model of the giant cell nucleus, then drag their gene sequence into a virtual one to determine what genetics suggested about Neanderthal hair color and skin tone.

At the display of the flute-like object found in a known Neanderthal site, *Of Flutes and Flowers* allowed visitors to play a virtual Neanderthal flute by blowing into the iPad and fingering the flute on the touchscreen to change the notes. Afterward, in the Lab, visitors performed a virtual version of a science experiment (gel electrophoresis) combining real pipettes and colored water with the app-simulated ultraviolet light, seeking evidence suggesting the cause of death was disease.

In front of the *Predator or Prey* display, visitors compared marks on the app that might be made by different animals with marks found on the Neanderthal bone replica in their hands.

At the Neanderthal Tool case, visitors used the app to turn a rock into a replica of a Neanderthal weapon, damaged a virtual bone, then compared that damage against the Neanderthal bone replica, seeking evidence suggesting the cause of death was murder.

Finally, a bonus activity was made available at the Dating Game exhibit, providing visitors with a simulator for playing with environmental conditions to determine the requirements for turning a bone into a fossil.

Each facilitated *CSN* journey was documented afterward in one shared document on Google Drive. This documentation captured which stations were selected, how long visitors spent at each one, the number of adults and children on the team, and any facilitator observation. Some observations highlighted what was working ("Interested in scanning bones, loved the music portion"). Other observations captured where *CSN* needed improvements ("Visitor didn't understand the fossil process. Needed a better understanding of gel electrophoresis").

In addition to the raw data, the interns were also tasked with writing blog posts. Reading their posts, we could see how nervous they were the first time they had to facilitate, but also how prepared and supported they felt by the Museum staff and their peers. They appreciated the significance of what we were asking them to do. "It wasn't like performing," one teen wrote. "This was a test of me being able to convey information that people have dedicated their careers to and I wanted to do them justice." All the teens eventually worked their way past the awkwardness of those first interactions until their confidence reached the level of their skill: "At first, interacting with strangers was very awkward and we messed up a lot. However, after a few more tries, we started getting a better hang of it and halfway through the day, we split up and facilitated on our own."

We could see in their entries examples of how running public prototypes helped facilitators, for example, to better understand the unintended impact of their role: "I have noticed that most visitors don't believe that the tool marks match the ones on the bone but change their answer once they noticed I'm not telling them that they're right." And they identified the unexpected challenges one can only learn by interacting with end users: "Children defocus the microscope, they jammed the pipette, ask difficult questions and give weird answers."

They learned to understand the complex family dynamics that determined dwell time: "There is a great difference between parents who are as excited about the experience as their child and those who aren't. Parents who aren't often beg their child to . . . quit the experience. Parents who are as enthusiastic as their children make the child want to learn more and they do not care about how much time they waste during the experience."

The blog post also provided us program leads with contextual evidence for the data being collected. For example, one pair of interns said what they enjoyed the most was the last step of the experience, when the Detectives must decide who or what killed the Neanderthal. "They've only collected a small amount of evidence, and the answer isn't very clear, so the kids have to make their best guess, without 100%. It's really amazing to see kids analyze the evidence and really think."

In the end, over eight day-long sessions, the interns engaged with 238 visitors (130 adults and 108 children), composed of eighty teams of Neanderthal Detectives all recruited within the Lab. Throughout, visitors created useful data by completing the printed station sheets, recording their interpretation of the evidence they collected; more than half finished every sheet, making a final recommendation about whether the bone discovery was important enough to warrant further research (with all but one team advocating to halt commercial construction on the site to protect this new discovery).

As there were different activities for visitors to select, their decisions in aggregate became a source of data regarding which ones struck them as the most appealing. The interns mixed and matched that data in different ways, to look for patterns and suggest meaning we might draw from it.

The interns analyzed the activity data to help us all better understand the visitor experience, not just which ones they chose but how much time was spent on each one. We had expected *CSN* to last twenty to thirty minutes, with visitors selecting three of the eight available activities. We thought that would be enough time to solve the mystery, close the case, and earn whatever swag we were offering that day. We could not have imagined visitors would want to spend much more time than that. The data, however, told us a very different story.

Not only were visitors completing an average of four activities (with many completing as many as eight), visitor dwell time was ranging all the way up to one hour. One teen reflected on their surprise upon viewing this data with "people are more patient than we think." In addition, one would expect time per team to increase as their number of activities increased, and this was true, in the aggregate. But what was also true, and much more fascinating, was the range of time; whether a team did three,

Number of Activities Completed Per Day

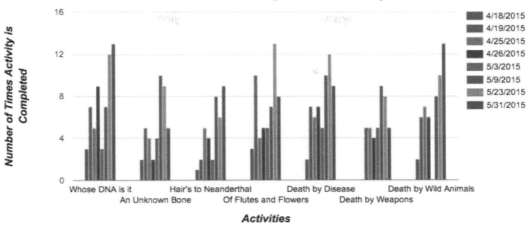

Figure 2.6. Example of data analysis from public pilots. *Author*

Dwell Time vs # of Activities

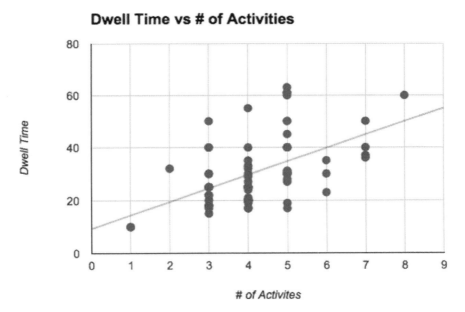

Figure 2.7. Dwell time versus number of activities. *Author*

four, or five activities, they might take anywhere from twenty minutes to three times that. It seemed *CSN* was adapting to meet the needs of each individual group.

The youth had successfully learned the Neanderthal content, trained in public facilitation, and developed skills in both iterative design and prototyping. By the end of their internship, they had successfully combined all they learned to put *CSN* to the test. It passed with flying colors. After a year of effort, we could see that visitors were accepting the *CSN* invitation, sticking through to the end, and spending more time and doing more than we had ever imagined. And through two months of prototyping, we iterated the script for the facilitators and developed a list of updates for our app developer.

As we closed out the internship, it was time for us to move from asking if *CSN* could work to asking a different question: how can we integrate a new experience into our existing infrastructure? To answer that question, we turned to two different types of internship programs: MEEP and Saltz.

Phase 3: Summer Public Prototyping and Evaluations

MEEPers are college students who participate each summer in the Museum Education and Employment Program. They develop tours around the museum based on their own interests and engage visitors at mobile touch carts loaded up with hands-on objects.

Meanwhile, the Saltz Internship Program was designed for high school students. They too worked on mobile carts equipped with artifacts, specimens, models, and more to facilitate science conversations.

Nick, who managed both programs and was also Senior Coordinator of the Lab at that time, felt he could bring *CSN* into both programs. His plan was to move the start of *CSN* out of the Sackler Lab and onto a mobile cart that could be positioned in different locations around the Hall.

Meanwhile, a graduate student intern from New York University's Digital Media Design for Learning Program, Tom Sarachan, led the evaluation, observing and interviewing both *CSN* participants along with the Saltz interns and the MEEPers.

We tasked Tom to determine three things over the course of the summer.

The first goal was to determine whether *CSN* is an experience that could work well if moved out of the Sackler Lab and onto one or more carts stationed in the Hall of Human Origins. He determined that it did indeed work, that moving the experience from the Lab to the Hall attracted a different type of visitor. While these new summer visitors (over two thousand within fourteen non-consecutive days) were spending an average of one-third the time spent by the spring *CSN* Detectives, they seemed just as satisfied. Using the framework of the academic John Falk, Tom speculated that those stopping at the cart seemed more likely to be experience seekers, curious but eager to see other things as well, while those in the Lab may have been more likely to attract explorers and hobbyists who wanted to study a specific topic in depth.

The second goal was to determine whether the learning goals we developed for the *CSN* experience were reached. We wanted visitors to increase their understanding of the topic of human evolution, appreciate how and why scientists collect data to understand the human evolutionary story, and engage in a deeper level of inquiry with a museum exhibit. Tom found that *CSN* was fairly successful on all three accounts. For example, two-thirds of visitors gave correct answers after completing the "Whose DNA Is It?" activity and over 80 percent of visitors understood by the end that Neanderthals had red hair. In the end Tom determined visitors came away with a new understanding of Neanderthals.

Finally, we asked Tom to help us assess overall user satisfaction, determine pain points, and write up a design document that could be used to create the final iteration of *CSN*, including modifications on the print materials, adding signage and a flashlight to the cart, and tech revisions and bug fixes on the mobile app.

Phase 4: The Roll-out of Crime Scene Neanderthal

After that summer, we delivered our new design document to our internal design team and external app developers. We planned to fully integrate *CSN* into our high school and college student on-the-floor visitor-facing services. We could see how visitors would soon stop at a *CSN* cart, accept an invitation to become a Neanderthal Detective, solve some mysteries, then be on their way.

That was the plan, at least. But it never happened. From the visitor perspective, *CSN* never made it past the summer.

CSN, as a visitor-facing experience, ended unexpectedly, and rapidly, for two reasons.

The first was the implosion of our app developers. We had been working with this team for a number of years at this point, located within a larger media production company. One day we learned the entire app team walked, exiting the company. I had worked in New Media for over two decades but had never seen anything like it. Overnight, we lost our app developer. The media company tried to replace the team but not in time for the second reason *CSN* came to a close.

The funds that had been set aside to complete *CSN* were re-allocated through a department-wide reorganization. That's the sort of thing that happens without warning. It can be disappointing, but part of digital design, in museums as elsewhere, is knowing when to let a product end gracefully (a lesson I continue to learn).

OUTCOMES

We did not start down the path that grew into *CSN* because at the start we felt we knew all the answers. It wasn't like we knew the final project would be themed off of the television series *CSI*, or that we would offer visitor pathways based on physical, cultural, and genetic anthropology, or even knew which exhibits we would utilize.

No, we went into this project knowing we wanted to ask questions, like: Can a youth program produce a prototype of a mobile app that can inform the Museum's overall mobile app strategy?

In the first stage, co-designing with the high school students, we were just learning how to even ask that question.

In the second stage, through the spring internship, we were exploring whether the answers we landed on were right—for the visitors.

In the third stage, through the summer prototyping and evaluation, we were exploring whether the answers we landed on were right—for the Museum.

We sometimes call aspects of a digital development process a "sprint," as if it were a race to the finish line. From that perspective, it is easy to feel like we failed to complete the final lap, that we let down Julia, and the students, and the educators, and the graphic designers, and everyone who worked so hard on the project. However, I prefer to think of it as a relay race, in which it is the job of each project to pass that baton as far as possible down the line. Each successful pass should solve problems that ease the path for all who follow. As my close colleague Hannah Jaris reflected, "Sometimes it's not always physical assets that survive but changed mindsets, best practices, new understandings and questions that keep the baton moving." The goal is not always to get to the end but to open up possibility spaces for the next round of innovation.

In the end, I can't truly say whether anything about *CSN* had any impact on the Museum's overall mobile app strategy, which was our original goal. I just don't know. But I do know this: a new question emerged over the course of the project which perhaps became more prominent: How can we use a combination of digital media and youth facilitation to enhance visitor engagement and learning? Around that, we learned a lot.

The Sackler Lab did not end up with a new *CSN* app, but it did learn new lessons about how to bring digital tools into hands-on visitor programming.

The Saltz and MEEP interns did not roll out *CSN* carts and engage visitors as Neanderthal Detectives. But they did advance their understanding of meaningful ways to incorporate digital learning onto carts and increased their capacity to offer other digital innovations that were to follow.

Finally, visitors did not get to combine a visitor guide with a mobile app to enhance their experience of the Hall of Human Origins. But the specific techniques used around this Hall, and the same iterative design process, would soon be transferred to efforts in different locations, such as the Hall of Northwest Coast Indians, through a prototype for an AR Family Guide and coloring book, and across the museum in an AR game called *MicroRangers*.

The baton had been passed.

Comparison: The Acropolis Museum (Athens, Greece) and the Cité de l'Espace (Toulouse, France)

I hate conferences. I mean, I love conferences, but I also hate them. I dislike being away so long from my family, but what really drives me batty is sitting still for an hour or more while focusing my attention on one speaker. I understand the value of the format, but for others. Not for me. It's just not how I learn. Maybe that's why during a panel I will often seek comfort in multitasking, engaged with the public backchannel on Twitter or taking copious notes. But even if the speaker is the most dynamic in the world, engaged with work that I deeply admire, I often find myself too antsy to sit still.

That is why if you saw me at a conference during my six years at the American Museum of Natural History, participating in one of the more than forty I was fortunate enough to attend, chances are good it was out in the hallway. Whether at Museums and the Web, Games for Change, the Museum Computer Network, the annual American Alliance of Museums, or Games, Learning and Society, the place to find me is often chatting up presenters and other attendees, hopefully on a comfy chair or couch.

Not that I find it easy breaking the ice with complete strangers. That's where having a blog comes in handy. When I started at AMNH, I founded my museum-focused blog in part to give me an excuse to connect with people I admired in the field. And these conferences were excellent places to find people worth emulating.

At the Museums and the Web conference in Chicago, I was fascinated by the work of Maria Roussou, an Assistant Professor at the National & Kapodistrian University of Athens. She came to the conference to present a research study exploring how museums could personalize a visitor's experience before they even arrived. I invited her to sit with me and chat about the power of user-centric design, storytelling, and personas.

Maria is an evaluator and reviewer for the European Commission on research projects but also participates as a researcher in funded projects. One of those is called The CHESS project, which stands for the rather wordy "Cultural Heritage Experiences through Socio-personal interactions and Storytelling." CHESS brought many players together from around Europe: two research universities (one computer science department, one mixed reality lab), two French tech and design development partners, a German research center with a background in augmented reality, and two museums—the Acropolis Museum in Athens, Greece, and a museum in Toulouse, France, called the *Cité de l'Espace* (the City of Space).

Maria told me how CHESS initially launched as a computer science research project. The idea was to develop a system that supported a cultural experience for visitors that was both adaptive and personalized to their needs and wants. "It tries to solve what we call the cold start problem," Maria told me, explaining how the CHESS system worked. "Cold start means that the visitor comes in and we know nothing about them. How do you actually start a personalized experience if you know nothing about this visitor." At the core of this system was the use of personas.

Personas are a design technique that began in the late 1990s in the tech industry, then slowly spread into related design practices. A persona, on one hand, is a fictional character representing a typical user. But each persona is based on real data, both qualitative and quantitative. So it might be more useful to view personas as the personification of user research, to give a face to all those numbers.

For the Acropolis Museum, for example, CHESS developed six different personas, from a ten-year-old student to a seventy-one-year-old retired teacher. The other museum, used primarily by families with young children, only required two.

Once the personas were complete, a tool was required to match them against every potential visitor, to deliver each a more personalized museum visit.

A visitor might begin at home, answering a web-based quiz so the system could understand more about this particular person, not just demographic information but also things like if they read the political column in the newspaper or if they read the comics (or both). CHESS used their responses to inform the system about the way this visitor might want information presented. At the end of the survey, which could also be completed onsite within the museum, the system generated a profile matched against the available personas. "But you don't see this persona," Maria clarified. "This persona is a tool that the design team of the CHESS project created with the museum staff. We can't personalize to each and every individual. Everybody is different, so we had to make these personas."

Each visitor could now begin their museum visit engaging with a story that the museum had already prepared for the persona that most closely matched their interests.

For example, if the system learned you are intrigued by everyday life of ancient Athens, and you are at the Acropolis Museum, there is a story about a woman who talks about what she did, how she was married, how her son was killed during the Persian Wars, how she offered a statue to Goddess Athena (who is the goddess protecting Athens), and so on. The woman is voiced by an actress, experienced on a tablet or phone, who guides you around the exhibit. While the story has a beginning, middle, and end, it still adapts to each visitor. "You have control on the interface, so you can skip or continue or choose a branch in the story," Maria told me. "The personalization system in the background records these choices and will automatically take you on certain paths that it assumes interest you more based on your previous interaction with the system." As the visitor on this journey travels the exhibit, guided by her narrator, her experience always concludes with that offering to Athena. "This woman actually existed," Maria explained. "We can see her name inscribed on the little statue on the offering, but you don't see that until the end of the story."

One of the challenges they learned early on is that if the mobile device did not actively encourage visitors to connect with the museum collections around them, their attention would remain fixed on their screens. "This was a real problem, of course, for the museum," Maria admitted with a laugh. "So what we did in subsequent iterations is we tried to include in the narrative ways of looking at the exhibits, and requiring observation before you can go on."

For example, in a story about Theseus, the visitor cannot advance the narrative until the army is strong enough to fight King Minos. To do this the visitor explores the gallery to "collect" appropriate exhibit elements. "We tried these tricks to get people to look, to observe more carefully. I can't say that it worked fully but it was significantly better than what we had done before."

Augmented reality played a role as well. For example, when I think of ancient Greece I think about white marbled structures. But in fact this marble was painted with really bright colors, in blues and reds and golds. To bring this to life for visitors they laser scanned statues to create three-dimensional models. Then an artist applied marble texture to these models and worked with conservators and the chief archaeologist to draw on them. "So when you raise your tablet in front of the sculpture," Maria described, "you can see, superimposed, the same sculpture, colorized." It was interactive as well; visitors could tap on the model to reveal details, such as the artist describing the decisions made when applying the bright colors.

CHESS was based on the premise of creating a storytelling experience rather than a didactic guided tour. This meant that the process of creating the experience would differ from the one archaeologists, who provided the founding text, were used to. "Visitors, especially those that don't usually come to the museum, find object descriptions rather boring." That is why the team decided to bring in storytellers. The writers, of course, went in the opposite direction, imagining a journalist from the future, time machines, and more. The process between academic content and creative storytelling kept swinging back and forth. "It just seemed like it never stopped," Maria explained. "And we changed a lot. We evaluated again and again. There were many iterations." One thing that emerged was the use of humor. The approach tested well with visitors, and the archeologists felt comfortable with it, allowing the writers to use humorous contemporary examples to illustrate some of the important facts of the past. "We tried to find that balance after many iterations, and had to also calm our storyteller down a bit."

As our time was coming to a close, I asked Maria what her main take-aways were from the experience. "Storytelling really works," she shared. "People are immersed in an experience. They pay attention to something that they wouldn't see before." And she insisted this was true not just for standard museum attendees but also those who would not ordinarily make such a visit.

The second take-away was how informative it could be to engage museum and creative industry professionals in a user-centric design process. "The visitor studies world has talked about different visiting styles for a long time," she explained, "but actually putting a face on visitors, through the personas, really helped the design team to speak the same language." Often everyone has somebody completely different in their mind and ends up not speaking the same language. Maria saw how personas could change all that. "Personas may look like a simple tool," she cautioned, "but as a design method it really helps everybody talk about the same user. So the interdisciplinary design team talked about Natalie or John and they knew exactly what Natalie or John represents, wants and likes."

At the time I spoke with Maria, the CHESS Project had come to a close. It was funded as a computer science research project, to advance their understanding of how technology could engage visitors to deliver a more personalized experience that spoke to the way that they learned and engaged with content. It had not actually launched as a product and was not in use in any of the museums. "At least not yet," she added. "Ideally it should have been but there were so many issues in the process and it's so difficult to create these stories because of the many iterations and the work that's involved." If it was ever to move from research to a product that could be deployed to a mass market, a company would need to come in and take it over.

Until then, Maria was traveling to places like Chicago to share lessons learned with people like me and help advance digital engagement in museums.

TIPS AND STRATEGIES

1.   User research

    Think: *What is another way we could have gathered data on the needs and interests of Museum visitors? What is another way the data that was collected could have been processed to elicit meaningful insights?*
    Do: *Think about a space to which you have access. Design a way to track how people move through that space. Track at least five people as they move through it. Study your findings, look for patterns, and suggest one design change to the space that could improve their experience.*

2. Rapid prototypes

   Think: *Running* CSN *required a wide range of materials: facilitator scripts, a new mobile app, print materials, interactions with Hall exhibits, physical objects, and scientific instruments. What are different ways to prioritize which materials should be prototyped, how they interact with each other, and what balance of resources should each receive?*
   Do: *For your next prototype, explore different ways to explore how physical objects and digital tools might interact.*

3. Public piloting

   Think: *Why do you think visitors spent less time with* CSN *in the summer than in the spring? How could the lessons learned here be reflected in the design?*
   Do: CSN *offered the pilot first through roving interns and then through a fixed station (a parked mobile cart). Design a piloting session that explores different ways to present a pilot and study how the various approaches might influence the collected data.*

4. Iterative design

   Think: *The entire experience of* CSN *was iterated over the course of its development process, but each individual "sub-mystery" had its own story development arc as well. What documentation process could have been used to capture any significant pivots or improvements to allow those individual design stories to be told?*
   Do: *Often iterative design decisions need to be made by individuals who have to rely on others to make direct connections with end users. Both evaluation instruments and the analysis of the generated data have to be strong enough to communicate that user experience back to the decision makers. Be that decision maker. Design a series of user testing to be implemented by others with a process in place solid enough to allow you to iterate the next step of your design. (Consider pairing with another decision maker and take turns implementing each other's user testing plan.)*

5. Youth collaboration

   Think: *Imagine* CSN *had not engaged youth co-designers. How might the project have suffered? How might it have been improved?*
   Do: *Find a young person already in your life. Invite them to create something with you, all in one sitting. Constrain the design process in advance, get them to agree to those constraints, then practice supporting the young person's creative journey (especially when you like your ideas better).*

6. Team up!

   Think: *Graduate student interns played a key role in this and all case studies explored in this book. Should graduate student interns be paid, and if so how much? Where is the line between tasks that expand upon their studies (providing invaluable real-world experiences) and responsibilities that hint at exploitative unpaid or low-paid labor? How can you design an intern program that does not exacerbate existing social inequities?*
   Do: *Identify local academic institutions—both public and private—whose students could benefit from working with you. If you are one of those students, explore intern opportunities and, if necessary, create your own opportunities.*

7. Comparative project

    Think: *Regarding the Six Tools for Digital Design, what does The CHESS Project have in common with CSN? How does it differ? How might any of what you noticed apply to your own design work?*

Hall of Ocean Life: 8:59 a.m.

It's just a simple square box of a room—a two-story space with an inner surrounding balcony, a sweeping staircase, and an arced elevated ceiling—but I like to think of our Hall of Ocean Life as the Museum's largest diorama.

At the start of my day, on the way to my office, I sometimes take a slight detour on my route from the staff cafeteria, turning left at the vending machines, through a pair of nondescript doors, and enter the Hall, pausing, alone, beneath the blue whale.

The room is filled with the empty calm of early morning, before the visitors lining Central Park West are permitted to enter. I can feel the space around me, the air filled with potential, like a mechanical toy, fully wound, waiting for release.

The iconic whale, once made of papier-mâché, now modernized through fiberglass with its own Twitter account, hangs overhead, framed from behind by videos projected across the ceiling of the sky from a fish's point of view—a white sun dissolving in shifting waves through an ocean's blue—as if to suggest the room beneath it swims underwater.

Perhaps that's why visitors so often sit on the floor underneath, or just lay down and look up, sensing that somehow this room is different from the others, their orientation now shifted, as the familiar diorama display with its front-on view has been rotated ninety degrees, sweeping them all up—whale and visitor alike—into this upside-down scene.

But not yet. The visitors have not arrived. The Museum is not yet open. There is no reason for the full power of the room to be on display.

It's one minute before 9:00 a.m., an hour before the doors open wide but seconds before this Hall turns to life.

From the ominously dark giant squid locked in a deathmatch with a sperm whale to the colorful Deep Sea diorama with its bioluminescent life, the Hall's displays remain unlit. The piped-in acoustical landscape of ocean waves and gulls remain silent. The wall-sized video documenting marine expeditions to coral reefs and the smaller scattered clips of magnificent ocean life are not yet in motion.

Then, all at once, it happens, automatically like a player piano: the room's bright night-time lights darken as each diorama receives its own targeted light, the videos play, and ocean sounds fill the room. The way the light and the quiet switch with the dark and the sound is like the shift in perspective when a drawing turns from a vase to a woman's face. The impact washes over me in the speed of a blink.

As Museum employees, we know what question to expect when telling others where we work. We are always asked some version of: "Do they really come alive at night?" (Thank you, *Night at the Museum*!)

So, no, the dinosaurs are still dead. But that's not the point. There is real magic to find in the Museum. And this, I want to say and can never find the words, this and now is when it happens.

3

Designing Game-based Learning

In Summary | tl;dr

Subject: This chapter focuses on using the Six Tools of Digital Design for game-based learning.

Case study: The three case studies in this chapter focus on tabletop games, mobile games, and commercial off-the-shelf games. Specifically, it looks at the creation of *Pterosaurs: The Card Game*, a mobile experience called *Playing with Dinos*, and the application of the videogame *Minecraft*. All were designed to address the question: Can games and play create the motivation and mind-set for informal science learning?

User research: We dropped the ball here, presuming we knew the needs of our users. Whoops. That means we just took the gamble and rolled the dice, hoping what we designed was what our end users needed. Were visitors looking to bring augmented reality card games home? Were families looking to play games in the dinosaur halls? Were Minecraft players looking for science-based maps to play?

Rapid prototyping: Paper prototypes were used within two of the case studies. *Pterosaurs* started with a modified deck of cards produced through the web-based engine created for the game *Phylo*; these were then iterated, over and over, until they became the final deck. Playing with Dinos used paper prototypes to get the games quickly into visitor hands and then, later, to ensure it was accessible to all during playtesting.

Public piloting: Certain qualities were identified that were needed among visitors for a successful public pilot of Playing with Dinos. We did not want to introduce a playful experience to people who were not expecting it. We needed a context in which visitors were open for, and even seeking out, something new. We discovered that the Night at the Museum Sleepovers attracted the perfect audience to pilot new games.

Iterative design: The use of Let's Play videos were iterated over the course of the three case studies. Let's Play videos were used for both *Pterosaurs: The Card Game* and two of the three *Minecraft* programs. They were used to support the youth to develop language to talk about their work to others, but eventually they were produced to teach the public how to play the final products.

Youth collaboration: Youth were co-developers across all three types of programs, but the balance of power they shared with the adults around them was different in each one. In *Pterosaurs: The Card Game* the youth took the lead on many aspects of the game design, while the adults led on the overall game design and made final decisions. In Playing with Dinos, the youth never had any say in the overall user experience—they were only focused on their individual games (which were added to the larger pool of games created by adults). But within each individual game, the youth had total control until it was passed to the Museum for copyediting and content review. Finally, the youth created nothing in the first *Minecraft*-based program (FoodCraft), had total control in the second program (Minecraft at the Museum), and shared that control in the final program Minecraft & Human Microbiome.

Teaming up: In the creation of *Pterosaurs: The Card Game*, we worked to gain buy-in with our in-house collaborators. With the Exhibitions Department, we focused on how both their science research and commissioned art would see more use through their inclusion in the game. With the team associated with the Museum's OLogy site, we focused on how the game could be a centerpiece of their support of the related exhibit. With the store, we focused on the opportunity to move Museum-related units. And with the scientists, we focused on the opportunity to help us "get it right" and spread science content of importance to them. Similar efforts went into building relationships for *Playing with Dinos*, both internal and external. For example, one internal partner was the Sleepovers program. We needed a place to prototype the games with families primed for a new experience; the Sleepovers needed new, low-cost activities to add to their programs. The external partners were graduate students from New York University's Game Center. We needed game designers who could quickly create new, solid games; the students needed an opportunity to apply their skills in an inspiring, real-world context.

Comparison: The chapter concludes by offering, for comparison, an exploration of the White House Game Jam and a mobile app developed for the National Zoological Park in Washington, DC.

CONTEXT AND GUIDING QUESTIONS

When I had earlier decided to pursue a position at the American Museum of Natural History (AMNH), I knew there was much I would need to learn, about informal science education, about teaching with collections, about place-based learning, and more. However, I had one powerhouse skill already under my belt that I was itching to explore within a museum: game-based learning.

I can still recall when it all first began, as I struggled to understand the apparent contradictions I was seeing. I had just left a Global Kids workshop in which the high school students were deeply engaged in exploring the plight of former child soldiers in Uganda. Their interest level was high and their concerns sincere. Yet I knew many would return home to plug into their gaming consoles and play military-based first-person shooters, in essence training themselves to become virtual child soldiers. I was asking, with no judgment intended, if there was something odd going on here and how we might unpack it.

In response, we created Playing For Keeps, an innovative new approach to youth media development and afterschool programming. The teens meeting after school would learn both game-design skills (iterative design, playtesting, game mechanics) and content knowledge (based on a global topic of their choosing). They would work with professional game developers to collaborate on a web-based product strong enough to compete as a free game on the open market. We wanted to see if we could use game design as a new vehicle for developing teen leadership skills on global issues and if they could enact that leadership through the medium of digital games.

Most of the students had backgrounds in the Caribbean. They brought their cultural heritage into play, interviewing family for memories or culling their own memories. Half wanted a game about access to education, the other half about health care. We decided to combine the two into one. The game we created (with generous funding through a grant from Microsoft) was called *Ayiti: The Cost of Life*. *Ayiti* (a creole word for Haiti) was built through a curriculum co-developed with a team from GameLab. Their Director of Game Design, Nicholas Fortugno, co-led both the curriculum development and the game-design process. A former teacher himself, Nick understood not only how to connect with the teens but arrived with a deep knowledge of game mechanics. So while we worked with the youth to conceive a narrative about a rural family struggling to survive in the face of abject poverty, it was obvious to Nick this would be a worker placement, turn-based game. In the end, playing *Ayiti*, while sad and illuminating, could also be fun, in the sense that losing everything can generate motivation to try again and again.

At the time, efforts to create games that address social causes or for social impact were quite the unicorn. I collaborated with a former colleague Suzanne Seggerman and new lifelong friend Benjamin Stokes to launch an effort that came to be known as Games for Change. Suzanne brought a deep network and a passion for exploring social issues through gaming. Benjamin was driven by the potential for social-impact games to energize the non-profit sector. I mostly wanted a place for my students to share their creations, like *Ayiti*, and attract funders to afterschool programs like our own. At the centerpiece was an annual festival that showcased games that were designed for more than just to entertain. Over the years, it grew to encompass games for social change, games for health, games for learning, and much more.

Still, building a space for youth to create social-impact games always felt like an uphill battle. Global Kids' Executive Director, Carole Artigiani, at the first Games for Change Festival, said that asking a principal to bring our gaming program into her school felt like "asking her to bring porn into the classroom." Nowadays, of course, youth design games everywhere—in schools, libraries, afterschool programs, and in their homes. Two decades ago, however, we had to ignore popular prejudice driven by media hits on *Grand Theft Auto* to stay focused on putting out into the world a model of what we knew was possible. We needed to get recognition within a community like Games for Change, which we did when it received the first Games for Change award. *Ayiti* became an example of a game which was as fun to play as it had impact, without feeling a need to sacrifice one for the other. An outside evaluation from the Center for Children and Technology even found that over time players increased their understanding that addressing poverty was complex and required a multipronged solution. I would like to think those high school students who collaborated on *Ayiti* helped, in some small way, to move the needle for a whole generation of youth game designers.

When I entered the world of museums, I brought all these interests with me: how game design can attract youth and develop their interests and skills; how youth co-designers can produce media for an organization; how partnerships between educators, game designers, and evaluators can produce something together they could never do on their own; and how games can educate and inspire its players.

So, yes, I was excited to see what it would mean to infuse game-based learning into AMNH. The Museum, however, was no stranger to games, whether for visitors or in youth-facing educational programming.

When I considered "gaming" as a form of public engagement, I could draw from the Museum's rich history of innovations in visitor engagement: the magic lantern (or lantern slides) that projected images on screens for crowds of educators in the late 1800s, diorama design that captured a dramatic moment to immerse visitors in a different time and place, and self-guided audio tour devices.

Gaming did not enter this list of innovations until relatively recently. In 2011, the Museum offered *Accomplice*, a scripted live-action roleplaying game. A year later the Rose Center for Earth and Space hosted an indie gaming event, its centerpiece played on the immersive screen of the Hayden Planetarium (with a non-player character voiced by Stephin Merritt of the Magnetic Fields). Later that year, the Museum's annual anthropology film event—the Mead Festival—expanded to include a culture-based games arcade, to probe "how, and if, games can illuminate and add to Mead's great legacy of how media newly engages people in understanding disparate cultures while asking the eternal question: What makes us human?"

All of these steps were impressive, and innovative. Most, however, were one-time events, or experiments, not part of an ongoing set of public offerings. When I entered the Museum, a visitor was most likely to encounter a game in the context of a temporary special exhibit, such as the Microsoft Kinect-based *Fly Like a Pterosaur* activity; eventually exhibits like this would close, go on the road, and the game would become just a memory. The most robust and ongoing gaming experiences lived within the Museum's website for children, OLogy, offering bite-sized game experiences most often used within a classroom to teach science.

Moving from gaming for visitors to gaming for youth learners, I looked to the application of games within youth-facing afterschool programming where they are just one of many pedagogical tools to be used in a classroom. A number of Museum courses brought in commercial games, like *Skyrim*, for the construction of virtual dioramas about the disappearance of Neanderthals. Other programs created their own tool, like in the Virtual Worlds Camps, in which youth researched cretaceous marine life, then built their own creatures in a predator/prey relationship. Worthy experiments, all, which could inform an ongoing digital learning strategy.

The year before I was hired, I had seen Ruth Cohen, the Senior Director of the Museum's Center for Lifelong Learning, present on a panel at Games for Change, entitled "Games and Cultural Spaces." She said the goals for something like gaming at the Museum were three-fold:

- Learning made personal
- Extension of experience onsite and online
- Access for all learners, lifelong learning

Ruth said their objective was to "tie the content that comes out of the exploration of exhibition topics to educational experiences for youth that will deepen their involvement with and understanding of the subject matter, have that happen online beyond the exhibition, and experiment within exhibitions to reach learners of all ages." I left the session thinking, Sign me up for that!

My arrival at the Museum felt like the perfect time to explore the next step in the impact of gaming, both for visitors and within the educational program, not just to have more games, but to explore the myriad ways games could enhance the museum experience, open up possibility spaces, and learn what might emerge.

We distilled this effort down into one guiding question: *Can games and play create the motivation and mind-set for informal science learning?*

WE PWN SCIENCE GAMES!

To get started, I interviewed people I admired for my blog, deep thinkers from a range of fields, to hear their perspective and get their advice on games and play in the context of museums.

In the world of academia, when it comes to games and learning, James Paul Gee is a legend. His 2003 book *What Video Games Have to Teach Us About Learning and Literacy* set the stage for a whole generation of ludology (the academic study of games).

"I have always been taken by the fact that, at art museums, what you do is you walk up to the picture so you can read the little caption, then you walk back so that you can look at the picture," he explained to me at the start of our interview. "That gives you a hell of a lot of exercise, but it's pretty stupid."

As a linguist, Jim views museums as a very textual experience. And the problem is we have always misunderstood textuality. "Language in text is given meaning through the experiences that you've had in life, right?" In other words, if you have not had the experience, you lack the context to understand its meaning. "Just like with a videogame, you understand its manual because you played its game." So when visitors enter a museum without the experience needed to draw meaning from it, additional text from within that domain, such as a sign by a curator next to a piece of art, will just make that visitor feel stupid and push them further from the experience. "This has always been to me one of the big problems with museums."

"The digital revolution brings us the capacity to move beyond this textuality," he argued. A game, for example, can provide someone with multiple perspectives, not just an official authoritative one. It can give them opportunities to deepen their understanding of the objects they're seeing, including the words associated with the objects and texts, and create experiences they can draw from once they encounter it in person.

Museums, according to Jim, are not just required to prepare people to be able to make sense of them. They are also obligated to design experiences within the museum which are future-oriented. "That is, they can take them out in the world and think in new ways and use them. Because that's what human experience is about," Jim explained. "So, then the question is for me: What sorts of experiences are you giving people?"

That is why, when reporters ask Jim if this experience or that experience in a museum is a good game, he tells them they are asking the wrong question. "You want to ask: Is it good interactivity?" In other words, "Is it a good interaction with objects in the world and words, such that I feel I'm a participant in this and I'm gaining something that I can be future-oriented with for my own development. It is the interactivity that is crucial."

Jim gave me a lot to think about. I took away two key points: the value of games lies in their ability to prepare visitors in advance to make meaning from their museum visit and to convey experiences that help them later to make sense of their lives.

I turned from the ivory tower to the world of commercial games, speaking with Jeffrey Yohalem. Seeking solace in games as an escape from his schoolyard's homophobic bullies, Jeffrey would later find his voice as lead writer for videogames. He won the Writers Guild Award for his work on Ubisoft Montreal's critically acclaimed *Assassin's Creed Brotherhood* (selling over seven million copies in its first year) and would go on to be nominated in the category for a history-setting five more times.

Jeffrey explained to me how games can embed good learning pedagogy. "A well-designed game teaches a different skill with each mission and then combines the skills as kind of a test of what you've learned," he told me. "Ideas should never repeat, but always evolve." Learning how to play the game is itself a type of learning, and one that can be transferred to other domains. "Adventure games taught me to never give up," he shared as an example. "If you face a locked door, there's always a window to climb through or a key to find that will get you in."

High-end commercial games offer rich, immersive worlds for players to explore. So how could we at museums compete?

"Focus on strong, personalized teaching," he replied. "Lead us through the experience in a linear, focused way." Since the modern world is bombarding us with noise, he explained, if we want to teach, we have to create a space in which we can focus on key messages. "Surprise us with those messages. Look at the general knowledge of the mainstream world at that moment and teach us something we don't know."

To create that personalized experience, he encouraged me to leverage technology: smartphones, tablets, augmented reality devices. "Create an overlay on top of the exhibit experience, allowing us to display or hide key facts about what we're seeing." We should create a space which feels good to the senses, that is mysterious or exciting.

"Tech should feel like a luxury that personalizes our experience," he concluded, "not a distraction or something that requires work to understand," as that would just add to the noise around us.

I found Jeffrey's advice encouraging, and a good reminder about digital media in general: it should seamlessly integrate into the user experience.

Finally, I spoke with someone often called the Shaman of Play: Bernie De Koven. Bernie changed my life before I even knew he existed. I grew up adoring giant earth balls, and parachute games, and other awesome activities at camp and in gym class whose design was drawn heavily from the 1970's New Games Movement. Bernie was a leader within New Games. A generation of young gaming academics in the 1990s rediscovered his early writing and spread the lessons he had imparted in books like his 1978 *The Well-Played Game*.

Bernie inspires people to approach the world playfully. But that doesn't mean he thinks there should be game layers on top of everything. "I have felt for a long time that the game is within," he explained. "The play is within the thing that we are addressing, not outside." Look at whatever you are doing from the sense of play and wonder, he directed me, and you will see that fun is the core of that experience. "And if you try to make it more fun by dressing it up or making it look sillier, painting clowns on it or whatever, you miss the point."

Instead, he wants to see people lead from the joy they already feel. "Let that inspire others," he said. "Let that joy that you have discovered in whatever it is that you are trying to teach—about bones or chickens or dinosaur eggs or whatever, you know?" Why do people become paleontologists? he asked, rhetorically. "Because of the puzzle of it, and the reasoning that goes on. It's just so much fun for them. As an educator, it's not like you are trying to make paleontology fun, it's that you are trying to bring the fun to the surface so it's more perceptible."

When Bernie thinks about where museums get it right, his thoughts turn to the places in children's museums where kids can just play. "And they can play for hours, and perhaps only learn one little tiny thing," he told me, "and they are perfectly content."

"As a museum, you'd want to be able to follow the impulses of the player," he concluded. "You want it to be guided by not the information as much as by the desire to play, by the fun that's inherent in it."

Bernie left me with a powerful lesson to mull over: if I want visitors or students to learn about something, I should present them with an opportunity to discover how much joy it might bring.

So how to turn all of this good advice into concrete action? There are so many different things one might do with games, play, and game-based learning. What was the right space to carve out for the Museum? Which would build on our strengths while advancing the role we aimed to play in society?

To focus our thinking, we created an infographic designed to publicly declare our intentions to lead in this area, setting expectations for the impact we aimed to achieve. Next to an image of a gaming console mashed up with an active chemistry set, the graphic boldly declared at the top: The Gaming of Science: A Manifesto.

Figure 3.1. Header from the gaming manifesto. *American Museum of Natural History*

Beneath that the infographic split into two columns. On the left we had "The State of Science Education," which shared statistics mapping the scary delta between the acceptance of natural selection within the scientific community and the general public's unwillingness to embrace Darwin's theories. That section led down to "Educators Get Games," sharing facts demonstrating how educators are responding to gaps like this through using games. For example, it reported that 95 percent of teachers use digital games that were designed specifically for educational use.

Meanwhile, the right-hand column showed, in parallel, "The State of Video Games," sharing the now old news that everyone is playing videogames, including the statistic that 71 percent of parents believe game play can be educational. This box led to "Games Get Educated," the intentional inverse of "Educators Get Games," to suggest how the two are approaching a state of convergence, highlighting which disciplines studies had shown could be learned from videogames.

Continuing down, the convergence was achieved through one column across the width of the manifesto: "At The AMNH, We Get Science." This section gave space for our science credentials to shine, with statistics listed under the headers: We Do Science, We Spread Science, and We Teach Science.

The next section made the case that science learning could be supported through games, through the development of science skills and conceptual understanding, through introducing players into scientific discourse and creating a personal identification with science, and through generating a motivation to learn.

That was followed by Games Get Youth, which highlighted the three ways we understand youth intersect with games: they played games (97 percent of all teens), they designed games (more than a half million at that point in Scratch), and they lived games (YouTube videos, fan fiction, and more).

With all of that as the buildup, it was now time to declare what we at the Museum were going to do about all this. "To advance science understanding" it began, then listed:

- We teach games and talk games.
- We play games and design games.
- We research games and critique games.
- We game science.

We then ended with a perhaps too cute but still sincere rallying cry, deploying the gamer phrase for declaring total victory: "WE PWN SCIENCE GAMES!"

And if that wasn't clear, we visually concluded with a formula to sum it all up and suggest it was a mathematical certainty: the AMNH logo plus a picture of a microscope plus a Nintendo game controller equaled "21st-Century Learning."

We iterated its design, honing its message tighter and tighter, but it never got beyond the draft phase. It would remain an internal document. And no, it was certainly not a mathematical certainty. If we wanted to be a leader in asking if and how games and play could create the motivation and mindset for informal science learning, we would have to build our reputation one project at a time.

The infographic, however, suggested the project areas we would need to address: teaching not just with but about games, talking publicly about their potential, playing games with learning outcomes and teaching youth to design their own, researching games as a subject of scientific study and critiquing science-based games, and exploring how citizen-scientist projects gamified the scientific process.

Over the next few years, we would take on each of these areas. In the following, we will dive deeper specifically into where those gaming efforts intersected with digital engagement and how they were developed through the Six Tools for Digital Design, focusing, in order, on tabletop games, mobile games, and commercial off-the-shelf games.

TABLETOP GAMES: PTEROSAURS: THE CARD GAME

At first, card games were the furthest thing from my mind. My son had yet to get into the collectible card game *Pokémon*; I had yet to get into the deck-building card game *Ascension*. Cards to me only meant Poker, Solitaire, or War—nothing that might have any bearing on the Museum, science learning, or digital engagement. Or so I thought.

I caught my first glimpse of a new world through our Digital Playground. At first, three colleagues and I met once a week to explore one new digital tool and explore its educational applications. Over time, it became a museum-wide seasonal event that might attract up to one hundred staff from around the campus, over a few slices of pizza, as their colleagues demonstrated something of interest. A new science visualization tool for space shows. A database being explored by the research library. An augmented reality Mars rover. A programmable ball. Anyone was welcome to spend two minutes presenting their tool of interest, but the bulk of the time was focused on the hands-on explorations and one-on-one chatting that followed, at each of a half dozen or so stations.

Bone Wars is not digital, so I don't know how it snuck its way onto the agenda, but this game of "Ruthless Paleontology" was a quick hit. The game is based on the truth-is-stranger-than-fiction early history of paleontology. You start by selecting a colorful public figure from the era (many associated with AMNH) and fighting against your paleo-opponents as you collect bones in the field, build dinosaurs for museum exhibits, and finally, during the controversy phase, destroy your rival's prestige while building your own.

This game is playfully mean. This is no live-and-let-live Euro-style *Settlers of Catan*. This is a pure American PREPARE TO BE DEFEATED fun-fest. "Oh, you thought that skull belonged to a Camarasaurus? Ha!" Perfect for parties. Lots of laughter.

A fun game, yes, but did it have value in the classroom? The core mechanic of the game—matching physical characteristics of the acquired fossils against real dinosaur descriptions—is strongly aligned with the paleontological practice of comparative anatomy. I might read on one card that a *T. rex* had hollow bones; do I have any heads in my hand with hollow bones? *Bone Wars* requires the players to pay close attention to both the content and practices of concern to the real scientists. A perfect match.

One passionate science educator, Nathan Bellomy, who had a minor in the subject, said that just to play it teaches you the history of paleontology. He saw it offering a nuanced take on the process of science. What could have simply become a simple game of matching anatomical characteristics used excellent game design to offer a much deeper, complex, and engaging experience.

It was time to take this commercial game and put it to the educational test. A few months later we recalled the game when developing the curriculum for Capturing Dinosaurs, a program in which youth would use three-dimensional scanning and printing technology to reproduce their own dinosaur models based on specimens from the research collection. We decided to use *Bone Wars* to introduce the history of the field *and* to introduce the practice of comparative fossil anatomy. And it worked. The youth loved the game (so much so that much of their free time during lunches was spent playing yet another round). We also learned that the post-game processing and framing of the game was crucial to move the youth from the sensational aspects of the history toward the ethical lessons learned as the field matured *and* the comparative fossil anatomy components.

One way we encouraged this deeper understanding was through a digital badging system which offered a badge associated with the game that required a reflective post. The following is one example from a successful submission which demonstrates how playing the game in a social context and then personally reflecting on it allowed at least this learner to make the connections we were after:

> The bone wars benefited the field of Paleontology, since it established ethics of the field from the early stage (This probably is the most important thing in science). It is important that correction of studies should be taken as an effort to advance in science, instead of a personal attack.

What I saw within Capturing Dinosaurs was that playing card games had clear educational outcomes—transferring content knowledge and offering an introduction to a set of skills—but there is another area of impact I wanted to understand as well. I wanted to figure out how to follow the lesson from Bernie De Koven: How was a card game helping its players discover the joy within comparative fossil anatomy?

I began to see how, yes, of course they were playing a game but, at a broader level, playing the game introduced a sense of play into their informal science learning experience. The game created what is often referred to as a "magic circle." Based on a concept first proposed by Johan Huizinga, Katie Salen and Eric Zimmerman expand on the idea in their seminal book *Rules of Play: Game Design Fundamentals*. In it they make the case that "to play a game means entering into a magic circle, or perhaps creating one as a game begins" and that "the term magic circle is appropriate because there is in fact something genuinely magical that happens when a game begins."[1]

What I wish I could describe here is that magic. The play allows youth to step out of their "student" or "learner" roles and be more creative in their interaction with the content and each other. They take on roles and engage in behaviors that are not necessarily aligned with their time outside the game (I recall one youth, who liked to make "stupid" jokes and then get teased for it, relishing his ability to "tease" back through his aggressive gameplay). Players can be competitive, in a safe and agreed upon way, that lets them show different sides of their personalities and bond through the interactions. It can also raise the emotional stake of their experience—one youth grew upset when stuck with a bad hand; he didn't care so much that he lost but that the game never gave him a chance to win.

The point I took away was not so much just to play more games in our programs. I thought, rather, the point was to figure out the complicated process of creating magic circles within our programs to encourage what a sense of play can engender among youth learners, in their relationship with the content, the instructors, our Museum, and each other.

And then I came across *Phylo*, and that was (pardon the pun) a game changer. I was asked to travel an hour or so north along the Hudson River to lead forty youth in a different type of game within the gorgeous Black Rock Forest. There I met youth who were staying all week as part of an intensive introduction to their year as part of a program in which they do research alongside Museum scientists. After spending the morning laying traps for turtles (in order to tag them, take blood samples and measurements, and add the data to an ongoing research study), I was tasked with giving them something fun and educational to do.

With the assistance of my son, we introduced them to the card game *Phylo*. *Phylo* challenges players to build food chains, pay attention to climates and terrains, and avoid ecological pitfalls. My son and I played a demo game, to model how it worked, and then gave each of the groups their own copies. The youth were exhausted after a day of hiking, but you would never have known it from watching them play.

While playing, one girl yelled, "It's *Pokémon*!" And, in fact, that is part of *Phylo*'s origin story. Its website opens with the story about how this project began in reaction to "the following nugget of information: *Kids know more about Pokémon creatures than they do about real creatures*. We think there's something wrong with that."[2]

"We" is in fact David Ng. This is where I get to the most intriguing thing about *Phylo*, which is not the game itself but who made it, and how, and the opportunities it opened for us to make our own.

David Ng has a doctorate in immunology and supervises the Advanced Molecular Biology Laboratory at the University of British Columbia, providing science learning experiences for both the general public and scientific communities. In 2010 he initiated a game development process to develop a *Pokémon*-style science game, *Phylo*, that can be modified by science museums and other institutions to address their own content. Developed through an innovative, online, crowdsourced initiative, he brought together game designers, artists, programmers, and scientific institutions to create not just a game but a game development platform. This platform allows players to customize their own decks, building it from any cards within the system or designing their own cards. The website provided all the instructions one might need to modify the game rules, create the copy and image assets for each card, and upload them into the system so they can be downloaded and played by others.

I reached out to David to learn more about how he used crowdsourcing to create and sustain this project. He explained to me that crowdsourcing, technically, is a term that describes a kind of out-sourcing of tasks, where informal, undefined groups of people participate, and usually with incentives that are outside of traditional means (e.g., payment, accreditation). "In other words," David said, "it's a way to galvanize a community towards a project that they simply believe in, and in doing so, you hope the community is large enough that many small acts of contribution can lead to a greater whole."

For *Phylo*, crowdsourcing was utilized primarily for pragmatic reasons. "To create an amazing biodiversity trading card culture under conventional conditions would simply be an intensive, all-consuming, cost-prohibitive, and frankly unrealistic endeavour for a small lab." He knew it would re-quire expertise from many different areas, including biodiversity science, visual art, gaming, website design, computer programming, and education. In the end, crowdsourcing was a low-stakes way of "having a go."

At the same time, David put funds aside to push the project in desired directions. One was in-centivizing natural history museums to make their own decks that could be sold in their gift shops. He thought of these funds as art commissions. "My lab decided to step in, and see if we can offer grants to pilot this possibility," he told me. "The intent here is to see how this might work with less risk to the participant given that my lab will front the funding." As a small lab, a five thousand dollar commission was realistic, generating data on the relative merits or dangers of such an investment. "The end effect is to assess whether future hosts might feel confident that their own investment is worth it."

Then came something I was not seeking, nor expecting, but was delighted to hear. David asked: "Can we commission the American Museum of Natural History to make a deck?"

Two months later I replied to David's offer and told him we were excited to accept. We already had plans in the works for a new gaming program. Producing an AMNH-themed *Phylo* deck would be a perfect project for the teens to take on.

This new youth program was called #scienceFTW! In the world of online gaming, FTW is short for "for the win." Adding a hashtag at the front, and the exclamation at the end—well, perhaps I was just trying too hard. Based on our experience bringing science-based tabletop games into our youth pro-gramming, we decided to build a new program around the idea with two twists: (1) the youth would be playing with scientists with expertise in the content behind each game and (2) the youth would collaborate with a professional game designer to design a new game in the *Phylo* system that would also be sold in the gift shop for an upcoming exhibit on pterosaurs.

The program launched. It was led by Julia Zichello (who also managed the Sackler Lab), with sup-port from J. Shepard Ramsay, an intern from New York University with a passion for game design. We drew in scientists from across the disciplines to play games and speak with the teens. For example, one guest scientist was Alex de Voogt. Alex was a researcher and assistant curator of African Ethnology. He researched, among other things, the dispersal of board games as cultural artifacts. Alex called on us all to join him in a circle sitting on the floor. He then proceeded to pull out one deck of cards after another—from Spain, from France, from Japan—each time challenging us to notice what stayed the same, what changed, and why. He was demonstrating how by studying the cards you could learn about what they might suggest about cultural diffusion. Then he taught us how to play the Japanese game *Koi Koi* on a deck of Hawaiian hanafuda cards. One student commented, at the end of that session, what she had learned: "It doesn't matter what you put on a card as long as it has purpose."

After weeks of bringing in scientists to play commercial tabletop games about paleontology, virology, astrophysics, and more, we felt the youth were ready to co-design a new game using *Phylo*. Rounding out our team of educators was an external professional game designer, Nick Fortugno, for-merly of GameLab, now founder and chief commercial officer of Playmatics. Nick, who often arrived via skateboard, co-developed the curriculum with Julia, and, with Shepard, taught the game design components.

Nick taught the teens how to identify and critique play mechanics within a game, and how to think critically about how games can incorporate science topics and practices. Eventually, Nick felt the teens were ready to use all they learned and apply it toward a card game about pterosaurs.

Each year the Museum creates one or two new special exhibits. Years of work go into each one, they open for a period of months to give visitors an excuse to return to the Museum, then they are sold, like a product, to other museums, and travel the world, some for as long as a decade. Given the lead role played by Museum paleontologists advancing world knowledge about the earliest verte-brates known to have evolved powered flight, the time seemed promising for the Museum to launch an exhibit dedicated to recent findings about these Mesozoic-era reptiles.

Two of the higher priced items when developing a science-based card game are the original art assets and the resources to ensure it is scientifically accurate. Luckily, special exhibits are designed by the Museum's Exhibitions Department. They are already pouring tremendous resources into creating new, striking, scientifically accurate, and up-to-date assets for the exhibit. I hoped they might see their use in the card game as getting extra value out of their investment while contributing to something that might be sold in the exhibit store.

I met with Martin Schwabacher, the exhibition writer, and together we played a round of *Phylo*. I explained how we would develop it within an education program and that we had a professional game designer adapting the game mechanic to fit our unique Mesozoic edition. To my delight, he was intrigued, and found the idea to be viable. They had commissioned almost three dozen pterosaur illustrations, whose rights they could contribute for free. Martin recommended some modifications to the *Phylo* game mechanic to make it fit the known science around pterosaurs. Each *Phylo* card includes a climate, and only those sharing climate could be linked in a food chain; Martin sharply observed that we could replace that feature with one based on eras of the Mesozoic, so a creature living in the Jurassic could not consume a creature that lived only during the Cretaceous.

Informing his team of this opportunity, he identified our next step. "The biggest challenge would be to flesh out the deck with organisms lower on the food chain, such as plankton, krill, shellfish, fish, various fish and plant species, as well as selected dinosaurs, plesiosaurs, ichthyosaurs, and of course a diverse selection of pterosaurs, which would be our stars. Fleshing out this list would require research into what each species of pterosaur ate (and what ate them), and research into finding inexpensive illustrations of the selected species." Who could guide us in such research? Martin recommended we reach out to John Maisey.

Special exhibits are not only designed by the Museum's Exhibitions Department, but through extremely close collaboration with Museum curators and scientists. Working on a game associated with an exhibit meant that we were always just a few doors down from a world expert on the subject. And when I say a "few doors" what I really mean is an elevator, past at least one cluster of visitors blocking passage through a Hall, some stairwells, more hallways for sure, and finally on the other side of a secret (to the public at least) doorway that, when opened like Dorothy leaving her home for the first time to step into Oz, revealed a magical world of science.

One of the scientists on the Pterosaurs exhibit was John Maisey. John was officially a curator of fossil fish, in the Division of Paleontology. He had edited an entire book on Santana fossils, which would inform the exhibit, complete with gorgeous plates and information on insects, plants, fish, and pterosaurs from Brazil. As with Martin, John was happy to consult on the project. He would provide us with both art assets we could use or connect us with someone who could. Throughout he would also assist to make sure the science in the game was not incorrect. For example, he recommended we not include a particular ray-finned fish called a Lepidotes which, as he explained, were "not likely to have been eaten by pterosaurs unless they had can openers!"

With the team fully recruited, it was time to work with the youth to create a pterosaur-based *Phylo* deck. We transitioned to the topic by taking the teens to the fourth floor halls that contain pterosaurs, with replicas flying overhead and fossils behind glass. They took notes, drew cladograms mapping the evolution of pterosaur traits, and sketched the fossils.

After their research, the youth were shown a list of pterosaurs that were to be featured in the upcoming special exhibit. Not all would fit into the card game, so there were impassioned discussions about which to include (much love was shown, for example, to the massive Quetzalcoatlus).

To prepare for the first playtesting session, all of the cards were produced in *Phylo*. That is, while we were building a game to be digitally distributed through the *Phylo* system, we were also leveraging it as a development space to create our prototype decks. At first it was like making a themed version of *Monopoly*. We were not looking to design new rules, just "reskin" the game around our content and see where it might break. And with the new Mesozoic content added in, we had definitely broken it. "The students thought that we had engineered it like that," Shepard, the graduate school intern, later told me. "I found this hilarious, because it's the process that all games go through."

At the end of our first playtesting session, the board was filled with different problems with our game and suggestions for how they could be fixed. Some cards were hard to play. Some had too many rules. And some generated new thematic ideas—like a meteorite event that knocks out an opponent's entire food chain.

To get to this point, all of the youth played the game—over and over and over—taking notes along the way, working on different teams. One team mapped out the game numerically, as a system, to identify its flaws. *Phylo* is based on building food chains, but not all chains are equal. Chains are built on matching features whose availability is not equally distributed throughout the deck. So the likelihood of being able to play any particular pterosaur card (at the top of a chain) might differ from one pterosaur card to another. So the point value of that pterosaur card should reflect how hard or easy it is—statistically—to build its required food chain. The more options, the easier it is to play, and cards that are easier to play should be worth less. Two teens mapped out the entire game to determine the final point value of each pterosaur card, building this chart by laying out the cards and exploring all possible options.

Figure 3.2. Mapping out the entire game. *Author*

As a result of this process, we were able to determine the point values, identify broken or challenging cards, and ensure the final pterosaurs' point values were properly balanced.

Another group focused on the event cards, determining that there should be less restrictions determining when they could be played, that they should be played lower on the food chain, and suggested a wide range of brilliant new ideas. My personal favorite was "migration" which causes a pterosaur to fly in the reverse direction. Since the direction a card faced indicated its owner, this event card allowed a player to steal a card from an opponent in a perfect marriage between content and game mechanic.

A third group focused on the colors of the different cards and reviewed the official copy for the upcoming AMNH pterosaur show to find interesting facts—"flavor text"—to insert into the cards.

All of their feedback was processed by the team, entered into *Phylo*, then printed out for the next round of testing. The teens could see how their feedback and contributions directly changed the play and design of the game, and led to the next round of playtesting. Their excitement and sense of ownership was palpable. "That is stuff I actually typed," one teen explained. "That is, like, unreal!"

After many rounds testing and iterating the design, and playtesting it with scientists visiting the course, everyone gave their sign-off. The students liked it. Julia, the scientist-educator, gave her approval. Nick, our game designer, thought it was ready to go.

While the cards were being copyedited and graphically designed within the publications section of the Education Department, I worked with the Museum's stores, of which there are six onsite plus one more online. With the funds secured by David Ng, and agreement by the stores to sell and promote them, we now also needed what we called a "fancy" design. That meant we needed a printing solution that could produce a limited number of decks (which we found in China) and a design for the box itself.

The team doing all of this graphic design is the same team responsible for the Museum's website for kids, OLogy. We worked with their team to create a digitally distributed print-and-play version of the game, allowing any child or educator to print the cards for free. Along with the cards, this mini-site offered small quizzes about pterosaurs and a video featuring two teens teaching the game by playing it with narration.

It felt like such a privilege to have access to so much rich content being developed by the Exhibitions Department for the upcoming show. The original pterosaur art was gorgeous. The scientific insights were compelling. The hardest part was having to turn down some amazing opportunities. For example, animations were created to show how pterosaurs moved to be shown on screens in the exhibit: how they walked, took off, flew, and landed. I had never seen anything like this, and I was not alone. But, alas, cards are static, right? So on that I needed to pass.

During this time, I traveled out of state to go to a museum conference. After a few days it was time to head to the airport to fly back with my supervisor, but I still had a few minutes I could use for a quick dash through the expo hall. I saw a colleague from the Museum running our exhibitions booth and she insisted I not leave before meeting an old friend. I insisted I had to dash or miss my plane, but there he was, Jeremy Kenisky. I was polite and accepted his card. I received many cards during my time at the Museum, but none were as consequential as that one. I still own and treasure it to this day.

On one side, to be expected, was his name, title, and the logo of his company. He asked me to turn it over. It featured a colorfully stylized image of a beetle. Jeremy handed me his phone, the augmented reality app already loaded, and told me to look at the card in my hand through his camera.

I was familiar with QR codes making animated three-dimensional models appear, but this was a new idea for me. Through the camera I saw my hand and the card it was holding. On the card was not a clunky QR code but an attractive piece of art, that stylized beetle. I was delighted when I first saw that two-dimensional beetle disappear to be replaced with a photorealistic one, appearing to stand on the card, in my hand. But that was just the set-up.

Designing Game-based Learning

The moment that insect crawled off the card and up my arm I was no longer thinking about the wonders of augmented reality. I just wanted to get that insect off of me!

I had never before experienced a piece of augmented reality so seamlessly integrated into an embodied experience. It was just a few moments long, but it was elegant. And made an impact.

I needed to test it on another. In the taxi on the way to the airport I showed my supervisor, Preeti, and watched her flinch as I had. Waiting online to check in for my flight I called Jeremy. By the time we boarded the plane, he was hired. He was going to take *Pterosaurs: The Card Game* to a whole new level. This was our first project with Geomedia, the multimedia design company we would later work with for both *Crime Scene Neanderthal* and *MicroRangers*.

We sent Jeremy the finished designs of select pterosaur cards and his team augmented them with the amazing animations I had earlier turned down. When a player held the card in their hand, when viewed through the app, the pterosaur took flight. It had no effect on the game play. Nothing changed on the cards or how they were used. But it added a promotional feature we could add to the box: "Download the free *Pterosaurs: The Card Game* app from the App Store and watch 6 of the pterosaurs come to life." It also gave me a low-cost way to explore how to leverage the Museum's assets for augmented reality, something that would soon pay off in other projects.

The Museum really got behind the game. A press release was issued just about the game: "AMERICAN MUSEUM OF NATURAL HISTORY DEVELOPS PTEROSAURS: THE CARD GAME TO ACCOMPANY SPRING EXHIBITION." It opened with a playful approach to spreading the good word: "Pikachu, make way for *Pterodactylus antiquus*. The American Museum of Natural History is putting all its cards on the table introducing a new trading card game in conjunction with its exhibition *Pterosaurs: Flight in the Age of Dinosaurs*, which opens on Saturday, April 5." The teen developers were invited to play the game with reporters at the press preview for the exhibit, and staff from Global Business Development (which licensed exhibits to other museums) interviewed the teens.

The pop-up pterosaur store was enthusiastic about the exhibit-related product. They created a prominent display so those exiting the exhibit could not miss this new type of opportunity for taking a piece of the exhibit home.

Finally, the Exhibitions Department went all in. Beautiful, round stickers, about a foot in diameter, were produced to promote the cards. Inviting visitors to "Keep flying!" they were posted all around the exhibit. In fact, the first one was on the entrance to the exhibit, in clear view as visitors queued to pass over their ticket, making the card game the first thing experienced upon entering.

Figure 3.3. The sign greeting visitors to the exhibit. *American Museum of Natural History*

While producing a variety of pterosaur-related videos displayed throughout the Hall, the Exhibitions Department also created what was essentially an interstitial advertisement for the card game and its augmented reality component, perfectly priming visitors for their upcoming encounter within the store. "For more fun, purchase *Pterosaurs: The Card Game*. Or download them for free."

With the youth program concluded, the exhibit launched, the game in the store, the app available for devices, the print-and-play version on the OLogy site ready for free download, the game was in good hands.

All I had to do was make sure the store had enough units to keep the game in stock.

With the successful launch of *Pterosaurs* behind us, it left me with a scratch to itch: what else might we do on a mobile device?

Mobile Games

The doors open and my family scrambles in. We find four seats together, in the middle of the subway car. We squeeze in and prepare for the slow, weekend service into Manhattan.

"Take out your phone," my daughter insists. "Let's play a game."

I know what kind she wants to play, and my wife and son agree. I open the app.

"What mood are you in?" it asks in text with bright colors, providing options. We select "Observant."

It next asks, "Where are you?" and I select "Traveling."

Four options appear, seeking more information: Car, Plane, Train/Bus, and Walking.

I make my selection and it asks, "How many people are playing?" I select four.

Good. Now we're ready to go. The app now knows our mood, location, and party size. It can serve us a game.

We reject the first one offered with a "Naw," and I hit "Show me another game."

"OK. How about this?" the friendly text reads, like a waiter seeking the perfect dish for our table. Then it asks, "Will your journey pass through a tunnel at some point?" For sure, between every station. I click "Yes."

"Ok!"

The name of the game appears, *Time Tunnel*, along with a description: "An underground numbers game for 2 or more players." Everyone is nodding, so I tap "Play this game."

First, the introduction. "Dark and terrible secrets lurk within our Earth, things that should not be seen. But how long will you be in the dark? Have a guess!" I tap the next arrow.

"When you enter a tunnel, guess how long you'll be in there. Say your number, in seconds, and begin counting down . . . who will be closest?" I tap next and over the next few screens the simple rules are explained, culminating in: "When you re-emerge, whoever is closest to zero but still counting wins."

We put down the phone and play. Every station is another round. As we enter each tunnel, we are each deeply engaged in our counting. The tunnels are longer than I expect, and I am often out early, but we're laughing and having a good time together.

Ten minutes later, someone asks for a new game. I take the phone back out and it offers "Play Again" and "Play Another." I tap for another game, and it asks, "Is there a route map somewhere nearby, with stops or stations marked on it?" And we're off and running on our next Tiny Game adventure.

I learned about Tiny Games from a Kickstarter campaign. Promised to be a "smartphone app bursting with HUNDREDS of games designed to fit right into your life no matter where it takes you," this British project surpassed their goal with pledges of £30,787. "Answer a couple of questions and the app will pick a game just for your situation, company, mood, and nearby props," it promised its supporters. "It will smoothly take you through the rules and then you'll be off and running, maybe literally!"

The campaign was launched by Hide&Seek, a British game-design firm dedicated to designing "new kinds of play." The games in the app were designed by a wide range of interesting game designers, many of whose work I knew and admired from the academic and indie game spaces, including Bernie De Koven. Apparently, what was once old was new again; I could see Bernie's inspiration all over this.

When the app arrived, I loved it right away, for many reasons.

First, it solved the screen problem. For many, bringing a digital screen into a social interaction turns a device into a divider. With Tiny Games, the screen acts as a facilitator, bringing people together and then, once its job is done, it gets out of your way. This intrigued me as a model for bringing screens into family engagement.

Second, the playful narration and user experience was key. The content of the app is just a collection of meta-tagged game instructions. In fact, Hide&Seek actually published book versions of the games. The games in print still work, but the reading experience falls flat, especially when compared with the punchy, irreverent, encouraging tone of the app. While the book is a great resource, the app makes you want to play. And if we wanted to bring play into the Museum, it would need something to set the tone.

Third, Tiny Games may organize the games into categories—like Home and Travel—but the design of the experience is content and context agnostic. The games can be about anything, to be played anywhere. Name your hall; name your exhibit. Any could get its own set of Tiny Games.

Fourth, the design of the app is modular and infinitely expandable. You could launch with five games but expand to five thousand. That was a model well suited to be launched through the creativity and energy of a youth program.

Fifth, it was so lo-fi it hurt! It's just text, game design, an algorithm, and good writing. So financially it was well within reach.

Finally, Tiny Games embodied my philosophy of games. In fact, Tiny Games was less about the games it contained than about an invitation to revel in the exquisite joy of play. Very Bernie De Koven.

Each year we took advantage of Regents Week in January. High school classes are canceled to make time for those students taking Regents tests, such as in science or global history. That means all students have to stay in town—no spring break trips for them—but are unscheduled most if not all of the week. Regents Week became our annual time to run high-risk, low-resource youth programming to drive innovation. We decided to run a three-day program during this week called Playing with Dinos, in which teens would learn game design, engage with the dinosaur Halls, and then create their own Tiny Games.

Unlike a book or a movie, there is no legal way to protect a game design. You can, in fact, protect the exact language within a set of rules, or trademark a product name, but the game mechanics themselves are free to repurpose, by anyone. However, I was hoping we might re-use certain elements of the app, and in any case wanted to eliminate any blurred lines. I wanted Hide&Seek to be fully on board.

One problem: Hide&Seek had closed just a few months earlier. Hide&Seek was founded by Holly Gramazio and Alex Fleetwood. As it would turn out, Nick Fortugno, the game designer who recently led *Pterosaurs*, knew Holly and made an introduction. She was generous with her time, and we spoke. She thought it was a great idea to use Tiny Games as an instructional tool. And if we had any game design questions, we could ask. But when it came to intellectual property issues, Alex controlled all the remaining assets from their now defunct company.

Holly made an email introduction between us. I replied to Alex with a compliment that I could stand behind:

> Tiny Games is a fantastic model of using a mobile device to connect people with each other and the spaces around them in a playful way. It elegantly and effectively serves them up a game to play, and the game can be learned super fast and played for a short time.

I described our vision for a Regents Week youth program as "both an educational project we are running for three days in January AND a prototyping process to help us better understand different opportunities for gaming the museum experience." This was the first time I had articulated the question behind this project; it was less to launch a Tiny Games–inspired app, per se, than to expand our awareness of ways games could help us re-think the onsite visitor experience.

Then for the ask, four of them. The first two were for the youth program.

1. Could we reference Tiny Games as the inspiration? ("That's super fine," he replied.)

2. The original Kickstarter campaign produced a PDF of all the games. Could we use them in the curriculum? ("We're okay with you using a relatively small amount of content," he agreed, "say, no more than 20% of everything you create.")

Excellent. Now for the final two questions, related to the prototype of the app.

3. Can we also adapt some of the games from the PDF into our app? ("See above," he wrote, in agreement.)

4. Could we use or adapt the supporting language of the game narrator? Here we got some well-deserved pushback. ("Also okay in small amounts," he offered, "but we'd really encourage you to find your own tone with it!")

I ended by sharing our plans for after the program concluded:

Come February we will share our prototype with folks within the Museum thinking about the next generation of mobile experiences. I am hoping they will be interested in further pursuing this idea. If so, then I would like to be back in touch with you to discuss potential crediting and/or IP issues, to the extent there are any, should the Museum wish to pursue this further.

We were off and running. Playing with Dinos was on!

The elevator pitch used in the promotions for the free offering promised that participants would create "a prototype for a new way to engage Museum visitors with our Halls (specifically our dinosaur Halls) and each other, inspired by Tiny Games."

To run the program, we needed a science educator and a game designer. Nathan, who was an extraordinary educator, stepped into the first role. He had developed and led the digitally infused youth programs before I had even arrived at the Museum, so I was confident he could adapt to the hectic day-long design processes we were about to undertake.

For the game designer, we ended up hiring a whole team. I had met Debra Everett-Lane a few years earlier, when she was Senior Writer & Designer at ESI Design. Debra had reached out through her role as one of the lead designers of the Come Out & Play Festival, an annual event featuring street games that turn the city into a giant playground (co-founded, in fact, by Nick Fortugno). Debra wondered if we could turn the Museum into a site for the next round of play. I made some connections for her with the Public Programs team and together they found an opportunity. Debra and Greg Trefry, another co-founder of Come Out & Play, coordinated a range of game designers to provide activities at a special family event on sharks in the Hall of Ocean Life. People ended up playing games like "I'm a Shark, You're OK" and "Sharkvolution." It was a blast.

Given her background in public games, and the positive experience we had at Shark Day, it seemed like working with ESI Design to create Tiny Games would be a perfect fit. Debra and other Come Out & Play designers had even developed a Come Out & Play Jam, an event where youth gathered to rapidly learn game design, then produce games to be played outdoors.

As we say in Yiddish, it was *beshert* ("destiny").

Working with her game jam curriculum as a model, Debra and her ESI colleague Jess Fiorini adapted it for creating Tiny Games at the Museum.

Now we needed an app, something that would allow us to rapidly create text-based instructions with a playful user interface and a backend algorithm for suggesting games based on a player's criteria. Given our simple needs, we did not actually require an app—just a mobile experience. A website optimized for a smartphone would do just fine. We worked with Mikael Colboc, a web developer in the Education Department in the team responsible for educational products, like the OLogy website. Working with Mikael and his supervisor, Karen Taber, we created a form-based backend for entering and editing game copy and a playful mobile webpage frontend to serve them all up.

The curricular team gathered to work out how to strike the right balance between the content (dinosaur and Museum) and the game design (training and production). We started by defining the educational objectives of the Tiny Games.

People who play the game will
- become more familiar with AMNH dinosaur Halls.
- understand something new to them about dinosaurs.
- learn new ways to engage with friends and family members within a museum.
- have a deeper appreciation of how play can provide a pathway to engagement within a museum.

We then identified the educational objectives of the youth program.
In addition to the educational objectives of the games, youth developing it in the program will

- gain a basic understanding of game design principles.
- gain a deeper appreciation of the Museum's Halls and curatorial approaches.
- contribute to broadening the Museum's onsite education strategies.
- contribute to the Museum's knowledge of how to integrate new digital tools into exhibit-based experiences that create new pathways for visitor engagement.
- expand their twenty-first-century learning skills, like collaboration, evidence-based thinking, through learning how to use digital tools to design a mobile learning experience for others.
- enhance their problem-solving skills.

All that in three days? We didn't call it high risk, low resource for nothing.

A few weeks later, for six hours a day, over three days, we combined paleo education with a game design jam. The class explored the Halls of Ornithischian and Saurischian Dinosaurs. They were there to observe and ask questions. Nathan would prompt them, but only when necessary. What do you see? What jumps out at you? What's this kiosk for? The youth took pictures and notes. They learned how the very structure of the Hall is designed around a cladogram (a family tree), arranging the exhibits by evolutionary relationship. Back in the classroom, they studied fossils and learned about the history of paleontology and early theories of fossils like biotic succession, "The Great Chain of Being," and Lamarckian evolution.

This paleo education was interspersed with a 101 on game design, the latter led by Debra and Jess. The teens learned the key steps—ideate, rules, playtest, critique, iterate—and then the special design needs required for building Tiny Games at and for a museum. Once the dozen teens had the training under their belts, they were given design constraints. Their games had to be the following:

- Easy to learn and play
- Playable without Museum staff support
- Short in duration (five to ten minutes)
- Appropriate for all ages
- Limited in prop requirements (if any)
- Playable in the museum
- Focused on Museum CONTENT!

ESI Design was contracted to not just co-teach the program but also contribute a few games of their own. They provided a model to help the youth understand both the core elements of each game and how they could all fit together. This is one from ESI called *Walk Like a Dinosaur*.

Name: Dino Tales
Intro: A game of storytelling and secrecy
Players: 2+
Mood: Brainy, Creative, Social, Funny, Silly, Cooperative, Inspired, Dramatic, Curious

Rules:

1. Who's first? Choose a character:
   Absent-minded professor
   Hero adventurer
   News reporter
2. Go to an area of the dinosaur hall by yourself, where no one can see you. Choose a dino there and learn as much as you can about it for one or two minutes.
3. Call everyone else over to you. Don't tell them who your dino is, but they should be able to see it.
4. As your character, tell a magnificent story about your dino. Stick to facts as much as possible, but also have fun with it. Other players can ask questions.
5. Everyone looks around and tries to figure out which dinosaur it is. The first to guess correctly wins and becomes the next storyteller.

Fact: Did you know that Protoceratops fossils scattered in the Gobi Desert may have inspired the stories of the mythical griffin?

As Hide&Seek had given us permission, we at the Museum also adapted a few from their app. The following was adapted from their game *One Elephant*:

Name: Counting Dinos
Intro: An observational race to count to five.
Players: 2+
Mood: Brainy, Quiet

Overview: In this game you'll look around for one lone dinosaur, then a pair of two dinos, then a set of three dinos, and so on.

Rules:

- In this game you'll look around for one lone dinosaur, then a pair of two dinos, then a set of three dinos, and so on.
- You must count aloud to five, but can only call a number when you spot that many of dinosaurs.
- You can't count with dinos another player has already used.
- All count out your own numbers at once, following your number with the dinosaurs counted (such as "Two *T. rex* Skulls!").
- No need to take turns: this is a race! The first player to reach five is the winner.
- How high can you count if you all cooperate?

Fact: In 2006, researchers at the University of Chicago estimated that over 71 percent of dinosaurs remain undiscovered!

To create their own, we took the teens through two game design sprints. Formally, design sprints can be a five-day affair. Adapted for our purposes, our sprints had to deploy design-thinking methods (co-creation, rapid prototyping, evaluative testing) under time pressure to solve a problem.

For the first four-hour sprint, the "problem" was engaging visitors at a location within the dinosaur halls (their choice) who are in a certain mood (choosing from our list) with a new Tiny Game. With a game design worksheet in hand, each team of randomly built teams had forty-five minutes to brainstorm ideas, internally playtest at least one of those ideas within their group, and further develop and refine their game through filling out the worksheet.

Each team then presented their game, using a paper prototype, while the others played it and presented feedback. Each group took their own turn. This playtest session was followed by a round of iterating the game design, playtesting again internally, then entering a second round of playtesting. This was followed by a second round of iterating the design. The sprint ended with each team presenting their final game to the full group.

Some of the playtests were done using the mobile app. The text would be entered into the backend and then devices were taken into the Hall by the youth and given to visitors to try. The team of students also had a feedback form to complete, with questions like "What happened during the playtest? What did players think about your game? What suggestions did they have for improving it?" They captured information like this:

- "I did it to a random person. It was scary but fun to talk to a complete stranger. He was friendly."
- "People actually got into it."
- "Sometimes people can't think of anything."
- "Some were trying to modify the rules to make them really more concise and clear."

Figure 3.4. Museum staff playtesting *Playing With Dinos. Author*

In the end, we were all pleased with many of the Tiny Games developed by the teens. This one, *Name Race*, creatively took advantage of how the tile layout of the floor could turn the hall into a playing board:

Name: Name Race
Intro: Which dino name will take you farthest?
Players: 2+
Mood: Active, Competitive, Social, Funny

Overview: A race through dinosaur names in the Hall!

Rules:

- Each player picks a dinosaur and remembers, writes down, or takes a picture of its two-word Latin species name—the longer, the better.
- Next, line up at one end of the Hall.
- For every letter in the dinosaur's name, move one tile forward—if you need to step to the side to avoid an obstacle, that doesn't count as a letter.
- If you want, you can walk like your dinosaur!
- Whoever's dino name takes them the furthest wins!
- When you're done, gather at the opposite end of the Hall and share the name of your dinosaur with other players.

This one, *Dinoccuptaion*, not only has a great name, but a totally wacky idea that combines careful observation with out-of-the-box creativity:

Name: Dinoccupation
Intro: Ask yourself: What would that dino do for a living?
Players: 4+

Overview: Take a good look at the dinosaurs and see if you can figure out what occupation they would be best at.

Rules:

- The person with the lightest shirt or darkest shoes is the Judge.
- The Judge decides which dinosaur to use and who comes up with the best "dinoccupation."
- Every player but the Judge creates a story about what pretend job the dino would have and why. Look at the dino's features and signs for inspiration!
- After a few minutes, players form a circle to explain their career choices.
- The Judge picks the best one.
- The winner gains a point and becomes the next round's Judge.
- Whoever has the most points after five rounds is the ultimate dino career specialist!

Fact: Many dinos had feathers, which might have been an adaptation against the cold.

In total, we filled *Playing with Dinos* with eighteen games, with great titles like:

- Don't Pet My Fossil
- I Lost My Dino, Again

- Don't Wake the Dino
- Fluffier than a *T. Rex*
- Is It Dead Yet?
- Don't Turn Around!

As part of the agreement with ESI Design, after the program they delivered a report summarizing what we had done and providing feedback on such things as the game design process and the potential for *Playing with Dinos*.

Through the process of designing their own contributions to the mobile experience and working with the youth to do the same, they shared lessons learned. Some examples:

- Tiny games are a great platform for engaging people and delivering content.
- They are well-suited to a museum visit, because they can be played quickly, can be played almost anywhere you are in the Museum, and easily adapt to a variety of audiences.
- The games made good use of the dinosaur halls, engaging with a variety of content and spaces.
- The game design process for tiny games worked well and led to the creation of games that were playable and fun.
- It's easy to make a tiny game, but more difficult to make a good tiny game that is really fun *and* conveys content well.
- A variety of game types is important for meeting the needs of different audiences. It was clear from playtesting that not everyone enjoys the same kind of game.
- The success of the tiny games is a good use case for integrating games into the museum experience.

Based on these observations they recommended we extend the content throughout the entire museum, leveraging geolocation data to deliver site-specific games.

For producing a proof of concept, the three days felt like a success, while, educationally, it had engaged the teen co-developers in science learning. Now we needed a way to pilot our eighteen games with the public. If only we had a regular venue at the Museum that brought in families looking for something extra, not only open to new activities but expecting an out-of-the-ordinary experience. In fact, we had just that: A Night at the Museum.

Also called Sleepovers, these evening events for families were inspired by both the Ben Stiller movie of the same name and the children's book it was based upon. Once or often twice a month, the Museum would close at its regularly scheduled hours and then, soon after, it would come alive . . . with hundreds upon hundreds of little kids in pajamas running around the Halls with their flashlights and stuffed triceratops. These are kids who already know the Museum but want to experience it in a new way, chaperoned by adults who paid quite a bit for the opportunity to sleep on a hard cot under the blue whale in a room that never quieted down before midnight.

They expected to be wowed, and the Sleepovers delivered: a flashlight-lit dinosaur Hall scavenger hunt in the dark, live animals in the theater, and more. Sacheen Sawney and Pierce Lydon, who managed the Sleepovers, were always on the lookout for low-cost enhancements to the night that my programs might provide. Sacheen was super organized, approachable, and always committed to ensuring each Sleepover guest had a special experience, while Pierce regularly published comic book reviews on the side and brought an edgy punk rock aesthetic to the Museum. Just like the Sackler Lab, the Sleepovers were an ideal place to pilot new prototypes with visitors. Sacheen and Pierce needed innovative ideas, and my programs could deliver.

We had earlier built our relationship through three-dimensional printers. Our five Makerbot desktop printers were on a three-tiered cart we could roll out into any hall that Sacheen and Pierce wanted to deploy us. In advance we would print the small bones that make up a finger (the phalanges) of a dinosaur on display, then challenge the PJed tots to search the hall until they could figure out which one it came from. Meanwhile, the three-dimensional printers would be building new copies, which always drew a crowd. The kids would learn about allosaurus claws, glue-gun their printed phalanges together, then spend the night poking each other with their new dinosaur claw.

When I suggested to Sacheen and Pierce that we bring *Playing with Dinos* into the Sleepovers, they loved the idea. A table would be set up to inform the evening's guests of the opportunity, with instructions for bringing it up on their smartphones and paper copies of each game for those who preferred the unplugged experience.

Emails were sent in advance to all attendees to remind them to fully charge their device if they intended to participate. At the event, the promotional material was designed to set the right expectations for the visitors. We needed them to understand this was both something in development *and* that we needed their participation to make it work:

When Was The Last Time You Played with Dinos?

Come play in the Hall of Saurischian Dinosaurs!
Grab your mobile device and be the first to try
a new, top-secret visitor experience.

Playing with Dinos *is still under development.*
After the game, please share your feedback!

At each Sleepover we had survey instruments to capture feedback from the visitors. We invited teens back from the program to administer it and then join the Sleepover if they liked (with a friend). At the same time, we had data analytics on the backend to learn such things as which games were most popular, how many games each party played, and for how long.

Figure 3.5. *Playing with Dinos* Sleepover promotion. *American Museum of Natural History*

We learned, at just the first Sleepover, at least 259 people played at least one game organized into eighty-four different groups. Twenty-four games were replayed immediately after the game was concluded, while an additional twenty-three teams clicked to play a different game immediately after the end of a game. Roughly, around 150 games were played and a little more than 50 percent of groups (forty-seven out of eighty-four) played more than one game.

We decided Sleepovers were a great place to keep piloting the experience, but we needed more games. Luckily, a graduate student intern currently working with us on another game stepped up to take the lead. Coming from New York University's game design program, Eric Teo volunteered to work with Carl Farra (another intern with us from the same program) to run a Game Jam. Like a design sprint, a Game Jam brings diverse people together to solve a problem through game design. But unlike with a design sprint, no one leaves until everything is completed. Eric and Carl proposed to me that they invite their fellow classmates into the Museum and, adapting the game development tools we created for the teen program, they would see how much they could add to *Playing with Dinos*. For them, it was a great exercise to apply their game-design skills for a top-notch organization around world-class content; for us it was a no-cost opportunity to significantly expand *Playing with Dinos*. It was a perfect win-win. Proceeding with the understanding that the Museum would decide which games made it into the app and could edit them anyway we wanted, the Dino Game Jam was off and running.

Over a dozen students came. Within the first thirty minutes they were already playtesting their new ideas with the public. Five hours after they had begun, these Dino Jam teams rapidly prototyped forty new Tiny Games. The new collection included some wonderful titles, like: "My Dino is better than your Dino," "Stomp stomp. Who's there?" "Congasaurus," and "Ninjasaur!" Once these games were delivered to the Museum, they were further refined and edited, then iterated after more rounds of public prototyping through the Night at the Museum Sleepover. In the end, thirty-two more games were added to *Playing with Dinos*, bringing the collection up to a grand total of fifty games.

Eight months after Alex Fleetwood had given us permission to adapt Tiny Games for the Museum, I could finally send him an update on the project, and a final round of thanks.

> Alex,
> Thank you once again for giving us permission last December to take inspiration and borrow some content from Tiny Games.
> We have since run a three-day workshop with high school students in January and a game-jam with graduate students in game design in April. Through the two we produced around 50 games which have now been tested through our sleepover programs, and have been played by around 600 people, to great effect.
> We also have made a version of it to be used by conference attendees to explore the use of games in museums, which has also been great, and we always mention Hide&Seek and Tiny Games.
> Thank you once again for the inspiration.

Commercial Off-the-Shelf Games

Commercial off-the-shelf games (known in the industry as COTS) are the kind of games that if you want to play one you would first need to literally walk into a store and pick one up off the shelf. Nowadays the ability to download a game has eliminated the requirement for shrink-wrapped packaging, but the concept remains: big-budget games made by commercial game designers.

When I first arrived at the Museum, they had already deployed a COTS game for learning. *Skyrim* is an action role-playing game, first published by Bethesda Game Studios in 2011. Designed as an open world (a design supporting exploration and non-linear gameplay) it offered an excellent environment for educators at the Museum, specifically Nathan, to use as a three-dimensional, interactive diorama engine. For the course, What Happened to the Neanderthals? youth would research the topic and construct their findings within *Skyrim*'s virtual world.

This was an emerging educational technique at the time, popping up in classrooms and libraries all around the world, using commercial games like *World of Warcraft* and *Second Life* to teach a wide range of academic subjects and topics. Few COTS games, however, could match the educational potential being reached in a small indie game that had recently been acquired by Microsoft: *Minecraft*.

What to say about *Minecraft*? I could write a chapter about *Minecraft*. I could write a book on *Minecraft* (and many already have). For our purposes, here, suffice it to say that *Minecraft* is wildly popular. The *New York Times Magazine*'s cover article on the topic (which, incidentally, featured my son) summed up its reach and impact in the title: *The Minecraft Generation*.

Popularity, however, is hardly enough to get a game into a classroom. *Minecraft*, it turns out, is not just an open world, like *Skyrim*; its primary mechanic of gameplay is creating. The name of the game says it all: in *Minecraft* you "mine" for resources, then "craft" them into a wide range of objects which can then be combined in an ever expanding number of ways. That means an educator on any topic could build nearly any experience they would like within their students' favorite game. Or, better yet, they could challenge their students to take on the building task themselves, and with glee.

Before coming to the Museum, I had developed a successful program at Global Kids for the Brooklyn Public Library in which we created an experience based in *Minecraft* to explore past and present social inequality (based around Panem, the fictional world in *The Hunger Games* series). I knew the Museum might provide a fertile ground to explore how a game like *Minecraft* could enhance the museum experience.

Our first attempt, during my first Regents Week at the Museum, was a day-long experience called FoodCraft. It was designed around the special exhibit at the time, *Our Global Kitchen*. Working with the curator, Eleanor J. Sterling (Chief Conservation Scientist at the Museum's Center for Biodiversity and Conservation), we identified content areas we might explore, hot topics to avoid, and the subtlety and distinctions we could not overlook. More importantly, she said it might be cool to focus on exchange and trade. We took that as our inspiration to explore through *Minecraft*.

I reached out to the same team I had brought into the Brooklyn Public Library, led by Joel Levin. Joel, a New York City school teacher, founded the company TeacherGaming, the educational innovator known best for having developed the sanctioned educational mod of *Minecraft*, called *MinecraftEdu*. We shared with him the questions underlying this program, and what we hoped it might teach us about gaming and exhibits:

- What roles can digital games play to extend the reach of an exhibit?
- Is the goal to reproduce the content from an exhibit or its overall experience?
- Should the game be designed to teach the material on its own, using the language of gameplay, or create a "need to know" that drives the learner to the exhibit?
- Is the ideal method through game play or game design?

We brought Nathan as curricular lead onto the team and soon had a program description ready for recruitment:

> In FoodCraft, youth participants will explore the science and politics of food through playing the video game *Minecraft* (no previous experience required) and the new AMNH exhibit *Our Global Kitchen*. More specifically, challenges to food production, preparation, trade, and transportation will be encountered in historical and present-day simulations, such as a pre-Columbian Aztec marketplace, illustrating the vital and complex role that food plays in our lives.

Meanwhile, Joel and his team created what's called a Map—the custom-built environment within *Minecraft* for the course to interact with. There were two maps, actually. The first map offered an Aztec-style, pre-Columbian market and the second the same location but in the present day (or close to it).

The map—and how the curriculum planned to use both it and the Museum exhibit in the program—were designed to meet the following learning objectives:

Youth will be able to

- articulate the different elements of a food system.
- identify some of the factors that influence the food system and their consequences, based on experiences within both FoodCraft and *Our Global Kitchen*.
- explain how a videogame can create a "need to know" about content in a museum exhibit and how a museum exhibit can provide needed content for a videogame.
- enhance their abilities to problem solve through collaboration in a digital environment.

At the same time, the program was designed to advance our own institutional objectives for digital learning:

- Increasing pathways for personal connections with physical objects in a digital age
- Digitizing assets in a modular, interoperable, and scalable manner
- Establishing new partnerships that strengthen AMNH brand
- Positioning the Museum as a digital leader and innovator
- Making AMNH a transmedia narrative
- Strengthening cross-departmental partnerships and resource flows
- Increasing use of Museum content in formal education

On the day of the program, the youth came into the classroom and entered Joel's *Minecraft* map. They chose their farm plots, got to work, and learned the local economics of the centralized marketplace. After lunch they went into the exhibit, with a special focus on its farming and global shipping content. When they returned to *Minecraft* everything had changed; a shipping port opened, bringing global goods into their marketplace, disrupting the local economy. And their farms had become industrialized. How would the teens respond? What did they learn in the exhibit that might help?

"I like how we worked with video games and we learned a lot," reflected one teen at the end of the day. "I think it's a good sense of 21st-century learning and we should do that more."

We agreed. Building on the framework of FoodCraft—connecting exhibits around the Museum with *Minecraft*—we launched a twenty-five-session program simply called Minecraft at the Museum. We intentionally kept the content out of the name as we wanted to both explore a wide range of topics and also leave space for the youths' interests to direct some of the program. With an expanded program scope, we also expanded the team, bringing in Museum educator Rebecca Saunders.

The program was divided into three parts. In the first we delivered experiences in both *Minecraft* and in the exhibit halls. Youths explored topics like geology, sustainability, and dinosaurs. With each pairing we challenged them to tease apart the embedded pedagogy. How was the experience in the game designed for learning? How was the experience in the Hall designed for learning? We aimed to teach them about a wide range of science content, how learning experiences are constructed, and how they could develop their own science learning experiences on the Museum's new *Minecraft* server.

Largely, we wanted to learn what they could teach us about how a videogame could be used to engage youth learners and what it might afford science education.

In the second part, we gave them administrative control over the Museum's *Minecraft* server and challenged them to build something that could teach others. They split into three groups, worked hard, and came up with different approaches to teach science through *Minecraft*. The first, the *Minecraft* Museum for Cretaceous Ocean Life, used a museum as a model. The second, about Vikings, created an interactive simulation, a form of roleplay. The third, about flowers, was an amusement park ride around a giant model, offering a different form of simulation and allowing us to experience something at a different scale. All the youth knew this was just an exercise—learning how to design an educational experience, learning how to collaborate. And it was an exercise for all of us in exploring different modes of science learning in *Minecraft*.

For the third and final part, we challenged youth to pick one topic and then work together to teach it in *Minecraft*. They chose "natural selection." So how can you teach evolution using *Minecraft*?

In *Minecraft*, there is something called "buffs." Buffs are features that can be given to a character to change its abilities. For example, some let you see in the dark, jump further than others, breathe underwater, etc. Using the random distribution of buffs, the youth challenged players in their map to race across various biomes to see how adapted they were to their environment and if they were "fit" enough to survive. Originally, they wanted buffs to occur as players entered each new biome—to represent a species evolving and becoming more or less "fit" for their new environment—but they couldn't work out the mechanics in time. So, instead, the player received all their buffs at the beginning—not ideal, but effective enough as a prototype.

In the end they created a video about their build. We posted it on YouTube.

The parts were now in place to create something for the public. We had learned how to teach teens to use *Minecraft* for science education. We had figured out ways to integrate exhibit content within a gamespace. And we had learned how to use map and video creation to produce assets that could be shared with others.

We developed a third program called Minecraft & Human Microbiome for students in the Museum's Lang Science Program. Lang is a remarkable mentorship program that supports youth from when they enter in middle school until their high school graduation. They engage with a wide range of courses and in the end design their own research projects. Brian Levine, its manager, was interested in trying something new with his students. He carved out time in the schedule and lent us an experienced Lang Educator, Brittany Klimowicz. We brought in Chris Vicari, a talented graduate student at Teachers College, to lead in the development and teaching of the *Minecraft*-related elements. He would also lead an evaluation of the program.

During this period, everyone was focused on the new exhibit, *The Secret World Inside You*. It explored the evolving science around the complexities of the human microbiome and what it revealed about human health. This seemed like a great topic for *Minecraft*, since we could play with scale to simulate various microbiomes that players could explore.

Figure 3.6. Teens in *Minecraft*. Author

Designing Game-based Learning

Partnering with Joel Levin once again, we supported the course through a *Minecraft* map custom-made to resemble a human body. Once in this map Lang students explored the diversity of microbes across the human body, roleplayed as white blood cells and antibiotics to protect the body from foreign invaders, and more.

We challenged the students to design and build activities that focused on a microbial topic of their choosing. Inspiration from trips to the exhibit, visits to Microbiology Labs, and feedback from scientists and their peers were all incorporated into their designs.

They came up with games like the following:

- Superbug: "Use antibiotics against life-threatening bacteria and learn about antibiotic resistance. As you fight against harmful bacteria be careful not to hurt the bacteria that are good for you."
- Defend the Human: "In the arm, you can use microorganisms like *Micrococcus luteus*, that live on human skin and help the immune system fight off infection. Or you can play the role of *Staphylococcus* to try to invade the body."
- Gut-Brain Axis: "In the neck, you will play the role of either serotonin or serotonin-inhibitor, racing your opponent through the vagus nerve that connects the brainstem to the abdomen, while learning about the relationship between microbes, the gut-brain axis, and depression."

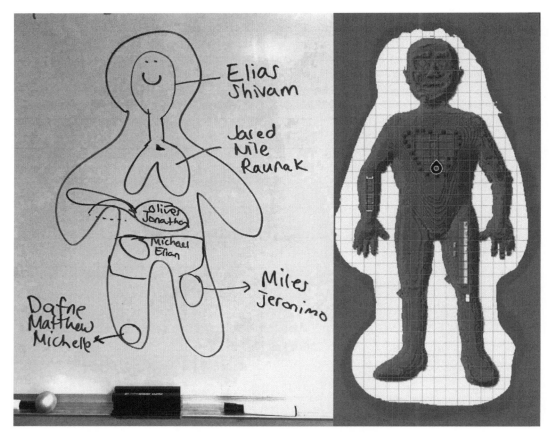

Figure 3.7. A *Minecraft* map custom-made to resemble a human body. *Author*

After this summer program, Joel and his team implemented the designs from the Lang students. Then, in the fall, the students returned to validate what they created and then develop Let's Play videos and other educational resources to accompany this microbial *Minecraft* world. Let's Play videos are a type of video walk-through of a game; a player chats about a game while they are playing it, adding personal commentary throughout. It is sort of like a cooking show, in that viewers are watching someone take on a task, for both entertainment and as a source of new ideas and inspiration. Susan Perkins, the Museum's curator of *Inside You*, even came to record her own Let's Play video, with her fiancé (a photographer at the Museum) and his daughter.

The OLogy website then created a microsite inviting children around the world to "play games in some of the areas of your body where microbes live." The site offered the videos of each game produced by their teen creators, Susan's video, and the *Minecraft* map itself containing all of the games. The *Minecraft* page then lived within the broader ecosystem of OLogy content based on the *Inside You* exhibit, supporting families to go deeper before or after a visit or for classrooms who might never be able to come in person.

OUTCOMES

We entered this stream of work driven by our guiding question: Can games and play create the motivation and mind-set for informal science learning?

After the *Minecraft* Lang course came to a close, Chris Vicari focused on completing his research developed over the course of the program. He had observed and interviewed the students, administered surveys, and analyzed both their *Minecraft* activities and their Let's Play commentaries. Some of his findings included the following:

Minecraft Let's Play videos served as evidence of youth's deep understanding of science content. Students emphasized a clear understanding of its connection to real-world science.

Minecraft helped students connect to microbiology. Students clearly articulated their microbiology knowledge as they described how their in-game experiences fit within a broader microbiology context.

Minecraft helped students articulate microbiology knowledge. By probing student content knowledge and requiring them to illustrate connections between the course material with the *Minecraft* activities, students articulated their microbiology knowledge via rich descriptions of their experiences and used microbiology terms to describe their in-game actions.

Minecraft helped students understand the iterative design process. Playtests and teacher feedback strengthened student understanding of the design process and how ideas can change over time. This was exemplified by their engagement and experience using *Minecraft* as they willingly continued improving, testing, and iterating on their designs throughout the course.

His research suggested that, yes indeed, games and play can create both motivation and mind-set for informal science learning. His findings were consistent with everything else we had seen within *Pterosaurs: The Card Game* and *Playing with Dinos*. Provided with the proper context, whether teens in a classroom or visitors in a Hall, we saw how games could act as a vehicle to engage people in science.

This was reflected as well in each of the outcomes that extended from these distinct projects. *Pterosaurs: The Card Game* begat more exhibit-based games that were sold in the Museum's stores. *Gutsy*, also connected to the *Inside You* exhibit about the human microbiome (co-designed this time by Susan Perkins), would quickly outsell *Pterosaurs*, moving thousands of units. A second card game, *Killer Snails*, inspired by research within a special exhibit on poison, would raise twenty-five thousand dollars through Kickstarter and go on to win game industry awards. For a time, this was generating good buzz within our scientist and curator community; I was approached in the hallways and staff cafeteria with exhibit- and research-based game ideas while the store would inquire if we had any new products for them to sell. However, an infrastructure was never established that could embed a tabletop game into the exhibit-as-product pipeline; that is, in the five- to ten-year lifespan of a traveling exhibit (always premiering, of course, at AMNH), someone needed to make the case that a tabletop game could earn a strong enough return on investment in a hosting Museum's store. While we had modeled the possibility, no one asked for the mandate to make this disruptive innovation a sustaining one.

Playing with Dinos led to an unexpected offshoot: as a pedagogical tool for teaching about games and museum design. At three game-based learning conferences, and at one museum conference, I led workshops for attendees. Our learning objective was to explore how gamifying a museum changed the way visitors connected with exhibits and the people they came with. But we needed a museum. So at each conference the first activity was to build a museum about the conference itself (out of previously "accessioned" conference memorabilia from years past). As it was being built, a few attendees were tasked with creating Tiny Games to drive engagement with the new exhibits, utilizing a blank instance of the *Playing with Dinos* toolset. Other attendees created traditional tours. Once the museum was "complete," we would open it to visitors (i.e., the session attendees) who took the tour, played the new Tiny Games, or wandered about on their own. Afterward, while processing the experience, we discussed how attendees explored the exhibit and how the inclusion of games inserted unique affordances into the museum visit experience.

Looking back at this series of programs that deployed *Minecraft* for learning, and how they eventually produced material for both Museum visitors and students through OLogy, let us return to where we started, in particular my conversation with Bernie De Koven. These *Minecraft*-based programs were already underway when I had the chance to speak with him. I wanted to know what he thought.

First, Bernie noticed that we were providing youth access to information in a way which modeled how cool it was to just know it. "You're presenting it in a way that says, 'Look how much fun it is to have this information.'"

Second, Bernie liked *Minecraft*. He described it as "an inherently good tool, a fun tool, an enabling tool because it allows kids to play." He spoke of it like a laboratory for exploration and building and creating. He saw it as a natural fit because it generates "the same kind of mindset that you want kids to have when they are investigating the natural world, the world of science." Of most importance, given my particular context, Bernie saw it presenting "the kinds of things that you hope that they are going to experience when they come into the museum."

Bernie concluded by admiring our program's "synergy between the form and content." We had avoided any sort of gamification incentive structure. Instead, "it comes out as a way of playing with something, a way of discovering the play that is inherent in the thing itself."

All of the learning from *Pterosaurs*, *Playing with Dinos*, and *Minecraft*-based programs about the potential of games and digital design became the foundation for one of my most significant projects at the Museum: the augmented reality mobile game, *MicroRangers*.

Comparison: Smithsonian Center for Learning and Digital Access and National Zoological Park (Washington, DC) and The Bronx Zoo (New York City)

When I first met Grace Collins, they were the Digital Media Project Manager at the Smithsonian Center for Learning and Digital Access. The work of the Center was broad, with the potential to touch all nineteen Smithsonian museums, nine research centers, and the National Zoo. The thread within Grace's work was implementing educational technology in digital environments, which included interactive media and games. Grace took quite seriously their role as game evangelist within the museum sector, speaking often on the topic at conferences.

At a Serious Play gathering in Pittsburgh, we sat down to explore their perspective on what digital games, and specifically game narratives, afford museum-based learning.

Grace had just finished a presentation and reiterated to me its five main takeaways.

First, it is time to stop arguing over whether game-based learning is worth exploring. The academics have done enough research and by now it should be considered a settled matter. "We can have conversations about efficiency, economics, and design strategy," they said, "but we know that game-based learning is effective when done right."

Second, while some emphasize how learning occurs through a game's mechanics (what a player does within a game), Grace focused on the power of narrative (the story a player enters within a game). To Grace, narrative is how games educate and persuade. "We've seen it do this in other forms of media, and we're seeing narrative maturing in games now."

Third, each medium defines and bounds the narrative experience. A narrative in a movie is constructed differently than a narrative in a book. Therefore, narratives cannot be freely transferred from one media to another. "Each time we explore the same narrative in a new type of media," they argued, "we are essentially redefining the entire experience." That means narratives developed through games must be developed from scratch, around what games afford as a medium, and by people who understand how to tell stories within that medium.

Fourth, and this is precisely why digitally oriented positions are so critical for museums, "If we do not have staff working with our digital collections, we won't be able to fully explore the different facets of our collections." Without that expertise, the full stories behind those objects can't be told.

Finally, for museums to develop expertise in digital narratives, they need to increase their efforts to experiment with and publish digital media, including digital games. "This means that museums will need to hire more digital content creators."

Grace told me about a recent game jam that had been held at the White House to prototype new videogames that teach complex topics in history, English, math, civics, and science. "We tackled the subject of evolution in marine environments," Grace said, about their team. "It's a topic that has been addressed many times before by natural history museums."

The White House Game Jam was inspired by a call to action made by President Obama a few years earlier. "I'm calling for investments in educational technology that will help create . . . educational software that's as compelling as the best videogame," the President said at the time. "I want you guys to be stuck on a videogame that's teaching you something other than just blowing something up."

In response, more than one hundred game developers plus thirty-five teachers, learning researchers, and students gathered together for forty-eight hours. They were split into twenty-three teams, powered by pizza, to rapidly prototype new approaches for educational software.

Grace's team needed to abstract scientific concepts and wrap them in a narrative that would appeal to a broad group of gamers. "We had the player exploring an ocean-covered Earth in the far distant future, examining creatures that had evolved over time, and piloting an underwater sea vessel that could mimic adaptations to solve puzzles." The team's educators ensured their content was accurate and tackled questions of pedagogy. "At the same time, we allowed the game to create a fantastical experience that would be impossible to replicate in a physical museum." And, as Grace saw it, this fantasy narrative is what had the power to connect players with the game's scientific content.

The producers of the White House Game Jam hoped that many of the prototypes would have life beyond the game jam. Some of the games, it was anticipated, would be developed into finished products while others could go as-is right into classrooms.

Games, according to Grace, are more than just products museums might produce. They offer a whole new way of thinking. Hearing the word "game," many picture a board game like *Monopoly* or a videogame like *Super Mario Brothers*. But games are so much more than discrete objects. "I would argue that games are directed, narrative experiences fit within systems," Grace explained. "The rules define the interplay between the system and the player."

Therefore, taking this broader view, we can understand a museum visit, itself, as a game and a visitor as a player. "We must then ask ourselves: what 'game' are we having our visitors play and why? Do these 'games' amaze and inspire?"

This is not about gamifying the museum visit, per se, like adding a scavenger hunt to the museum's app. This is about re-visiting the entire museum experience from the lens of game play and what games afford. "Thinking in this way can provide us with a new perspective on what a museum experience should be."

Chatting with Grace reminded me of when I first encountered an app for the Smithsonian's National Zoo. At first I had dismissed it. I soon learned how wrong I was. Chastened by how hastily I had judged it, it served as a reminder to never fail to consider the Six Tools for Digital Design.

Normally I am eager to approach any new exploration of digital media released by museums as an opportunity to learn. I often ask myself: Is it engaging? How is the learning content integrated with the experience? How does the experience reflect the character of the institution, and in what way? And, more often than not, why didn't I think of that first?!!

I learned of the new Zoo app when a colleague at work emailed a notice about something new called *Shutterbugs: Wiggle and Stomp*. The app was designed in collaboration with the Smithsonian Science Education Center, which promotes authentic, inquiry-based kindergarten through twelfth grade STEM learning, and Filament Games, which consistently releases games for learning which I consider best in class.

The email introducing *Shutterbugs* came with the following description:

> The Smithsonian Science Education Center has created a free learning game that can be played online or downloaded to a tablet device. *Shutterbugs: Wiggle and Stomp* is aligned with national standards for science education. Children ages 3–5 can play the game to learn how to describe movement and motion while visiting exotic animals from the Smithsonian's National Zoological Park.

I went to the app store and downloaded it to my phone. The visuals were beautiful—anyone would be proud to show this to a supervisor or funder and say: "Here's what we got for our money"—but I could not tell if it actually taught anything. Or if it was any fun. I feared I was just looking at yet another educational product using the language of games to mask something that was really just traditional education.

The title of the game comes from the narrative—the player is at a zoo and is challenged to take photos of animals on the move. Along the way the player is asked to describe animal movement and motion, often acting it out on their own.

When I played it all I saw was a quiz. Each question was essentially the same, as the animal options and movement changed with each screen. Which animal is swimming, or jumping, or kicking, or running? It was adorable, yes. But was it actually a game? More importantly, as James Paul Gee had advised me, was it a meaningful interaction?

I quickly dismissed it. I wrote back to my colleagues the following: *I found it really disappointing. All it is is an animated quiz with nice graphic design but weak user interface and educational design. But I am glad they made it.*

I could not have been more wrong. I was viewing it through the lens of my own perspective, not that of its intended audience. I was viewing the app as if it lived on its own, not recognizing how digital experiences are often much broader than the digital tools that support them. Finally, I was viewing the app as the fixed end of an experience, not the start of something that could be adapted and remixed by its end users.

I first began to question my approach when I returned home and, the next day, introduced the app to my children. At the time, my daughter Miri was four years old and my son, Akiva, seven. Saturday morning, before Miri's ice-skating lesson, I told them both I had a new app for them. I wanted to see how they'd respond to it.

Over the next two hours, they each on separate devices completed every animal and action in the app, collecting stars for each. Completing an animal rewards you with a coloring page you can print out, with your name, the name of the animal, and its associated action. This motivated Miri to learn for the first time how to wirelessly print to our home printer, which she soon mastered and was able to do on her own. She colored more than a half dozen of the animals, using the animal in the app as her color guide.

Once the coloring was complete Miri cut string to hang each one above her bed (she slept at the time in the bottom of a bunk bed) to make what she described as her own zoo.

My son, meanwhile, completed the app but cared little about printing and coloring. Instead, he printed and nicely cut out a personalized certificate provided at the end of the experience, and then helped his sister do the same.

The next day we just happened to have plans to visit our own local zoo, the Bronx Zoo. To prepare, Miri cut down her zoo and collected them all together. She explained she was bringing her drawings along to use as a checklist. She wanted to mark them off when we found each animal. (I don't think she understood we were going to a different zoo than the one in the app, or perhaps that different zoos have different animals.) Miri then printed out additional animals that I knew would be at the zoo; she used her time in the car ride to color those in.

My son had a different plan of action. To prepare for the trip, he powered his iPod. Akiva wanted to create his own collection by photographing the day's animals and note their actions, with plans to later print them out as a project. That narrative within *Shutterbugs* of taking photos of the animals was ignored by my daughter but it became the primary point of identification for my son.

Once at the zoo, my daughter marked off the first animal she saw, a sea lion, but, when she learned I did not have a mobile printer (!) and we could not print out her new animal, she set her collection aside for the day and instead used her drawing pad to sketch animals she observed.

My son, however, took photos all day. I hadn't seen him take photos like this for over a year, when we last went on a hiking trip. I was amazed at how motivated he was. He chose his subjects carefully, reviewing them afterward, deleting the bad ones, and later proudly narrating the collection to the family later at dinner. "This is a stork eating," he said. "This is a penguin swimming." The app was no longer involved in any way, but he had picked up and extended what it had modeled: pair an animal with a movement.

Meanwhile (yes, there was more) we picked up a child-sized pamphlet while walking the Bronx Zoo entitled Animal Activity Trail. It presented the same type of information as the Smithsonian's app—animals and their actions—but rather than present it as a quiz-like game it offered a simplified scavenger hunt, sending us to the various locations around the park where you might see the animal and its activity. It also required parent-child interactions as the pamphlet, unlike the app, did not scaffold the experience with audio guidance. We never actually saw a designated animal at its location—for example, a running ostrich—but the pamphlet suggested ways children could mimic the action. The suggested running game—such as sprint as fast as you can in five seconds—and the variations we came up with became Miri's preferred activity until we left the park.

I was intrigued by how much there was for me to unpack, just comparing the *Shutterbugs* app with the print guide (both focused on the same learning content)! Analog versus digital. A quiz versus a scavenger hunt. At-home learning versus in-person. Self-directed learning versus parent-supported.

The main lesson I chose to take from this was to avoid judging an app on its own. It needs to be evaluated within the ecology of activities and relationships it will be inserted into, and only then through user testing and iterative design.

How did the design of *Shutterbugs* support (or discourage) my children's creative exploration of the content, both within and outside its digital confines? How did its design support (or discourage) interactions with their siblings or parents?

I am also left with a question worth pondering: How did a zoo app played at home provide better motivation and scaffolding to learn about animal behavior than a location-specific pamphlet that included the live animals? And are there ways either could be improved by being integrated with the other?

TIPS AND STRATEGIES

1. User research

    Think: *What ways could we have developed user research to explore visitor needs that could be met through a game or a playful experience?*
    Do: *Identify an end user's needs and then develop a game that can meet them.*

2. Rapid prototypes

    Think: Pterosaurs: The Card Game *focused on creating prototypes for play among the developers; Playing with Dinos focused on creating prototypes for play with the public. What are the strengths and limitations of each approach?*
    Do: *Reverse engineer something you already made digitally. Create a physical prototype, ideally with paper, to explore solving something you already solved digitally. Test it with users. It doesn't matter what you learn from the test. The important thing is to ask yourself: What did you learn about testing it through a physical prototype?*

3. Public piloting

   Think: *Users of a pilot have to be in the right mind-set in order to participate. Come up with three good examples of a bad mismatch between a pilot and its context. For example, piloting a ball-tossing game in a china shop. Or testing a social game among strangers on a crowded public city bus.*
   Do: *Design your next pilot to require testers to approach it with a certain state of mind. Then create the right context to generate that state of mind.*

4. Iterative design

   Think: *How did the three Minecraft youth programs iterate their design from one course to another? What other directions could they have gone, building on lessons learned, to have engaged more of the public?*
   Do: *Think about iterating not just within but across projects. Pick one project that incorporated a lesson learned from an earlier project. Building on those two, identify a new lesson and iterate something new in this series.*

5. Youth collaboration

   Think: *What might have happened if the Museum youth were empowered with the responsibility to run a public Minecraft server? What could have gone wrong? What could have been epic?*
   Do: *Design a learning experience using an existing game co-developed with a young person who knows that game and its player community much better than you.*

6. Team up!

   Think: *In your mind swap some of Pterosaurs' in-house and outsourced team members, from in-house to outsourced or the other way around. In what ways would that have changed the process of creating the game, and the game itself?*
   Do: *For your next project, build a team with at least one member who is discounting their costs or contributing their efforts for free. Identify what might motivate them beyond the financial.*

7. Comparative project

   Think: *Playing with Dinos used a game jam as a process for generating new games. The White House Game Jam used the process to create prototypes of new game-based educational experiences. What is similar about the two events? What was different?*

NOTES
1. Katie Salen Tekinbas and Eric Zimmerman, *Rules of Play* (United Kingdom: Books24x7.com, 2003), 95.
2. *Phylo*, accessed November 23, 2021, https://phylogame.org.

Car no. 9

Elevator buttons can serve as vertical maps in their stubborn dedication to the Z-axis. The best vertical map in the Museum is found in car no. 9. I take it most days after visiting the staff cafeteria, toasted bagel with butter in hand, heading from the lower level (LL) to the fourth floor (4F), where I can enjoy my morning breakfast alone with the dinosaurs on the walk to my desk.

Elevator no. 9 is not for the public. It feels like the love child between a service elevator and a moving van. Its walls, towering twelve feet high, are perennially draped in protective sheets of cloth, as if it were moving day, every day. The industrial ceiling lights glare down like those in a school cafeteria.

This is the kind of elevator with two doors, the front one (F) facing east (toward Central Park) and the rear one (R) facing west (toward the Hudson river). There's usually a ragged empty chair by a raft of buttons that require a Museum badge to activate. Each set of doors have a separate set of buttons, and that's where things get interesting.

One column is for the front door, its buttons numbering LL to six. The second column is for the rear, numbering LL to nine. Together, they serve as a Rosetta Stone to the architectural soul of the Museum.

At each of the first four floors, the front opens on a momentary snapshot of a different public exhibit.

The first floor (1F) opens and closes on a giant millipede working its way through a 1940s diorama of a larger-than-life forest floor.

The second floor (2F) opens and closes on a triple-hinged wall blocking the elevator exit (with an exhibit on its visitor-facing side about Asian culture) that must be swung out slowly into the Hall, saloon-style, on its creaky hinges, its single wheel tracing the curved path etched over the years into the wooden floor.

The third floor (3F) opens and closes on the ticketing area for our current special exhibit, each running for nine months before hitting the road like a hard-working immigrant to send money back home to the family.

The fourth floor (4F) opens and closes on the transitional space between Ornithischian dinosaurs and extinct mammals, the floor mapping a diagram about amniotic life.

Above those public spaces, the fifth (5F) and sixth (6F) reveal the hallways traversed by scientists moving among labs, offices, and collection spaces.

I can exit on every floor on the front side, but the rear is another story. My museum badge provides me no access. I can only glimpse beyond its poker-faced doors if someone enters from that side. Which they never do, at least not while I'm around. But the display screen above the buttons offers a few clues.

Here's what the display reads for the first few floors as I travel up from the basement toward my office, each glowing number replacing the one before it: LL, 1R, 1F, 2R, 3R, 2F, 4R, 3F, 5R, 4F, . . .

Okay, that's starting to get weird, right? First of all, the front and rear doors are not paired together, opening at the same time, but are sequential, like beads in two separate rows. As if that's not odd enough, the sequence appears to be out of order. Going up, 2F follows 3R, then 3F comes after 4R? Shouldn't it be the other way around? And why is 5R after 3F, suggesting there's two floors between them?

The confusion in these questions is why I love this elevator, as it reliably generates the cognitive dissonance required to introduce newcomers to the broader reality that defines the building.

Which is simply this: there is no building. Rather, the Museum is a campus composed of more than two dozen. Sure, to the outside observer, the Museum appears to be one large contiguous building, draping itself down Central Park West from 81st to 77th Street, where it then wraps around the corner to stretch to Columbus Avenue. But ever since building one was opened in 1972, the Museum has never stopped expanding, each addition coded on security maps with a number signaling its order in the architectural family lineup.

Most can be accessed by the public but contain additional floors, both below and above, which might be revealed to observant visitors attuned to elevator button maps. (Some even contain half-floors marked as "mezzanine" like in that movie *Being John Malkovich*.) Other buildings are tucked inside and away from the street view, nuzzled between other buildings, and can only be accessed by staff with badge access and the knowledge that a single non-descript door in one building goes not to a cozy broom closet but a vast building with floor after floor dedicated to ornithology, or a collection of whale bones, or a genomic research center.

The hallways are often interconnected between the buildings like a human-sized Habitrail, for both visitors and staff alike, designed to gloss over the subtle changes in room acoustics and air flow. Oh, and ceiling height. That's why the buttons for the front door of car no. 9 run from LL to six while those for the rear reach three floors higher: the elevator is nestled between two buildings, each relatively the same height, but one with shorter—thus additional—floors.

Car no. 9 is the cartilage connecting the outward-facing building five with the inner building thirteen, the Fisk building, housing most of the Paleontologists and their dinosaur research.

So when I find myself exiting car no. 9 on the fifth floor, I'm always aware in the back of my mind that just a few feet behind me a scientist is hard at work studying a dinosaur fossil, on the eighth.

4

Designing Augmented Reality

IN SUMMARY | tl;dr

Subject: This chapter focuses on using the Six Tools of Digital Design for developing a mobile augmented reality game.

Case study: The case study in this chapter focuses on *MicroRangers*, a mobile game that used augmented reality to invite visitors to explore exhibits across four Halls to combat threats to global biodiversity. It was designed to address the question: Can games and play create the motivation and mind-set to promote public awareness and deep understanding of the critical impact of biodiversity on human health?

User research: The online service IFTTT (If This Then That) was used to generate user insights for *MicroRangers* by providing access to photos posted by visitors on social media. The main insight was gleaned by looking beyond the content of the photos to observe instead the practice of taking those photos, noticing how visitors used the process to construct meaning from their visit. It led us to ask: How could we design an experience that guides visitors to use the cameras in their pockets to play with the Museum?

Rapid prototyping: Youth were provided with transparencies, markers, and photos of each museum exhibit so they could develop paper prototypes to explore how visitors would experience both the augmented characters and the MicroGames. They used cardboard iPads and hand-drawn stand-ins to simulate the augmented reality components. They then acted out the different game characters (with costumes, unanticipated accents, and descriptive names) utilizing all the material they created in an after-hours in-Hall beta test.

Public piloting: The prototypes for *MicroRangers* were piloted with different audiences.

1. **Families:** At the *MicroRangers'* Game On! Event we focused on families, who were expected to be one of the primary audiences for the game. We unexpectedly learned there are key differences between families who came to the Museum to play the game versus families who discovered the game while already on their visit.

2. **Members:** Members of the Museum received special coins. They represented a category of visitors highly committed to the institution who return often looking for ways to enhance their visit.

3. **General visitors:** Visitors pulled out of the ticket line allowed us to better understand how the game might be played for people who were visiting the Museum for the first time and are unlikely to return any time soon.

4. **Lang students:** This was a unique group of highly committed young people who were most likely to visit the Museum with their families and come often.
5. **Master of Arts in Teaching:** These New York City teachers allowed us to better understand how the game might be used by a secondary audience of school classes on field trips.

Iterative design: There were many design changes iterated during the development of *MicroRangers*. A list might include removing the flatulent buffalo to keep the game on one floor, replacing the augmented reality target cards with challenge coins, simplifying the game by eliminating the "concerned citizens" as active characters, and replacing live videos of the teens with animated characters.

Youth collaboration: *MicroRangers* was developed with the crucial involvement of two different afterschool youth programs. In fact, one of the students from the first program went to college and returned as the teacher assistant for the second program. This brought many benefits. Having any students continue is itself a plus; they bring continuity, institutional knowledge, and an excitement for the project that can be contagious. Having a former student now be a teacher assistant is extra special. It means someone has developed sufficient leadership skills to step into a paid position; this models for the youth that they too might aspire to follow a similar path. It also means the teacher assistant for the new program requires less on-boarding.

Teaming up: The *MicroRangers* Brainstrust that was created invited key individuals from adjacent departments from around the Museum to inform the development process. It was designed to ensure the program was aligned with the needs of departments around the Museum, to avoid known pitfalls, to gain buy-in among key allies around the Museum, to lend legitimacy to the initiative, to stay on top of related Museum efforts, and to alert as soon as possible individuals and departments who needed to stay informed.

Comparison: The chapter concludes by offering, for comparison, an exploration of the use of museum-based augmented reality games at the Minnesota Historical Society in Saint Paul, Minnesota.

CONTEXT AND GUIDING QUESTIONS

I needed to meet Susan Perkins. Luckily, I had a card up my sleeve. Fifty-five cards to be precise.

Susan was a Curator and Professor of Invertebrate Zoology at the Museum. In earlier chapters I spoke about how she joined our *#scienceFTW* program as a guest, to play science-themed games with the youth and critique their content. Susan also advised our *Minecraft* program about the human microbiome and graciously starred in our Let's Play video for the body-shaped map produced by the Lang Program.

But before all that ever happened, I first had to meet her.

After my first encounter with *Bone Wars*, I kept my eye out for science-based tabletop games. At the time games with science content were usually siloed into "educational games," widely disparaged as featuring low commercial and gameplay value. That perception would soon change but, until it did, the field was small enough to make the strong ones stand out. *Bone Wars*, the card game about paleontology, easily stood out among its peers. For each new game that I found I tried to match its science content against an area of research at the Museum.

The publishers of *Bone Wars* published a game called *Parasite Unleashed*. With gameplay based on the life cycle of parasites, its slogan was "a totally gross, totally true card game." I had heard the Museum had a scientist active on Twitter posting about parasites. I tracked down her feed but, being unfamiliar with the science, could not begin to decipher it (e.g., "Parasitic nematodes are usually presumed to have same sex determination as *C. elegans* . . . but that's not the case"). I had no idea what she looked like, nor even where she worked. I mean, I knew she had an office in the Museum, but didn't know in which building.

In summary, I had no idea where she worked, what she looked like, and I didn't understand her science. I'll admit I felt a little intimidated at the prospect of tracking her down. Then I saw her name as a speaker at an upcoming content seminar and I knew this could be my chance.

The content seminars were one of my favorite behind-the-scenes events at the Museum. At the earliest stages of the development of a new exhibit, departments around the campus would be brought together to prepare for its potential arrival. Scores of us would gather, fill our plates with the catered lunch, then sit at tables for an intense round of twenty-minute presentations and conversations spread over the next five hours. Scientists—both those curating the exhibit and visiting guests—would present to their colleagues and introduce fascinating aspects of the latest science. They would raise new ethical issues and social implications, and explore other topics that might be addressed within the future exhibit. This is where, for example, many educational programs were first born, to keep the department aligned with the Museum's focus one or two years down the road.

The notice about the upcoming content seminar said it was an exhibit called *Inside You*, about the human microbiome. It said one of the exhibit's curators was Susan Perkins. The provided bio described her as a microbiologist with "three main research foci." One was the study of the parasites that cause malaria. The second was symbiotic bacteria found in blood-feeding leeches. The third related to patterns of genomics and geography, in relation to pathogenicity, of RNA viruses (and I still don't know what that means).

And there, on the schedule, between 2:10 and 2:30, on the topic of "parasites and symbionts," Dr. Perkins would be addressing "the different kinds of relationships (parasitic vs. symbiotic) that microbes have with their human hosts and the effects of an overly sterile world."

I decided I would make my move during the reception at the end of the day. I didn't literally have a deck of *Parasite Unleashed* in my pocket, but I had my line ready: "Dr. Perkins, I am curious if you've heard of a game called *Parasites Unleashed*?"

After the final presentation (on the ethical and social implications of recent studies of the human microbiome), I watched for Susan to be alone. Then, with sweaty palms, I approached her, made an introduction, then asked my question. I had presumed the word "parasite" might get her attention, allowing her to look past something as trivial as a game. I was wrong. I had deeply underestimated her. It turned out I had her at "game."

Susan was happy to talk with me about *Parasites Unleashed* but what she *really* wanted to discuss with me was *Carcassonne* (a game about a medieval fortified French town), *Killer Bunnies and the Quest for the Magic Carrot* (a game about . . . killer bunnies), and a whole host of other recent favorites. It turned out she was a tabletop enthusiast. When it came to games, she cared less about what they were about (their narrative) than about their gameplay (the challenges created for the players and the tools provided to solve them). The opportunity, however, to combine her personal interest in gaming with her research and curatorial work was an exciting combination. Over the years we would hold lunchtime tabletop gaming sessions in her lab, invite other colleagues (with some games spread over a year), and collaborate on a number of youth programs and science-based games—both analog and digital. The largest and most challenging game we created together, however, was *MicroRangers*.

A proposal was already underway at the Museum to the National Institute of Health's SEPA program for developing educational programs in advance of the *Inside You* exhibit. SEPA is the Science Education Partnership Award program, funding innovative school-based STEM and informal science education projects. The overarching goal was to promote public awareness and deep understanding of the critical impact of biodiversity on human health. I was invited to a meeting with Development to discuss its various components. One piece was public conversations with experts oriented toward teens. Another was a polling station to collect visitor information assessing their gaps in knowledge and what they'd want from future exhibitions. Another was the one Susan had been asked to develop: The Digital Biodiversity and Health Tour.

The idea of the tour was to take existing exhibits within the Museum's permanent Halls, identify themes that connected them with the proposed *Inside You* exhibit, and add it to the Museum's main app, *Explorer*. Fifteen stops on the tour would "allow users to explore the links between biodiversity and human health" and "show the user that a simple object or organism may hold the key to human health concerns in ways they never imagined." For example, in the Hall of Ocean Life, at the Kelp Forest exhibit, visitors would learn how hard it is for humans to digest seaweed . . . unless you are Japanese, whose microbiome hosts bacteria that possess genes that allow their human hosts to digest it. In the Hall of African Peoples, at the Pygmy Peoples exhibit, visitors would learn that due to a unique mouth microbiome, the Twa people almost never get cavities.

I loved the idea of using digital tools to add new life and meaning to our otherwise static permanent exhibits. And I loved the idea of connecting an experience across Halls. But I felt, if the goal was innovation, we could go further. Much further. In fact, Susan wondered if we could turn it into a game. I was authorized to lead this part of the SEPA-funded project and to work with Susan to make something happen. We were off and running.

In our first meeting Susan reframed the content, which she would own. She recommended we broaden the focus from human health (which would still make up the bulk of the experience) and frame it instead about microbes in general. I would drive the game design. We agreed we could do much more than just a walking tour on a phone while still meeting the same learning and institutional goals. And it just *had* to include augmented reality (AR). We decided I would design a youth program with the aim of producing a prototype for this currently unnamed project.

First we had to give the afterschool program a name. Later, by email, Susan suggested, "How about *Discover the Microscopic Museum*?"

I replied, "How about just '*The Microscopic Museum* (a game development program about microbial organisms and processes that are associated with AMNH exhibits)'?"

Marisa Jahn weighed in next. Marisa was the Executive Director of Studio Rev-, a non-profit studio for artists, media makers, and youth to work together to produce issue-oriented media. I had admired her recent work at the Queens-based New York Hall of Science, a geolocative game about imagining the future. I had been looking for an opportunity to collaborate and this project fit the bill, with her leading the app development education with the youth co-developers. Marisa said, "Let's go with MicroMuseum," and our program had a cool new name.

The guiding questions behind the MicroMuseum prototype grew from what it inherited from both the SEPA proposal and our current exploration of games. Throughout MicroMusuem, and its eventual transformation into the game *MicroRangers*, we were asking ourselves: *Can games and play create the motivation and mind-set to promote public awareness and deep understanding of the critical impact of biodiversity on human health?*

INSPIRATIONS

I collect many things. When I worked at the Museum, one thing I collected were sources of inspiration. Sometimes I came across new ways to learn something unexpected about the Museum. Other times I encountered something remarkable out in the world and wondered how we could adapt its innovations. I filed these all away in the file cabinet deep in my brain. Then, whenever I launched a new program or project, I didn't have to work hard browsing my files for related material. Like puppies in a pet store window, they would just leap up and beg me to give them a new home.

When it came to the design of the first *MicroRangers* prototype, there were four "puppies" that wanted my attention.

If This Then That, known as IFTTT, is an internet service that lets you connect something measurable with an automatic, internet-driven action. If the weather predicts rain, then text me "Bring an umbrella!" If the *New York Times* posts an article with the phrase "seltzer water," email me a copy. And so on. When I first discovered IFTTT, I wanted to see what it could tell me about the Museum and its visitors. Sure, I could follow the @amnh Twitter tag to see what people were sharing with their friends and family, but I wanted to know what visitors were doing when they thought we weren't watching. I found what I needed through IFTTT.

One setting allowed me to receive a regular email listing social media posts that originated within a defined geographic region. If I owned a small store, this would be hard to pull off; I'd be receiving messages from people all around the block. The Museum's campus, however, is vast—four blocks on one side and an avenue that parallels an internal hallway that it is often described as the longest in the city. IFTTT would have no problem capturing images within that zone.

So each day I received an email listing a few dozen posts—from Twitter, from Instagram—that included all photos shared from within the Museum (and, for some reason, the gym across the street). Every week a few would jump out at me, and I built a collection over time. As I added new ones, I looked for patterns.

They say a picture is worth a thousand words, so please forgive me as I abbreviate my descriptions:

- A selfie by a couple throwing terrified expressions at the camera while the skull of the *T. rex* is carefully positioned to hover overhead.
- A man posing with the seated statue of Teddy Roosevelt, both Instagram filtered to wear dog ears and noses.
- A pair of feet standing on the Planetarium's "Your Weight on the Moon" scale, which displays 45.7 pounds. "I don't think you guys understand the GRAVITY of the situation."
- A teenager in pajamas gleefully wrapping her arms around an enormous block of azurite in the Hall of Gems and Minerals. "No one has ever been happier than me hugging a slab of rock. #amnhsleepovers"

These four are examples of the museum as prop, in which the camera captures a visitor interacting with it, whether physically (like the Moon scale, Roosevelt, or the rock) or narratively (like the couple "chased" by the *T. rex*).

A second type of photo interacts with the museum by turning it into a setting:

- A family of five captured in midair, feet tucked under, arms splayed, outside the front entrance. The caption: "We complete the ground tour of Museum of Natural History. This jump under the honor of these completion."
- A selfie under the Hall banner "Asian Peoples" by three smiling women with the caption "We found our peoples!"
- A man is splayed across the floor in the Hall of Gems and Minerals. "I spent so much time here as a child. . . . Very happy to have a ridiculous picture of myself taken in this carpeted heaven. #memories #minerals #childhood #gayselfie."

Finally, another type of social media post comments upon or transforms the Museum through the juxtaposition of the image and its description:

- A photo in the Hall of South American Peoples focused on an indigenous woman bent over collecting sticks. "Yo! She's not wearing a shirt! #boobies."
- A photo of thirty small items on display in the Hall of Gems and Minerals, each with its own distinct and bright color. "Happy NYC Pride Weekend. #lovewins #NYCPride."
- A photo of the cheetah diorama in the Hall of African Mammals. "Pretty cool all the animals at this zoo kill themselves. #EarthDay."
- An artsy photo of a human skeleton in the Hall of Human Origins. "Came for the A/C, stayed for the men."

There is a lot to say about these photos, but what primarily grabbed me was how playful they were, among the visitors and with the Museum. And how performative, whether in the Halls or for the audience on social media. It left me wondering: How could we leverage these existing practices? More specifically, how could we design an experience that guides visitors to use the cameras in their pockets to play with the Museum? (And when I say "play with" I mean it in two ways, as in "play with a stick" to explore its affordances and "play with a friend" in order to make a connection.)

The second source of inspiration came from a board game: *Pandemic*. When it first came out in 2008, it was sort of a unicorn. It modeled a new way for players to collaborate and would inspire a new generation of collaborative board games (along with many expansion packs and sequels). Working together as a team of scientists, players unite against a series of virulent diseases breaking out across the world. It was "you" versus the game, in which "you" was the totality of all players. This was a perfect model of social interaction with the Museum. I wanted neither a single-user experience (in which everyone else in the player's party was either bored or forced into the role of observer) nor a competitive multiplayer experience (in which all members of the visitor's group had to play against one another). Instead, I wanted collaboration. I wanted friendly conversations among players. I wanted people to help each other. I wanted different people to lean in at different points based on different abilities and areas of interest. Sort of like, you know, a trip to a museum.

At the same time, *Pandemic* takes place on a board based on the map of the world. Oh no! An outbreak is spreading out of Buenos Aires, but a new virus just appeared in Jakarta! Can you get your players across the board in time? Of course, the Museum had a map as well, five in fact, one for each floor of the campus. Much of the visitor experience is designed *within* an exhibit; I wondered what an experience might look like *across* exhibits, turning the Museum map into a game board that visitors must traverse.

A third source of inspiration were the adorable and accessible digital toys from the Swedish app development studio, Toca Boca. Toca Boca apps are guided by a philosophy articulated on their website.[1] One describes broad accessibility: "Our apps aren't ever made for a specific type of kid, they're made with all kids in mind." Another explains how they are more like toys than games: "There's no failure, only play." Very Bernie De Koven. The possibility for infinite play.

Their apps usually start with a real-world theme and location—doctor's office, grocery store, hair salon, kitchen, house—and then offer the child player a simple app interaction (a finger drag, a finger swirl, etc.) that maps to an activity within the app (combing hair, stirring the pot, etc.). Each interaction is short—just a few seconds—and the feedback is immediate: drag your finger and make your customer's hair point left. Swirl your finger and make the water boil. And there is little to no language: no text on the screens, no spoken words (designed to reach across their initial European-focused market).

What inspired me about Toca Boca was their style of play. Very simple. Very accessible. Very aligned with the affordances of the mechanism. A phone knows when it is tilted; how can we make titling fun? A phone can track a swirling finger; how can we make swirling fun? A phone can track the speed of a tapping finger; how can we make tapping fun? This left me wondering: how could this quick, simple, and accessible style of play be integrated into a museum experience, in which the real-world themes and locations were defined by the various Halls?

The fourth and final inspiration came through a family trip to the Magic Kingdom at Disney World in Orlando, Florida. Walking through the park, a "cast member" was passing something out to visitors like us. We each received our own free deck of playing cards, a map of special locations around the park, and directions to the closest booth to register to play. At the booth, tucked into an out-of-the-way location behind "Ye Olde Christmas Shoppe," we learned all about *Sorcerers of the Magic Kingdom*.

Sorcerers is a game played throughout the streets and alleys of the Magic Kingdom. It uses *Pokémon*-style collectible cards featuring scores of Disney film heroes. Players use a card key at select locations to unlock a "portal"—revealing, for example, that a wall poster is actually an interactive video screen—to present the visitor the next segment of the story and allow the player to use their hero cards to fight Disney movie villains. From an outsider's perspective, players wait in line to watch videos in places like shop windows who then, after about a minute of video watching, hold cards up in the air before moving on. If no one is playing, it is hard to identify that anything is amiss, effectively hiding the game in plain sight. The videos are different for each player, based on their status in the game and their current narrative, and edited in real time based on the cards selected; for example, holding up the card Belle's Mountain Blizzard might throw animated snowballs at the video henchmen while Mulan's Dragon Cannon would instead shoot fire.

At the time I was amazed at the seamless way Disney had hidden the technology (in the cards and the video kiosks) to create an intuitive, location-specific, collectible card game. I was enamored with the idea that we might have our cake and eat it too—that is, one could add a game layer over a vast geography to motivate and direct guest movement yet have it be nearly invisible to those not playing.

It also used sophisticated technology, but the experience was not about the equipment. Virtual reality is often about the wonder of suddenly finding yourself in an immersive 360 environment, but it draws attention to the device required to support that experience. *Sorcerers*, in contrast, was about solving puzzles in a personalized, Disney-branded animated adventure. The behind-the-scenes tech tracking your movement through the park, your location in the narrative, the cards used for battle, the real-time rendered videos, how the game recognizes which card is being played—that is all made invisible to the player.

So the game is invisible to non-players while the technology behind it is invisible to its players. Now that is some Disney magic (which is just another way to say exquisite design).

So without a team of Disney Imagineers, scaled back to a Museum level, I asked myself: how can we design a game layer across the Museum that is known only to players, foregrounds the interactive narrative experience, and is richly informed by the geolocation of the player? At the same time, could we design something that allowed our visitors to slip seamlessly in and out of gameplay, so the players controlled the pace of the game (not the other way around) while the wonders of the Museum could always command their attention without being in conflict with game requirements?

When I left the meeting with Susan tasked with launching a youth program to build a prototype for a game about the impact of biodiversity on human health, these were the "puppies" that were barking for my attention. These were the lessons and models I was drawing from. I had no idea what the game would be about or what players would experience. But I was fairly confident visitors as a team would be using the cameras on their phones to play with the Museum using quick, simple, and accessible minigames while exploring a narrative that leverages locations in, and content from, all around the Museum.

MICROMUSEUM

MicroMuseum now had its team in place. In addition to Susan Perkins (the subject-matter expert) and Marisa Jahn (the educational-app developer), we also had Abbey Novia (a dynamic part-time science educator with the desired biology background) and Ruth Sherman (an enthusiastic graduate student intern from New York University). And we had Hannah, Program Assistant for Youth Digital Learning Programs. It's time to introduce Hannah.

Hannah Jaris has been with us throughout this book, but it's time she step out into the light. In the parlance of *Star Trek*, she was the Spock to my Kirk, the Riker to my Picard. She could run missions while I ran the ship. Or vice versa. Often, in this book, when I write "I" I am really thinking "we."

Together, the team designed the scope of the program and the educational objectives of the game:

> The program will engage 20 high school youth this spring in an afterschool program to collaborate with microbial curator Susan Perkins and educational-app developer Marisa Jahn to create a prototype of a game designed to explore the "hidden world" within our halls. The game will encourage its players to look for things that exist and operate at a microscale while developing an understanding of their ecological role across scale. The high school youth will play a key role selecting and working with the science content, shaping the game aesthetics, and co-designing the educational and gameplay experience.

We decided that visitors who played the game should be able to

- have a familiarity with a diversity of microorganisms.
- understand that microorganisms are part of a complex ecosystem across scales.
- envision how humans are part of that complex ecosystem.
- appreciate the overall importance of a healthy ecosystem.
- see the microscale within the Museum's macroscale.
- contemplate additional stories hidden throughout the Museum.
- visit less trafficked AMNH exhibits.

In addition to the educational objectives of the game, we decided that youth developing it in the afterschool program should also be able to

- co-design a Hall-based educational experience.
- contribute to the Museum's knowledge of how to integrate new digital tools into exhibit-based experiences that create new pathways for visitor engagement.
- expand their twenty-first-century learning skills through learning how to use digital tools to design a mobile learning experience.

Before the first session we needed to have a clear idea of the game design. Without that we would not know how to best direct the attention and energies of the youth. To begin we needed to understand the affordances of the materials around which we were designing the experience.

Yes, we knew we would use a mobile device, but how would we ask players to use it? Toca Boca suggested one model—quick, repeated, intuitive actions. But how would a player understand why they were using the app to do these actions? That is, when asked to solve a problem, how would the phone provide a path to the solution? Maybe we should pretend the phone is a scientific device, we wondered, a super science toolkit for seeing and studying the microscopic level, one that changes with each challenge, turning the screen on the phone into the view from the imagined device. For example, if the activity called for a microscope, then the phone became its lens. This decision allowed us to constrain the design of the activity to the real-world two-dimensional flatness of the visitor's phone, and design the Toca Boca–style minigames to match.

Another material within the game were the exhibits themselves. Most all were behind glass, preventing the visitors from touching them or moving around them. But like in *Where's Waldo?* we could invite visitors to use their phone's camera to look for relevant visual elements and capture what they found. The exhibits would provide real-world content for each challenge, suggesting the science to be explored and, from a narrative perspective, teaching its own distinct story for how we understand life at the microbial scale. The distance between the exhibits spread across different Halls could be used as a game design element. And perhaps the minigames could layer a game over the exhibit through the phone's camera, combining Toca Boca–style interactives with AR.

Along with the app on the phone and the exhibits in the halls, we also wanted an object for the player to hold, something to both use during the game and a souvenir to take home. Perhaps it might even be something to collect. We began by drawing from the world of baseball cards and collectible card games. In my mind, after *Pterosaurs: The Card Game*, I wanted to see what might happen if an AR target was incorporated into the game mechanic, not just as an add-on. I could still feel that wonder of watching Jeremy's augmented insect crawl up my arm, and the delight of holding a flying pterosaur in my hand. What would be equally awesome in this game and, more importantly, essential for playing it? Would each card augment a different scientific instrument, and the player would have to figure out the "right card to play" to solve each challenge?

Each of these materials, and the way they might interact with each other, would find meaning only within the narrative that tied them all together, that would justify the player's relationship with these tools and their need to use these tools throughout the Museum. We explored a few grand narratives. Microbiome signatures are used in forensics. So maybe, just maybe, someone came to the Museum, stole items from the collections, then replaced them with duplicates. Our job now is to travel the Museum to find the fakes by authenticating the real ones, by testing their microbiome signature.

Or maybe not. That would lock us into one scientific practice, repeated over and over. We wanted instead to explore a variety of science activities and topics. And why focus on something distasteful that really does happen—people stealing items from the Museum (albeit rarely)—rather than something more noble?

Instead of treating the Museum as . . . well, a museum (as items that someone might steal), we decided to use the dioramas for what they were designed to do, which is capture a moment in time and transport you there: roaming a Wyoming prairie teeming with tens of millions of bison, exploring a forest floor at the size of insects, hiking a mixed deciduous forest in late spring within the Great Smoky Mountains National Park. Now we could use the game to take you one step further—now that you were there, in Wyoming or on the forest floor, something was wrong (what exactly, we did not yet know). Your job, as the player, was to bring together the scientific tools and human resources to solve it.

So who are you then, the player, within these narratives, as someone solving these scientific mysteries? We imagined they were like Park Rangers but working on the microscopic level. Ah! MicroRangers. Yes, that could work. MicroRangers, operating at the microscopic level to keep the fictitious microbiomes within the scenes represented in our exhibits healthy and diverse.

We played with the idea of having visitors explore these mysteries like a detective, investigating the source of the problem, determining what tools to use, and recruiting the right scientists to engage. It soon became clear this was way too complicated. The mental bandwidth for a game played in the Hall can be fairly low. Instead, the narrative would introduce regular but engaged citizens (just like the visitors themselves) who identified a problem and called in the MicroRangers to help. Each situation would describe a system out of balance, in which something at the microbial level is having an impact at the human-scale macro-level, and the game would partner you with the right type of scientist to investigate and then resolve the problem. This simplified the narrative and gameplay while providing us with a wide range of real-world systems and science practices to explore.

The cards now were no longer augmented science tools. Instead, the cards augmented each of the partnering scientists, with one additional character to tie it all together: the Dispatcher. This is the character who is the player's guide (we never forgot this whole project was replacing the original idea of a Museum tour). The Dispatcher fields a call from the concerned hiker. The Dispatcher activates the player and sends them on their mission. The Dispatcher tells the player which scientist is right for each challenge.

We knew families would need to be able to pause the game at any time—to get lunch, go to the bathroom, or let an unexpected exhibit catch their eye. This meant visitors would need to be free from the urgency created by a timed experience. Instead, players would need to control the speed of their gameplay, slowing it down to a crawl when needed and speeding it up when desired. To address this we decided, like *Pandemic*, our game should be turn-based. So if time wouldn't add pressure to the game, we needed something else to create a nice arc of gameplay. Something had to make the later part of the game both move faster and feel more consequential, like the third act in a movie.

We imagined the challenges would appear in a random order and were treated as threats that could worsen over time (that is, over a certain number of turns). In the board game *Pandemic*, a virus appears. Once it appears in a particular city that location is more likely than others to get hit again. If a threat increases past a certain threshold in one city, then all adjacent cities get infected as well. In other words, if you ignore a threat it can spread. And if too many spreads occur, the players instantly lose the game. That means players have to constantly balance between resolving a challenge at a local level while attending to the health of the overall system. That gives every decision weight and meaning. You could resolve a local challenge but in doing so lose the overall game. As a result, a game mechanic with increasing threat levels turned each player's decision into a precious resource carefully considered and more valuable over the course of the game.

We tried to map that concept onto our own design. The game would begin in the Hall of Biodiversity. From there the player would move to different exhibits around the Museum. The nine exhibits would be grouped into three regions, three exhibits per region. Within each region, each site would contain a challenge related to either bacteria, virus, or eukaryote. Resolve an exhibit's threat and its scientist would receive a related power-up. End the game back in the Hall of Biodiversity with either three scientists with the same power-up (e.g., three bacteria power-ups) or three scientists with one of each power. This used game design to provide players with meaningful decisions—do we go to the seals exhibit or the bison? At the same time, if a threat was left alone for too long, the threat could spread to an entire Hall. If players lost a Hall, then game over. In this way players had to work at both the local level and game-wide level at the same time.

Susan helped to remind us how the narrative and gameplay had to align with the science we wanted to teach. The story needed to highlight that the threats at each exhibit all share an idea in common: a complex ecosystem is a healthier ecosystem, and a healthy biodiversity means that there are a lot of different types of organisms. When one organism starts to reproduce too fast it reduces the level of other healthy organisms that share the ecosystem. This is why removing invasive species increases biodiversity. So for certain types of microbes, like with the spread of a destructive virus, the threat will be identified as their having disrupted the balance of the ecosystem, and therefore reducing biodiversity. The balance is the key. This way players can still restore biodiversity by reducing the population of a virus (assuming at that point the virus was overpopulating and taking resources away from other organisms in the ecosystem). At the same time, we had to be clear not to equate microbes as always threats to biodiversity. Some distress calls must require the addition of microbes into the ecosystem or reinforce the positive effect they are currently having to untangle a mystery.

The key was communicating that problems at the macroscopic level (at the exhibit level) can arise from sources unseen at the microscopic level (the game explored within the app). We decided that our problem will always be an example of an ecosystem out of balance. The solution would always be found in restoring that balance (using each particular scientists' area of expertise, in the context of the narrative created by one Museum exhibit), with the player collaborating at the microscopic level with the scientist at the macroscopic level. Using this as a guide, Susan identified locations we might consider using within the Museum, the challenges we might encounter there, and the tools of science required to resolve them.

For example, at the African elephant exhibit in the Akeley Gallery of African Mammals, players might learn how elephants in captivity might get tuberculosis if *Mycobacterium* is passed from an infected human.

Susan found more for us to explore as well, about animals (gorillas and malaria, armadillos and leprosy, ticks and Lyme disease), rocks (goethite and iron-breathing microbes), and humans (using yeast to turn plant juice alcoholic).

Of course, this was all just pre-planning, the decisions made were just best guesses, us having fun swiping at low-hanging fruit. But would visitors actually like it? Would it teach them anything? Would they actually integrate it into their regular visit? We could not answer any of these questions until we had a prototype in hand, one we could test with the public. And for that we needed to partner with a youth program to produce it.

In order to make useful contributions, the teens would need training on the content and in their game design skills. As we developed their expertise in both areas, we focused them on fleshing out the content required by the prototype. We used the following production workflow to make sure everyone was on the same page and that our schedules were aligned—not just among us at the Museum, but also with Jeremy Kenisky and his crack-team of mobile app developers.

The youth program would begin with the two grey boxes at the top, with sessions introducing them to the science of microbiology and the exhibits throughout the museum. Activities would then divide. On the left-hand workflow you can see the development of the Toca Boca–style minigames, beginning with the youth and then passing the work over to Jeremy and his team to deliver. Meanwhile, the right-hand flow focuses on both the narrative (characters, plot, videos) and the app design (tying together the narrative and the Toca Boca–style minigames with the playing card AR targets). All of the activities culminate in the alignment of the youth program and Jeremy producing the beta, prepped for testing.

At least, that was the plan.

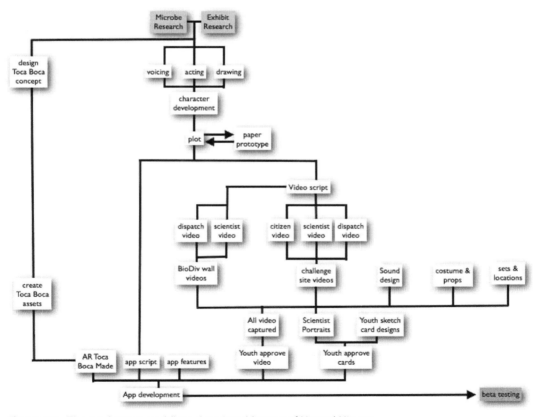

Figure 4.1. The production workflow. *American Museum of Natural History*

From the youth perspective, all of this went on behind the scenes. We kept their field of view narrowly focused on one step at a time. In fact, for them, it all began with a pint of ice cream.

I brought out some Häagen-Dazs, cookies and cream flavored I recall. I took out an iPad, turned up the volume, projected it to the screen, and pointed its camera at the top of the lid. Suddenly, a concerto began, played by a violist who appeared to be floating above the pint. I brought out a second flavor, maybe strawberry. Now a cellist joined in, floating above his flavor. The "idea" is that this concerto is a timer; when the song concludes the ice cream should be soft enough to scoop and serve. Which we did. And as we ate, we discussed the experience.

Why did the company make this AR app? How was it designed to enhance our ice cream eating experience (and did it)? What if it wasn't produced by a for-profit company but an indie artist virtually tagging these products with their virtual work—would we respond differently?

The teens described their experience as first being surprised—who would have expected a musician to appear?—which then transformed into wanting to know more about what was happening. It generated curiosity. We talked about how AR is a fun trick to capture someone's attention and develop their need to know more. But did it generate curiosity about the product or just about the technology itself? We challenged them to think about how AR could be used to capture people's attention and get them to want to know more about not ice cream but microbiology.

After exploring AR apps, both commercial (Ikea catalogs) and educational (the Asian Art Museum of San Francisco's *China's Terracotta Warriors App*), we traveled to the Hall of Ocean Life. It was after hours, so the Museum was closed to visitors. We had the vast hall to ourselves, turning it into our private classroom. It was time for them to come up with their own augmented minigames.

We wanted the teens to imagine the types of interactions and games that could be part of MicroRangers. Working in groups, they were challenged to choose an exhibit, learn about it, then offer a short pitch about how they might use an AR experience to inform others about the imagined microbial interactions within the depicted diorama. They explored kelp forests, Arctic algae, and deep-sea bioluminescent creatures. They came up with minigames (which they re-branded MicroGames) like adding ice cubes to save coral from bleaching or dragging microbes into a human's intestinal tracts to help them digest seaweed. While much was not even close to scientifically accurate, that was not the point; they were learning how to map a game mechanic onto a science-based narrative. They were just getting warmed up.

When next we met, we shared with the teens the list prepared earlier by Susan of the dozen possible locations around the Museum for missions within the game. We needed them to pare back the list, ideally to five. It was time for the teens to start making significant co-development design decisions, and they felt ready.

They weighed the pros and cons of each site and brainstormed interactive AR experiences around each one. This included narratives ranging from a fairy with a magical frog to a flatulent buffalo. They evaluated and quantified potential visitor interest in each location, the plausibility of each narrative-based scientific challenge, and the educational potential of each MicroGame.

After much debate and discussion—not just among themselves but with Susan, Abbey, and Marisa—they got it down to five sites and their related microorganisms:

- Frogs / Chytrid
- Mbuti Pygmies / Haemophilus
- Beavers / Giardia
- Water Buffalo / Methanogen
- Coral / Zooxanthellae

It was sad letting some of the other exhibits and game ideas go. On the other hand, it was exciting to start focusing so we could dig deeper into the design. Plus, it was good exercise to toughen ourselves for the job we would next have to take on: whittling down the list from five to just two for the prototype.

In youth programs like this—integrated with an iterative design process and the content needs that emerge—an instructor must be nimble and ready to pivot in whichever direction the process requires. One cannot simply create the curriculum in advance and just deliver it in a set sequence. Now that the five potential sites were identified, Abbey could rapidly develop the curriculum (with support from Susan) and deliver the next level of detail for the relevant microbial science. For example, What do zooxanthellae have to do with coral bleaching (and how do you actually pronounce their name)? What do methane-producing bacteria have to do with how buffaloes digest their food?

While Abbey increased the content knowledge of the youth, Marissa and I, with Ruth and Hannah, led the youth in exploring the narrative and gaming potential of each exhibit. The youth dug deep into their creative power, thought up new ideas for MicroGames, and imagined new characters and ways visitors might interact with the Museum. We provided transparencies, markers, and photos of each exhibit so they could develop mock-ups of how visitors would experience both the augmented characters and the MicroGames.

These efforts culminated in another after-hours in-Hall beta test, in which the youth led walkthroughs of their ideas, carried cardboard iPads and hand-drawn stand-ins for the augmented cards, and acted out the characters of the Dispatcher, Distressed Citizens, and Scientists, using costumes with unanticipated accents and descriptive names.

We revisited and evaluated all five based on three criteria: its potential for fun, for teaching science, and for its integration with a mobile AR activity. We also had to consider how the final two

Figure 4.2. Transparencies and exhibit photos to mock up the visitor experience. *Author*

would fit together: How would players move between the two locations? Did the two together offer a contrast in microbial content and science solutions? Could they represent in a pilot the vast potential that could be explored in a final product?

In the end, we landed on the coral and the water buffalo exhibit. Over the next month, we developed the MicroCrisis for each location—the microbe-based mystery and its assortment of characters, science, MicroGames, and the narrative tying it all together. Youth had to answer questions like *What do zooxanthellae look like?* and *What are the components of a water buffalo's digestive tract?* They wrote scripts for the characters, developed the MicroGames, and designed concept art for the augmented character cards.

We had everything we needed for Jeremy and his team to take our assets and turn them into a playable prototype. Well, almost. We just needed the video assets to create the digital characters that would appear in the player's hand, triggered when the app viewed the visual AR targets on the scientist playing cards. Fortunately, the Museum has a photo studio, with lighting, cameras, green screens, and everything else we might need. We held our own auditions within the course for our AR stars, costumed these new actors and actresses, then headed to the studio for the film shoot. The footage from the day would be triggered at key moments within the game and be seen in the palm of the player's hand like Princess Leia from the first *Star Wars* film ("Help me, Obi-Wan Kenobi. You're my only hope").

Figure 4.3. The augmented reality video shoot. *American Museum of Natural History*

The first character to appear in the game is the Dispatch Operator, who acts as a guide for the player, a cadet ready for the final test in order to become a full-fledged MicroRanger. "Welcome to your final training day, cadet! It's me, your MicroRangers Dispatch Operator. You've trained hard over the last 6 months to become a MicroRanger, working to keep the balance, one microbiome at a time. To graduate and become a full-fledged MicroRanger, you'll handle real MicroCrises with real civilians. Your first mission, if you choose to accept it, is to help this citizen with their MicroCrisis."

That citizen is the Dairy Farmer. "My water buffalo, which makes the best milk for mozzarella cheese, have been farting constantly! I tried to increase their milk production by feeding them grass like the cow farmers next door but the only thing that increased is their flatulence. Send help!" The player must travel to the Asian buffalo exhibit in the Hall of Asian Mammals.

When they arrive the player has a decision to make: Which scientist will they need? They can choose from P.H. Meter, an Environmental Specialist: "I will want to start by asking questions like, Has it been abnormally hot recently?"; Dr. Mike Robiome, a Microbiome Specialist: "I will want to start by asking questions like, Could the bacteria in the buffalo be affecting it?"; or Dr. Sue DeMonas, a Disease Specialist: "I will want to start by asking questions like, Have you or your buffalo been congested recently?"

Once the player selects the most appropriate scientist, Dr. Mike Robiome, he explains that as he works on the MacroScale, the player should "use your microscopic size to go inside its stomach. Actually, they have four stomachs—head into the first one, the rumen, look around, and figure out why its gut microbiome is out of balance." This dialogue initiates the diagnostic MicroGame: viewing the space all around the buffalo exhibit, now augmented with floating purple/black microbes, which are each cleared and caught through a finger tap as a timer counts down.

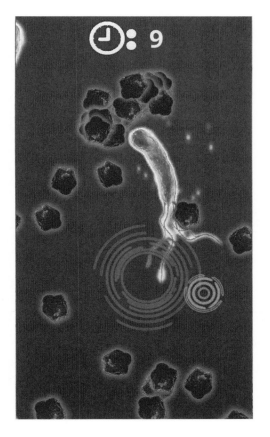

Figure 4.4. A screenshot of a *MicroRangers* MicroGame. *Author*

The augmented Dr. Robiome returns with his analysis: "It seems those microbes, methanogens, are the ones causing all the trouble." Referring to the Dairy Farmer's distress call, in which we learned a change in diet caused the buffalo's difficulties, our scientist explains what the source of the problem was and how the MicroRanger cadet can now solve it: "We need to help the farmer change the water buffalo's diet so it will use different bacteria to break down its meals. Let's see if a change in diet will improve the situation. Try out some *different* foods and see how the water buffalo reacts." The resolution MicroGame now begins: orienting the phone's camera over the exhibit's buffalo, the player decides which items to feed it, observing and evaluating the effect of each food source on its production of both methane and milk.

Once resolved, Dr. Robiome returns once again. "You figured out that high-quality foods like grains not only helped the farmer but you also helped the earth—methane gas from animals like cows and water buffalo is also a major source of global warming."

The Dispatch Operator congratulates the player and shares a final message of thanks from the augmented Dairy Farmer: "After you started feeding the buffalo grains, they not only stopped farting so much but the milk also makes the most DE-LICIOUS mozzarella! Here, have some!" And from there, a new distress call comes in, from a glass-bottom boat tour operator concerned about bleached coral. Time for the player to head to a new exhibit in the Hall of Ocean Life.

After delivering the videos to Jeremy, we focused the youth on other activities—like a behind-the-scenes tour of Susan's genetics laboratory, and swabbing public places in the museum for microbes (one teen's final program reflection included the following: "What surprised me the most was how much bacteria we found on the water fountain"). After a few weeks, Jeremy delivered all the assets we needed for a fully playable prototype. I took it for a test run myself, giving it a thorough walk-through in the empty Halls one day before the Museum opened. I wanted to make sure everything worked properly, both technically and as we had designed it. As you can see in the following, at the water buffalo in the Hall of Asian Mammals, the AR is enhanced by holding the white silhouette of the animal around the specimen in the exhibit; that allowed us, for example, to add animation to make it look like the real buffalo was snorting.

Figure 4.5. Holding the AR card target to the camera (left). Feeding the augmented buffalo (right). *Author*

It is always exciting to see something come together for the first time: holding the newly designed cards in my hand, watching the augmented videos of the teens appear to float above my phone, playing site-specific MicroGames. I could hardly wait for the rest of the team to see it and for us to do a formal walk-through with the teens.

Figure 4.6. The augmented reality *MicroRanger* cards. *American Museum of Natural History*

After two months of research and design the teens could finally see their ideas realized—augmented videos of characters they created, location-specific MicroGames, and more. They critiqued the prototype and prepared for a final presentation—a gathering of seventy friends and family members, to whom they presented both their behind-the-scenes creation story and the full walk-through. They collected player feedback along the way; for example, the wayfinding was still off, as it was not clear to all players how to get from the buffalo exhibit to the coral reef.

In our last afterschool session, we asked the youth to predict the future of *MicroRangers*:

"Kids will be begging their mom [to] play."

"The future for *MicroRangers* holds great things, but there will always be room for improvement."

"If it's a success, we might update the app with more events, games, and other locations."

To update the app, to move it from prototype to a gold release, a number of things had to happen. First was getting sign-off from the Museum. That meant showing the game to Lisa Gugenheim, Senior Vice President for Education. Lisa was high up in the ranks—technically my boss's boss's boss. I might meet with her, if I was lucky, once a season. Time with her was precious. Talking with someone at her level within the Museum was like talking with Yoda; you are always aware she is operating on a different plane of existence, can see things you cannot even imagine, and you're grateful for the brief time your reality overlapped with her own. If this walk-through went well, it could mean the project got passed on to the Development Department, who would look for a funder or sponsor to advance it. If it did not go well . . . that could be it.

At first, everything seemed to be going smoothly. We started in the Hall of Biodiversity. The game led us to the Spectrum of Life, an artistic interpretation of ecological biodiversity, created through over fifteen hundred specimens and models. We located the virtual "MicroRangers Home Base" inside the gorgeous hand-blown crystal of a microorganism. If *MicroRangers* was a board game, this would be the starting square. Using the app's AR feature, we "checked in" and were welcomed by the Dispatcher to our first training day as a *MicroRangers* cadet.

Before long the first MicroCrisis appeared. That is when I got concerned. The Dairy Farmer appeared, with his "My water buffalo . . . have been farting constantly!" Maybe I was expecting a "Kids will love this" response. Instead, I feared I was reading disgust on Lisa's face, a judgment that we had done something tasteless and off-brand. Or it all could have been in my head. We headed to the Hall of Asian Mammals, played the diagnostic MicroGame, then fed buffalo to resolve the MicroCrisis.

Designing Augmented Reality   **95**

Before we got to the end, Lisa had seen enough. She did not need to travel to the Hall of Ocean Life and experience the coral reef mission. She liked it, enough. She saw its potential. *MicroRangers* had passed one of its earliest and most important tests. And I learned a valuable lesson: in a prototype, lead with your strongest content (and next time please save the fart jokes for a later build!).

For now, MicroRangers was now out of our hands. Its future was driven by the Development Department. Six months later, I received an email with the subject "opportunity knocks." There was a relatively new funder who cared about the Museum, science learning, and "kids being able to blow things up" (as in disrupt afterschool learning, not arm them with actual explosives). We were informed we could use the funds to establish something that had earlier only been piloted. How often does that happen? And it could go under a banner like "Expand Mobile Learning Opportunities."

MicroRangers had found its funder.

MICRORANGERS

The second phase of *MicroRangers* was designed to take the proof of concept for the game—containing two missions—and expand it into a full-fledged product—with nine missions plus a culminating boss battle. This phase also needed to cover all the required product development components, like launch, communications, and a sustainability plan. And again it would be developed through an afterschool youth program, this time running for twenty-nine afterschool sessions in the winter and spring.

We expanded the team for the course. Abbey stayed on to write the curriculum, but a new instructor, Christine Marsh, stepped into Abbey's shoes to deliver it. Nick Fortugno came on board to lead the game design, with the active support of student intern Carl Farra (earning his master of fine arts in game design from New York University's Game Center). And to everyone's surprise and delight, Alejandro, the high school student who played the Dairy Farmer with the flatulent buffalo, now returned to the project as the course's teacher assistant (having since graduated and begun his college career studying science).

Before starting the new youth program, we had to complete a round of revisions on the game design. First of all, no more requiring players to get from one floor to another. Getting around just one floor in the Museum can be challenging enough! We kept the Hall of Biodiversity and its crystal protist as MicroRangers Home Base, along with the adjacent Hall of Ocean Life. To those we added the nearby Hall of North American Mammals (where a bison could adapt the narrative from our flatulent Asian water buffalo) and the lightly traveled Hall of North American Forests. It was not always easy to decide which Halls to keep and which to let go. It felt hard to include the anthropology-based exhibits, like the one with the Mbuti Pygmies; the science was fascinating but it was hard to negotiate the required sensitivity to cultural issues. Other Halls came with institutional challenges, like the Hall of Ocean Life often being closed to the public for special events (like a *Game of Thrones* season premiere party); in this case we decided the content was too good not to include and we would just add *MicroRangers* disappointment to the list that accompanies daily Hall closings.

In addition, Nick and Carl dug deeper into collaborative board games like *Pandemic*. They created a model for a fully fleshed out *MicroRangers*, one which required three MicroCrises in each of the three Halls. They also simplified the game flow; for example, the player would now be assigned one unique scientist per challenge, rather than have to pick from an existing set of scientists.

Upon launch of the new youth program, the team of youth co-developers went through a similar process as the youth from MicroMuseum: after learning content related to microbiology, to game design, and to the Museum itself, we set them loose. They gathered story ideas for each MicroCrisis, developing the new characters and designing one MicroGame for identifying the source of the problem and a second one to resolve it. Each team of youth took their ideas through critique sessions and multiple iterations based on the received feedback.

At the same time, Nick and Carl came up with the macro-game, only revealed over time to the players, that brings the gameplay and narrative through a dramatic arc. Playing a handful of Micro-Crises could be fun, but after a while it would lose some of its charge, repeating the same type of things over and over. Something was needed to introduce risk and drama in the gameplay story. We had earlier decided that what united each of the MicroCrises was that something was out of balance, that this lack of balance was having an impact at both the micro and macro level, and that the Micro-Ranger is being asked to restore that balance. What we had never addressed was who or what could be causing this imbalance.

To address this, we drew inspiration from the Hall of Biodiversity itself, and through in-depth meetings with the Museum's Center for Biodiversity. In the middle of the Hall, right before the entrance to the Hall of Ocean Life, where one can just begin to get a peek of the massive blue whale waiting on the other side, most visitors walk right over a roughly six-foot diameter circle. It is a plaque recognizing the five major extinctions in the history of the planet. It reads, in part, "Global climate change and other causes, probably including collisions between earth and extraterrestrial objects, were responsible for these events. Right now we are in the midst of the Sixth Extinction, this time caused solely by humanity's transformation of the ecological landscape." That was it. The "Sixth Extinction." That's what the players were up against.

The boss battle, only unlocked after players resolve a certain combination of MicroCrises, leads players to stand on the plaque and, facing away from the Hall of Ocean Life, hold the AR camera toward the Dzanga-Sangha Rain Forest exhibit. The outside of this replica of this Central African Republic forest are what we referred to as habit photos—oversized, brightly lit photographs that display the beauty and majesty of the natural environment. Coral reefs. The deserts. An ocean teaming with whales. The Dispatcher appears, sharing what is described as a simulation of where we are heading in the future if something is not done today. The delightful photos in front of the player are transformed through the AR camera into an apocalyptic hellscape. The coral reefs have bleached and died. Nuclear dumping has irradiated the deserts, setting them aflame. The whales fade from the ocean photo, as they are now extinct. As the player pans across the exhibit, one photo after another is transformed.

It is now up to the players, in the present, to restore the balance before it is too late. Players strategically complete the emerging MicroCrises that algorithmically populate the "board." If they fail, game over. The Sixth Extinction has won, and the MicroRanger can start over and try again. However, if they succeed at this level of gameplay, they unlock the final Boss Battle. A Boss Battle in a game is when a player is challenged to use all the new skills taught through the gameplay to take on a greater challenge, often applying what they learned in a new way in order to demonstrate mastery.

MicroRangers' Boss Battle took place within the Dzanga-Sangha Rain Forest exhibit. In this end-game phase, the distinction between the game's fictional narrative and the visitor's real-world challenges have become completely blurred as players debate decisions they should make to fight the Sixth Extinction. The game concludes back at the MicroRangers Home Base, where the Dispatcher congratulates the Cadet for having prevented the Sixth Extinction, as least for now, and for having graduated to a full-fledged MicroRanger.

Throughout the development of *MicroRangers*, we were facing a constant challenge: no pipeline really existed for what we were doing. The Exhibitions Department had their process well developed for ensuring their work was aligned with the Museum's goals, integrated with the activities of the Communication Department, connected with the Membership team, produced in partnership with the OLogy website, etc. I could say the same for Public Programs, or the high school science teacher program, and many others whose work reached across the Museum. Most of my work to this point, however, was fairly localized, within the afterschool youth program space; I collaborated with colleagues all around the campus, but often in ad hoc ways and often with individuals, not systems. For *MicroRangers* to have both a successful launch and to be fully integrated into our visitor offerings, it needed something more. Much more.

To get my hands around it, to get help, we created an advisory. We called them the *MicroRangers* Braintrust. Meeting monthly, it was designed to ensure the program was aligned with the needs of departments around the Museum and to avoid known pitfalls. It was also designed, in part, to gain buy-in among key allies around the Museum and lend legitimacy to the initiative. We also wanted to stay informed about other Museum efforts with which we would need to coordinate or leverage. Finally, we wanted to be alerted as soon as possible about individuals and departments who needed to stay informed.

The Braintrust included representatives from Information Technology and Exhibitions. It included scientists from Anthropology, Invertebrate Zoology, and the paleontologist and ornithologist who curated the Hall of Biodiversity. It included the lead from the Communication Digital Group, Matt Tarr, responsible for the Museum's *Explorer* app, so we could tackle shared problems together, like best practices for mobile wayfinding. I also admired Matt, someone who had successfully navigated the Museum for nearly two decades and drove innovation in his role as Digital Architect Director without covering over his collection of tattoos nor abandoning his skateboarder persona. The Braintrust also included the producer for OLogy, who would help guide the game's eventual web presence, much of the design of physical elements of the game, and ensure it was included within the educational print materials for the *Inside You* exhibit. We even included a Museum member, to represent family visitors.

At each meeting we would bring them up to speed on the development of the game, highlight changes, and raise questions we needed their help to answer. At the first session we asked, What is the most dangerous thing for us *not* to do? This list was lengthy. Do not underestimate the difficulty of getting the physical AR cards into visitors' hands. Make sure we can update the app if it is successful so we can add more content. Take into consideration unavoidable Hall closings.

We also explored complex topics, like how to represent the microbes. As the representative from Exhibitions said, "Part of what people come to the museum for is for things to look real." We went back and forth—will they have faces? How cartoonish can they look? How can we include visuals of actual microbes? We decided we could have it both ways: the protist-based Dispatcher could appear cartoonish while microbes within the MicroGames could appear more realistic.

It was challenging to explain the design of the meta-game, from a gameplay perspective, since we could not actually play it. Not yet, at least. But we tried to describe it to the Braintrust. Someone more experienced with modern tabletop games described it as a "very good crisis management game." But for others, it just sounded too complex. Could visitors really attend to so much information while walking through the Halls? I assured the BrainTrust we were not designing a game strictly for indie game players but, rather, simplifying mechanics proven successful in one space to adapt them for a general population within our Halls. Ultimately, it was acknowledged, we would learn if we had struck the right balance only by prototyping the game.

Concerns about the cards were a recurring feature of our conversations. Will it disrupt visitor expectations to require something physical to interact with an app? Will the floors be littered with discarded cards? Will visitors be able to find a card when they are ready to play? What will make them valuable or interesting enough to carry throughout their experience? Eventually Jeremy, our AR and mobile app developer, came up with a solution to some of these questions, by recommending we get rid of the cards entirely. Yes, we would still give visitors physical AR targets to hold in their hands, but it would no longer be pieces of paper. Instead, they would be metallic challenge coins.

When Jeremy first introduced the idea to me, I had never heard of a challenge coin. Apparently, there is a strong tradition in the US military that emerged in the twentieth century, using custom-made zinc-alloy castings or die-struck bronze. A commander, for example, might have one designed with their unit's badge or motto and present it to a member in recognition of a special achievement. In recent years they have been adapted in a variety of areas; the sample Jeremy sent me was a promotion for a tire store. It had a good heft in my hand. It felt good turning it around in my fingers. If it was good enough for a tire store and the Marines, why not the Museum?

Jeremy first raised the ideas as we worked to further streamline the narrative. He explained that tracking technology was improving, so the ability to use an image as an AR target was now feasible. His company tested images painted on coins and found it worked quite well. Choosing metal over paper, the MicroRanger target would be more durable over time. In fact, now it would be an even more attractive collectible to take home and display. We explored what a two-sided coin might look like—perhaps the Dispatcher image or game logo on one side, and a different scientist on the reverse.

This decision also aligned with another technical constraint Jeremy had raised: full-video in AR—the Princess Leia effect—was making the app just too large to download. For some reason an AR video of a person is much larger in file size then an animated character doing the same. To ensure a lower bandwidth for the app, it was an easy decision to make. We hated saying goodbye to the video of the teen performers, but the youth still had a role to play. We held auditions across all of the youth programs and those selected voiced the characters in the game. Within the Museum's audio booth, they took on the role of all of the new scientists, and we brought back our original performers to expand their roles. Now scientists started each interaction at an exhibit with an "observation" beat, instructing the player to use the phone's camera to take a picture of something they could see with their eyes (a favorite fish, an interesting tree marking, etc.). The scientists also absorbed the role of the concerned citizens; the concerns of boat captains and others were now communicated directly by the scientists. It was all getting tightened up.

The Braintrust liked the transition to the coins. They appreciated the weight and feel. They recognized the image could be customized—such as for a special event or using a limited edition, gold-rimmed coin for members. One person suggested it would be cool if there was a coin flip in the game (true—but we never did that). Another realized that the coin image could still act as an AR trigger even within another medium, like on the back of the exhibit's educator guide, turning the printed guide itself into a replacement for the coin (and we did just that). Eventually, the art for the animated scientists made it onto the coins. They looked beautiful.

At the third Braintrust, Matt Tarr announced the final decision about the relationship between *MicroRangers* and plans for the Museum's overhaul of the *Explorer* app. I had always hoped our new game might somehow live within the Museum's signature app. It would be so much easier politically. It would also integrate the game into an existing pipeline and address long-term sustainability and

Figure 4.7. The augmented reality *MicroRangers* coins. *Author*

management questions. At the same time, the *Explorer* app had its own schedule and technical requirements. It would be very challenging to keep the two aligned. Matt shared the decision with the group. "*MicroRangers* may not be in *Explorer* this year due to technical and budgetary reasons," he told them. "But it can be coded as something that can be integrated later." At least that was the hope. In the meantime, we still had common challenges we could explore together. The primary one was wayfinding: How could both apps get visitors from one point in the museum to another?

The current *Explorer* app drew from Google Maps's capabilities. Using GPS signals it would locate you on a map and then provide step-by-step instructions, one screen at a time, to get from a location on any one floor (e.g., fourth floor *T. rex*) to a different location on a different floor (e.g., lower-level subway exit). Matt knew we could do better and worked with me to experiment with different options through *MicroRangers*. At first we took a more radical approach—getting rid of the maps completely. Instead, we experimented with video. Microsoft had a new app at the time called *Hyperlapse* which we found intriguing. Reproducing a stop-motion technique, to make a hyperlapse film you walk from one location to another; the app then speeds it up while stabilizing the image. A three-minute walk from, say, the coral reef to the forest floor exhibit turns into an oddly compelling and smoothly delivered fifteen-second visual guide from one location to another. It was a nice idea—but when you consider all the different permutations from just the nine different MicroCrises to each other, in the end it was just not feasible.

MicroRangers' geolocating was eventually built off of a new beacon system Matt deployed around the Museum. These beacons were much more accurate than GPS. A Hall might have dozens of these tiny devices secreted away in unseen locations all around the room. Rather than GPS locating an individual as being within a room, the beacons could tell the app exactly where in the room the person was standing. *MicroRangers*' Dispatcher could now direct a player to "Go to the Hall of Ocean Life"; once passing through the entrance, the app could ring, request the MicroRangers Coin, then have the Dispatcher give the player an exhibit to find; upon arrival at the right exhibit, the beacon would trigger the app that the player was positioned to confront their next MicroCrisis. The beacons did not always work perfectly—apparently beacons are weak through water, which is what humans are bags of in no small measure—but it worked well enough. And when it did, when your phone knew exactly where you were, for just one moment reality and fiction blurred. It could feel like magic.

Over the course of the program, the youth provided continuous feedback on the game design and the overall experience. The youth identified ways to make it more "game-y," recommending more opportunities for players to gain points, earn rewards, and receive stronger feedback (with messages like "level cleared"). They suggested the game be broken down into different levels of difficulty, to appeal to both the casual and the expert gamer alike. They emphasized the importance of featuring real science, with real scientists, and real science content (*What are the names of these microbes? How are they shaped?*). Finally, they helped us set the right tone for the game, giving players just a bit of a challenge but being forgiving where possible.

Carl Farra, the graduate student working with Nick on the game design, created the print prototype of the game early on. It was a good design challenge for him to use paper and small objects to represent a game reliant on digital interactivity and physical movement in the real world. At the time I invited him to share his thoughts on the process. Carl highlighted for me three techniques he used that made this a successful prototyping and playtesting process.

Carl's first design takeaway he called "Play games and play with games." Recall that one inspiration for *MicroRangers* was the collaborative aspect of the board game *Pandemic*. That game also provided a model for motivating player movement around a map. So Carl played *Pandemic*. A lot. Doing so helped him to learn how to create meaningful choices for our players. "We needed to have an extra layer of things to do, an additional task between players and victory," Carl shared.

In *Pandemic*, players don't simply remove blocks to cure diseases, as that would be too one-dimensional, but they're also collecting different colored cards as well, and it's the cards that directly tie in with the victory condition. With that in mind, we came up with Research Points, which are tokens that would be earned as players managed threats around the board. In order to win the game, players must earn a certain amount of Research Points and place them in the Hall of Biodiversity. The amount of Research Points they earn varies depending on their performance in the various mini-games around the museum.

Carl not only played *Pandemic*—he modified it, in ways to simulate the constraints of *MicroRangers*. Thus, his advice to not just play games but to play *with* them. For example, he would play *Pandemic* but limit himself to the nine cities in North America (akin to the nine MicroCrises in *MicroRangers*). "Playing the modified game was very helpful in getting the prototype off the ground," he said. "I could sort of envision what it's like to travel between nine museum exhibits and solving problems, how long the game might last, and how many cards should be in the deck."

Carl's second design takeaway he called *"Playtest. A lot."* Carl played through his non-digital prototype thirty times. In just four weeks there had been ten different versions of the game, with major differences between them (such as the amount of points a player earned, or the speed at which unattended MicroCrises took damage). He played and tweaked and played and tweaked until he arrived at a design he was satisfied with, a design in which the math felt balanced and did not leave the game broken.

More importantly, he leveraged the power of working with different playtesters. When he played with me, he found I showed little interest in good game design on its own; instead, I focused on the context in which it would be played, attending to both how the game mechanics supported the narrative and how the game experience aligned with the expectations of a museum visitor. His classmates, however, would bring in a different perspective, trying to break the game and look for mechanical inconsistencies. "It might be tempting to just roleplay as all the players yourself," he told me, "but you will get a lot more objective feedback you hadn't thought about if somebody else is playing your game."

Finally, Carl's third design takeaway he called "Go all out." I think what Carl was saying here is that one must do whatever it takes to reduce the difference between the paper prototype and final play conditions. For *MicroRangers*, that meant picking up that paper prototype and go play it out in the real Halls, moving from one exhibit to another as he played. He simulated the way the app would increase the threat level of MicroCrises through a drawing app. The AR MicroGames were replaced with simple dice rolling on an app, to focus efforts at the global level of the game without losing how it was shaped by the success or failure at the local level. A deck of cards was deployed to indicate the status of exhibits under attack. "When you're making a prototype in a different format than what the actual game's gonna be, keep in mind that the experiences are going to be vastly different," Carl said. "Playing the paper prototype in the halls allowed us to reduce this discrepancy."

As a result of this prototyping in the Halls, the game improved in many ways. Experiencing how packed the Halls could be, and how tiring it became to move from exhibit to exhibit, rules were simplified, the game was shortened (players could win by resolving a smaller number of MicroCrises), and complex situations that were hard to understand were removed. At the same time, standing in the Dzanga-Sangha Rain Forest was just fascinating, and we kept returning to it. As a result, it became the location of the final boss battle at the end of the hardest level in the game.

The second youth program ended as the first, with a final presentation to friends, family, and colleagues, and with a design document for Jeremy and his team to implement. By summer we had a strong Alpha ready to prototype with the public. A team of graduate students led by Hannah Jaris spent ten hours conducting seventeen sessions with fifty-seven visitors out in the Halls. They set out to assess visitors' level of engagement and, afterward, how much science content was retained.

Designing Augmented Reality   **101**

The team would scope out the lines waiting to enter the Museum in the Rotunda. Their target: small groups of adults with tween or teenage children. The visitors were offered free entrance to the Museum and free tickets to a special exhibit of their choosing. The team's approach within each thirty-minute session was to observe the visitors with minimal intervention and then interview them immediately afterward.

Their findings were quite positive and validated that we were moving in the right direction. Visitors seemed to be learning science from the game. The vast majority (83 percent) claimed to learn something new and could repeat back information that aligned with our learning objectives. For example, one child reported, "corals get stressed, zoosomethings leave, and the coral loses its color." Bingo!

The visitors also reported that it was fun to play ("It was more fun to read and experience information in this way than read an old plaque") and that it enhanced their visit. More specifically, they said that the game made the museum visit more interactive, added technology in a modern way, and provided a focus for their visit. It "totally changes your museum experience" said one visitor, while another shared that it made their experience "more precise."

This was all great to hear, and we were sure to report the findings up the food chain to decision makers, the results serving as validation of our hopes going into the playtesting. However, equally, if not more, important were the lessons learned that would not have been possible without the playtest. Those learnings, however, were not for sharing up the food chain; they were critical feedback for both the game designers and the app developers.

We learned the game instructions given to the players by the animated characters were successfully guiding visitors through the experience . . . but only when visitors could hear them. Audio in the hall continued to be a challenge. The app was quiet for some reason, and it could be hard for multiple people to hold one phone to their gathered ears. One visitor advised, "The game has to be sure to address the needs of both auditory and visual learners." We had added captions along with the audio, but players needed more control over the speed at which the text was presented, and the ability to refer back to moments earlier in the dialogue.

While the majority of users claimed to learn some science-related facts, almost none of them could recall the terms. Should the game include a glossary? Or offer movies to reinforce the learning? We gathered valuable feedback about what visitors expected in their wayfinding experience (they wanted hints, and the freedom to look around as they traveled between the Halls), gained clarity in how to trigger the augmented characters, and identified problems in the user interface.

We learned even more later that summer, this time playtesting it not with visitors but with groups of both youth and adults who were quite familiar with the Museum. The youth were from the Lang program, the multiyear youth program described in the chapter on *Minecraft*. These youth knew the Museum backward and forward, and were invited to play with their whole family. The adults were from the master of arts in teaching program. Master of arts in teaching residents are New York City science teachers working with the Museum to earn their advanced degree.

Again led by Hannah, each playtest lasted ninety minutes. After a brief introduction to the project, their gameplay was observed, a survey was completed, and a post-play discussion was held. The findings built on what we were already learning—they thought it was fun, learned something new (95 percent), and said they were interested in playing again. In fact, when asked to stop playing so we could move on to the survey, almost everyone wanted to keep playing. That was a good sign that they were doing more than just kindly helping us out for the playtest; the game was igniting their internal motivation.

Equally important, it helped these seasoned visitors—both young and old—discover new things about the Museum. "I saw new things," said one master of arts in teaching program teacher, "and I've been here a LONG time!" And one Lang student shared, "[MicroRangers] went into depth about the corals that I would just look at and skip without looking at the info." This reinforced our need to continue to take into consideration perspectives from all types of museum visitors, from members that visit the Museum regularly to visitors only at the Museum for one day.

By early fall we had our launch plan in place. The Braintrust helped to develop and approve a strategy in which *MicroRangers* would gently roll out in late fall, both to leverage a series of family-oriented events scheduled at that time and to slowly integrate it into the Museum as we ramped up for the active end-of-year season.

We still had to schedule internal reviews with different departments—Memberships, Exhibitions, Visitor Services, and curators for all of the selected Halls—but we only had one final internal gate to pass: meeting with Lisa, the Senior Vice President for Education. This time, however, we had an advanced Beta in hand. And we would not lead with a flatulent buffalo.

At the end of our presentation, she said we were "spot on." She complimented us by recognizing that "remarkable progress has been made" and that we had "tackled some intense content." She did raise some concerns (*Will visitors be able to play the game on their own? Does the design of the Dispatcher make it appear to be a red pepper?*) and provided some recommendations of opportunities to watch for (*Could the game support visitor interest in science careers in addition to the science content?*). But this all meant she had accepted the primary ask we had brought with us into the meeting, that after a year and a half of co-developing with teens and partnering with experts inside and outside the Museum, using an iterative design process that drew from user research to rapidly prototype, and then publicly test a new digital experience with and for our visitors, *MicroRangers* was cleared for launch.

That did not mean, however, we were done. The opposite was the case, as we still had work to do both to finalize the Gold version of the app and then to develop that launch ramp. We continued to playtest and debug each new build of the game delivered by Jeremy and his team. The builds were iterated frequently. One technical challenge we faced was battery life. Using the camera so much, and its AR-driven image recognition features, was drawing more power than we anticipated. We also had the game default to turning the flashlight on when looking for the challenge coin. Back then Halls were littered with families camping in corners to plug their devices into wall outlets designed for the maintenance staff. Phones were not as strong back then and the Museum had not yet institutionalized ways to meet visitors' mobile power needs. If *MicroRangers* could not be played from beginning to end in one visit, it would fail. We created charts visualizing the battery level at every point of the game as we played and tweaked the app again and again until we got the game to draw what we saw as an acceptable amount of power.

The *MicroRangers* coins needed to be printed, working with a company that regularly produced challenge coins (both the standard coins and the special gold-colored ones for a members promotion). The *MicroRangers* landing page on the OLogy webpage was designed, including everything families and educators would need to play the game.

We worked with the store (as a location for visitors to collect coins). We worked with the Communications Department to create promotional ads to run both before IMAX movies and on the video wall at the cafeteria check-out. An article in *Rotunda* was prepared, Sleepovers was engaged, and the social media staff created a campaign.

We officially held the soft launch in December. We decided it was better to hold off a hard launch for a few months, to get any kinks out of the system.

Many projects, once they launch, do not have the resources to keep iterating. While we had no funds to change the app experience, we still had resources to tweak how visitors discovered and engaged with it. The first thing we did was explore how we might get some post-visit data. Working with both members and visitors (who received comped tickets and could skip the entrance line), we captured their email addresses and sent them a survey. This data in the early weeks suggested *Micro-Rangers* was ready for a hard launch.

According to the surveys, visitors valued *MicroRangers* as a way to connect with the Museum. The vast majority reported that playing the game was time well spent (88 percent), they would recommend it to their friends (94 percent), and that the Museum should offer more experiences like *MicroRangers* in the future (92 percent). This is the type of engagement data we had been seeing throughout playtesting, so it was reaffirming but not a surprise. Post-visit learning, however, had been a black box. We had no idea going into it what we might find.

All visitors, 100 percent, reported learning new scientific ideas, phrases, or vocabulary. That, again, was aligned with our earlier findings taken during their visits. What we could not know until now is what happened next. Did they forget about their new learning once they moved on to a new exhibit, or returned home and went back to their regular lives? Well, according to what they reported, nearly all (92 percent) shared that new learning with others. And a majority (58 percent) said when they returned home they did further research about something first learned through *MicroRangers*. Even if these numbers are inflated due to a tendency to overstate good news, this still suggested an impressive ability for the game to ignite a new interest and motivate action.

During the soft launch period, the Museum's membership magazine, *Rotunda*, featured a two-page spread about the game. I was delighted that they also saw value in not just promoting this new visitor experience but also how it was developed, and what that might mean for the Museum in the future:

> Museum educators collaborated on *MicroRangers* with teenagers, the app's natural audience, on everything from content and game design to early voice-overs for the game's characters—in large part, Joseph says, to show that the Museum is not just a place youth can come to learn, but one where they can contribute.
>
> "From the very start, we wanted young people to be not just participants in a focus group, but co-designers of their own science education," says Joseph.
>
> And while *MicroRangers* has already been a learning experience for the youth and staff who helped develop the game, designers say the ways people play the game will provide design lessons for the future. How users are playing the game and what activities and interactions they embrace or ignore will help to shape the experiences offered by future Museum games.
>
> "The ideal Museum visit is also the ideal game," says Joseph. "You connect with exhibits, connect with the people around you, and learn something new."

By spring we were ready to formally launch *MicroRangers* with two events, each for a different audience. The first, "Game On!" was a family-oriented event. Promotional coverage in the *New York Times* promised that

> on Sunday the museum will introduce MicroRangers at Game On!, an event that will award prizes, ranging from toys to a museum sleepover, for successful completion of different levels of the game. Staff members will advise players, and a telepresence robot—like a video screen on wheels—will roam the halls, showing teenagers (who were instrumental in MicoRangers' development) dressed as some of the game's scientist characters, soliciting visitors' help.[2]

The event was well attended, with one-third reporting that they came to the Museum that day just to play the game. Through an emailed post-visit survey, we learned that many even returned, as this response attests: "My 8-year old daughter made us come back the very next day to play again! She loves it."

We were surprised to learn that the size of the groups of players was determined by how they learned of the game; most players who came to the Museum just to play the game were smaller single-family units (two or three people in size) while those who learned about it within the Museum were larger or multifamily units (four to eight people in size). This was unexpected and suggested to us that different types of family players might have different needs. For example, a small family can easily work on one device while a larger family unit might find benefit in a game that can be synchronized across multiple devices.

The second event was strictly "no children allowed." At *Game Night Gone Wild*, roughly three hundred adults played *MicroRangers*, primarily in their twenties and thirties, cocktails in hand. The evening featured a wide range of largely analog games, with science themes, that could be played with scientists. It was a good opportunity to not just promote *MicroRangers* to Millennials, but other games from the Museum (like *Killer Snails* and *Gutsy*) and games used within the afterschool programs like *#scienceFTW* (*Bone Wars*).

In the first twenty weeks after the soft launch, we estimated, based on Google Analytics, that roughly forty-five hundred people had played *MicroRangers*, with each party averaging fourteen minutes per session. During this time, Cooper Wright, a graduate student from New York University in Digital Media Design for Learning, observed forty-nine missions among a total of 115 people playing *MicroRangers* at the Museum.

Cooper wrote mini-snapshots of visitor interactions with the game. They provided an on-the-ground view of how visitors were bringing the game into their visits. Here is one example, which Cooper used as evidence that *MicroRangers* was working across multiple youth age groups:

> I observed a nine-year-old boy with his five-year-old brother and dad. The five-year-old had the phone and was playing the game. Even though the five-year-old didn't seem to understand much about the game, he was engaged, which seemed to pull his older brother in. Clearly, the older brother would have been more adept at playing the game, but he let his younger brother have the phone. He would go away for a few minutes, look at something in the dioramas that caught his eye, and then come back to help his brother. When the dispatcher directed them to find a bobtail squid, the nine-year-old got excited and ran off to find it in the diorama. Then they played the games in the Case of the Bio-luminescent Blackout together. This is an example of the game engaging two kids of very different ages on different levels; it brought the older one deeper into the museum experience, even though he was not the one holding the phone, and it engaged the younger one through the user experience of the game play.

This and related efforts, again led by Hannah, produced our last set of general recommendations, to strengthen *MicroRangers'* long-term viability.

- Expand internal visibility to general visitors (more digital and analog signage)
- Expand external visibility (more social media, more events, teacher outreach, etc.)
- Create a new build of *MicroRangers* more deeply integrated within the Museum's digital infrastructure
- Add multiple language captions

Finally, we recommended Nick Martinez's high school and college interns, within the Saltz and Museum Education and Employment Program, run a new microbiology learning cart featuring *MicroRangers*. Previously we had a *MicroRangers* cart out in the halls, led by teaching volunteers (the same group, for example, who offered free tours of the Museum). This was not a group known for being digitally savvy, but eventually they effectively supported visitors to troubleshoot technical challenges with confidence.

Nick picked up the challenge of balancing competing priorities, between our goal to engage the public through a game and Nick's goal to teach the public through a hands-on cart. Eventually, he and his interns developed cart-based activities that were connected content-wise to *MicroRangers*, which justified using the interns to give out the coins and directing visitors to the app. The evaluation of the *MicroRangers* cart as a promotional tool raised many topics that improved the next iteration of the game: streamline the game's onboarding experience and reduce the script. Other recommendations were about the cart itself, like adding a charging station for visitors' phones or improving their current pitch line (*Would you like to hear about a free game?*).

By now, however, my team had to move away from both the app (there were no efforts in place to look for additional funds nor how it was delivered to visitors, which was now largely in the hands of both Nick's carts and Communications). But one quote from a visitor summed up everything we could have ever hoped to hear during this period. "As a parent, I hope this project is expanded," they told us. "Our family looked at the museum in a different way and they now have interest in learning more about microorganisms!"

If I was paying careful attention, every once in a while while reviewing my daily IFTTT email summarizing social media images posted from within the Museum, between photos of a terrified couple underneath a dinosaur and a pair of shoes taking their weight on the moon, there I would find some visitors, *MicroRangers* coin in hand, proudly posing in front of an exhibit.

OUTCOMES

The guiding question behind *MicroRangers* was: Can games and play create the motivation and mindset to promote public awareness and deep understanding of the critical impact of biodiversity on human health? Our surveys, interviews, and observations suggest that the answer was a solid "yes." At the same time, we cannot say for sure whether that understanding was "deep" or that players understood the impact was "critical." That would require further data to resolve.

It is clear, however, that *MicroRangers*, as a game layered onto a traditional museum visit, provided visitors with a new way to connect with permanent exhibits and motivated them to learn in new ways and, for many, to continue that learning on their own once they returned home.

Visitors continued to learn about the game through the *MicroRangers* cart. The promotional ads ran in the cafeteria and in the IMAX theater. Membership continued to promote the game to visitors. No one individual or department, however, ever took ownership over the entire *MicroRangers* experience (including the codebase, the game design, the learning objectives, nor visitor engagement). No one needed to, as no one was asking for it. Once the funds were spent, there was no sponsor requiring an update. No director needed data on metrics achieved for a seasonal report. There were infrastructures in place for long-term projects like a temporary exhibit or the *Explorer* app, but none formed around *MicroRangers* and it failed to be absorbed by any already in existence.

A year after launch, I prepared the following in a report to Lisa on "lessons learned" from *MicroRangers*:

- *MicroRangers* helped us integrate iterative design practices into our youth programs.
- It helped us explore games-based learning as informal science pedagogy.
- It is furthering our capacity to develop public-facing digital learning experiences with youth.
- It is helping us to explore if games can play a role most often associated with live facilitators or tour guides.
- It is furthering our ongoing efforts to educate the public about the human role on climate change.
- It is letting us explore in a more significant way if we can combine science content, Museum exhibits, and dramatic narrative into an engaging package that highlights scientists and their work in a heroic way.
- Finally, *MicroRangers* is teaching us how to draw from and coordinate the Museum's vast, often untapped, resources in the support of a public-facing initiative.

The new version of the Museum's *Explorer* app came out soon after *MicroRangers*. It featured *Avatour*, billed as an "augmented reality adventure, which lets users 'Be the Bear' in the Bernard Family Hall of North American Mammals by unlocking the animal's ursine 'Superpowers.'" It let visitors use their mobile device to see the unseen within exhibits in permanent halls and tackle small AR-driven challenges.

While the *Explorer* app still guides visitors through the halls of AMNH (now sans *Avatour*), *Micro-Rangers* ran only for two more years. It was never viewed as a resource that required ongoing funding and updating; rather, new funds were targeted at new digital experiences. Promotional efforts moved on to the latest offerings, and eventually the interns running the *MicroRangers* cart were assigned to other carts. Matt Tarr always promoted the idea that mobile apps should be developed not just with a launch date but also an end date; technology becomes obsolete or outdated and if there is no intention to keep resources flowing then a targeted sunset date is required.

In early 2018, that date arrived.

The *MicroRangers* app was removed from the Apple and Google stores. The five-foot-tall promotional floor banner no longer served any purpose, so one day I swept through the Hall of Biodiversity and carried it back under my arm to my office. In my heart, if not my mind, that is when *MicroRangers* came to a close. Without that banner there was nothing left to remind visitors the game ever existed.

Which, of course, as a digital experience, was part of the design. If we aimed to build a layer on top of the Museum that was invisible to non-players, its absence should also leave no footprint. I often find it also helps to never forget that digital is always ephemeral. I keep on my desk a floppy disk from 1982. It contains the first two programs I ever made: an incomplete cave-based text adventure and something I named "Programmer's Revenge" which allowed you to curse at your computer through an endless dialogue. I know their code is on that disk, but I will never again see them realized. I have no access to the hardware required to turn those 0s and 1s back into an interactive form. But I am glad I created that code, for it was a stepping stone to everything digital that followed. And I enjoyed playing each one. I keep that floppy on my desk as a reminder that everything digital I work on has a sunset date, whether I know it or not. I should not get too precious about the digital experience. All that remains in the end, when that code goes offline, is the impact it had on its end users, and the lessons learned that will inform whatever comes next.

A short post-script: what of all the user research that helped inform this project, all those photos scrapped from social media? For a while I printed them out and left them on the board behind my desk, as inspiration. But that felt selfish and too ephemeral. Then one day I walked through the main gift shop and came across a PinBox 3000, a do-it-yourself cardboard pinball machine. I built the machine, decorated it with visitor photos, and then worked with the staff in the Museum's research library. They accessioned it and put it in the collections so anyone can check it out, launch a ball, and lose themselves in the visitor experience.

Figure 4.8. The cardboard pinball social media visitor experience. *Author*

Comparison: Minnesota Historical Society (Saint Paul, Minnesota)

Between 2007 and 2018, if I happened to speak with a museum educator planning to run a mobile app youth program, I was guaranteed to hear one word: ARIS. ARIS described itself as "a user-friendly, open-source platform for creating and playing mobile games, tours and interactive stories." During its heyday I wanted to learn more. I spoke with David Gagnon, who directed the ARIS program for the University of Wisconsin-Madison. He invited along Jennifer Sly, the Museum Education and Technology Specialist at the Minnesota Historical Society in Saint Paul, to understand how they used playtesting to iterate how this accessible geolocative platform was integrated into their museum experience and educational programs.

ARIS differed in many ways from commercially available mobile locative platforms. First, it was developed for research and prototyping purposes by a university with a strong games-based learning program. The goal was to offer a toolkit of everything interesting at the intersection of mobile, education, and gaming. As they added more and more features into the platform, they wanted to make it available for anyone else to iterate and apply. For free.

Funded in part by the MacArthur Foundation and the Pearson Foundation, as more institutions began using it, they had to transform from supporting ARIS as a platform for rapid prototyping into one for production. David told me how this brought new constraints into their design process, required different staff, and different attitudes about how development happens. "It's been a learning curve for us," he explained, "to move from a platform that allows you to do anything you could ever imagine into doing less things really, really well in a really, really reliable way."

ARIS also stood out because it centered around narrative. It was designed to tell stories located in space. With the emergence in recent years of popular geolocation games like *Pokémon Go*, place-based narratives are commonplace. But when ARIS was developed, this was an uncommon experience. And design tools were hardly accessible. ARIS was designed to allow non-technical people to author their own mobile locative apps, stories, and games. Combine this all together—a free, easy-to-use, powerful tool for creating location-based stories and games—and it is little surprise how popular it became among museum educators looking for tools to engage teens in digital production within their halls.

Those features attracted Jennifer Sly to ARIS as well. "The rapid prototyping was great because we were nontechnical people," she told me, "and we were hoping eventually that young people could help us in our designs." The Minnesota Historical Society set out to use ARIS in two ways. The first was to develop an in-gallery mobile app specifically for kids on field trips. "We are hoping that we can put an iPad in the hand of every kid that visits our museum," she said. The second use of ARIS was to engage those teens in designing history-based games.

When Jennifer talks about an app to be used in her gallery, she does not mean as a virtual tour guide. She wanted visitors to be able to roleplay different periods of Minnesota history and try to solve local problems, both past and contemporary. For example, one of the exhibits is about mining. With the addition of ARIS, visitors could now record what they are doing in the mine, meet some virtual miners and talk to them about life in the mine, and help them solve problems.

David always loves hearing about ARIS and the mine. He described it as "one of the most playful, interesting and weird experiments I have ever been a part of." From David's perspective as a game designer, Jennifer has turned the physical museum into a game controller. In the physical exhibit, visitors load simulated sticks of dynamite into the wall and then push on a physical plunger to activate a sound of the explosion. With ARIS in hand, the visitor is role playing as a miner, trying to make a living. When that real-world plunger is activated, it connects to ARIS and its impact is felt within the virtual gameplay. For David, Jennifer's application of ARIS was using the objects in their museum to answer the question: What if we could turn the physical environment into a game controller?

"Playtesting has been really helpful for us," Jennifer shared upon reflection, "just because the things that we assumed would work didn't." She told me they had tested the experience with a thousand kids and figured they needed two thousand more before she'd be satisfied. Her recommendation to others who want to do the same? "Plan on an iterative design process."

The relationship between David and Jennifer, and between his design lab and her museum, speak to the power and importance of collaboration when developing and applying new tools for digital engagement. Being part of a community of innovation is essential. "I think we are all in the Wild West," Jennifer shared, "so I think everybody is learning at the same time." Not just about their successes, but where they struggle as well. "There is a lot of failure," she admitted, "so even if we can share the failures, there is a lot we can learn."

David finds that approach inspiring. He knows that if we were going to figure out what "mobile locative embodied narrative-centric media" is going to do we are going to have to take a lot of big risks. It's not "Let's do something really big together." Instead, it's "Let's take some risks along the way." For many years, ARIS was one of the tools that enabled those risks to happen quickly and cheaply, helping us all expand our understanding of what was possible.

TIPS AND STRATEGIES

1. User research

   Think: What is another way images could have been captured to generate insights on user needs and behaviors? What is another type of publicly accessible user data that could have been collected and analyzed?
   Do: Figure out a way to ethically and legally collect and analyze photos of your users.

2. Rapid prototypes

   Think: How might we have rapidly prototyped the Toca Boca–style MicroGames, without any digital development?
   Do: For your next prototype, explore how performing the game characters in person gives you deeper insight into who they are, their roles within the game, and their relationship with the players.

3. Public piloting

   Think: What are other types of audiences we might have reached out to for pilot testing? What might they have been uniquely positioned to help us understand?
   Do: For a current project or on your next one, identify specific questions you have that only certain types of audiences could help you to clarify. Find that audience and discover whether they could help you find the answers you need.

4. Iterative design

   Think: Much of the design was iterated through playtesting and piloting. However, the design was also iterated both within the Braintrust and through the approaches we developed for engaging visitors (events, membership, carts, a sign, etc.). Consider how the design of the experience can be iterated within those other spaces.

Do: Think about the materials required for a project. Remove one of those materials, replace it with something else, and explore how that affects the overall design.

5. Youth collaboration

Think: We clearly defined the domains where the youth had influence and where decisions were being made outside of their line of sight. Consider what might have happened if we had expanded youth input or decision making to additional areas (such as how the game would be promoted to the public, or the nature of the AR target). Inversely, consider what might have happened if we had constricted youth input or decision making; what might we have lost?

Do: We began developing MicroRangers with one group of youth but concluded it with a different group. Do the same. Notice the resources required to onboard a second group of co-developers as balanced against the benefits of working with the additional resources.

6. Team up!

Think: Can you imagine any ways that MicroRangers could have built its own sustainable pipeline or been integrated into an existing one?

Do: Consider a previous or upcoming project. List all the people (or groups of people) who are not directly involved in the production of the project but can either help pave the way for its success and/ or remove obstacles. Decide how to engage them—individually or as a group? formally or informally? regularly or as the need arises?

7. Comparative project

Think: Regarding the Six Tools for Digital Design, what does ARIS and its application within the Minnesota Historical Society have in common with MicroRangers? How does it differ?

NOTES

1. "Ten years of Toca Boca!" Toca Boca, accessed November 23, 2021, https://tocaboca.com.
2. Laurel Graeber, "Solving Mysteries at the American Museum of Natural History, Smartphone in Hand," *New York Times*, April 15, 2016.

A Room with a View

The Museum opens.

Patrons stream underneath the domed rotunda of building 12 (1935) to negotiate their admission tickets with Visitor Services. Viewed from above, five stories high, their snaking lines bisect the display of fossil casts dramatically pitting an allosaurus against a barosaurus (a photo opportunity few can resist).

From this height, the visitors to the main entrance at 79th street all look small. Built as the official New York State memorial to Teddy Roosevelt, its construction initiated a major northerly expansion of the Museum and the first one in over fifty years. The intended grandeur and solemnity of the tribute to our former governor (and son of a Museum founder) is reflected in the epic, thirty-four-foot-high paintings of world figures posed in the style of Roman statues. Visitors who tilt their gaze take in colorful, larger-than-life scenes depicting the president's leadership around the world, in Panama, in Egypt, in Asia. The three murals, some of the largest in the city, bracket Teddy quotes on nature, youth, manhood, and the state. "Only those are fit to live," declares one, "who do not fear to die." Another: "Keep your eyes on the stars . . . and your feet on the ground."

Few visitors, however, take Teddy's advice to look higher, specifically at the floral design around the ceiling lights overhead, accessible only from a catwalk above the rotunda's dome, like backstage at a theater, from which each can be carefully removed to change a burnt bulb, leaving behind momentarily a hole just large enough for a face to peer down at the crowd below and lock eyes with someone looking back up, in wonder, at this isolated face floating high overhead, like a pale moon reflecting the ghost of Teddy Roosevelt.

5

Designing Extended Reality

In Summary | tl;dr

Subject: This chapter focuses on using the Six Tools of Digital Design for developing extended reality (XR) experiences.

Case study: The case studies in this chapter focus on both 360 videos and virtual reality (VR) projects. The 360 video case study begins with media produced outside the Museum, then shifts toward creating an original 360 video project about paleontology developed both in and for the Museum. The VR case study explores A:B testing two very similar but distinct commercial VR properties: *theBlu* and *Ocean Rift*. All of these projects were designed to answer questions about the potential of XR to enhance the Museum visitor experience, focusing on logistics, functional aspects, and the aesthetic experience.

User research: Research was performed with visitors to identify topics they wanted to experience in 360 VR and their level of interest in each one.

Rapid prototyping: When we rapid prototyped a 360 video, we had to decide to cut corners to reduce the level of invested resources and speed up the production process. We cut corners, for example, by including a fictionalized tour to bookend the longer video that featured Museum staff pretending to be visitors, bloopers and all (like a security guard accidentally interrupting the shoot). We knew in advance there would be no reshoots of any scenes. Scripts for the scientists were mostly a path to traverse with talking points, around which they improvised their dialogue. Finally, we did not bring in extra lighting or audio tools for the shoot, and we kept the production staff down to two people. Even with all of these compromises, there were lines we knew we could not cross: the scientists were real, the Museum locations were real, and the dinosaur specimens were real. We also did not cut corners on the film editing, working with a top-notch film editor. In the end, the prototype needed to be a strong 360-degree experience with valid science content.

Public piloting: Often the design of the 360 videos was informed by evaluation needs. For example, 360 videos differ, in part, from traditional videos by providing objects and activities of interest in all directions, often at the same time. Some visitors reported listening to the narration of the scientist but looking, instead, at the bones on the shelves around them. That was part of the design. The evaluators, however, had no way at the time to know to what visitors were visually paying attention. As a result, we tried to exaggerate the action of the narrators' movements so they would be distinct and visible to the evaluators, such as when one walked up a ladder, or when another slowly circled the camera.

Iterative design: The iterative loops of the 360 videos were tied tightly to the needs of the evaluation. For example, we did not know if visitors preferred a social 360 experience or an immersive 360 experience. To evaluate their preferences, we iterated the visitor experience to shift between watching the Big Bone Room video split equally between each of those two approaches. We found visitors were engaged with each half of their video experience, and the only preference they had was based on the order of the videos (not whether it was social or immersive). This told us that the Museum could feel free to design toward either type of 360 video.

At the same time, there were things we chose not to iterate. For example, the 360 videos produced rather weak learning outcomes. We could have iterated the design to improve those outcomes, but we did not need to. The videos were just placeholder content that only needed to be strong enough for testing the broader guiding questions pertaining to the logistics required to offer the experience, the functional aspects of supporting visitors to engage with it, and the aesthetics of the visitor experience. In the end visitors were excited to peek behind the scenes, and 360 video offered an effective way to offer a "you are there" experience. That is all we needed to know. With that as a foundation, future efforts could focus on iterating content and its learning outcomes.

Youth collaboration: There were no youth programs associated with the 360 videos or VR piloting. We imagined that the original paleontology 360 video trip to the Big Bone Room might be used in afterschool programming (and reduce the requests to do so in person). However, we never piloted the video within any courses or worked with any youth to help develop the content. So . . . yeah.

Teaming up: One of the internal partners for the original 360 video was the Paleontology Department who by necessity must vigorously review and approve any work requests. To negotiate the relationship, we made sure to aim at all times to respect their need to control access to both their staff and their collections, clearly define the precise details of the ask and our time estimates, remain open to their ideas and be flexible about our own, hold out the mindframe to get them to "yes" and were prepared to shape the project around whatever constraints they required, and follow their lead.

Comparison: The chapter concludes by offering, for comparison, an exploration of the use of 360 videos at the Shedd Aquarium in Chicago, Illinois.

CONTEXT AND GUIDING QUESTIONS

The rapid speed of tech innovation can feel dizzying at times. The title of futurist Alvin Toffler's 1970s book introduced a term that captured this sense of dislocation: *Future Shock*. For those advancing digital engagement in museums, however, we need to move beyond a state of shock. We need to grow comfortable with the discomfort of digital disruptions. We need to make order out of the perceived chaos.

One attempt at order can be found in the term XR. Fans of XR intend it to be read "extended reality." I am no fan of using "XR"; it points to a problem without resolving it, in an attempt to avoid the discomfort found in a profusion of terms: VR, AR, MR.

Virtual reality (VR) looks like a user doffing a sensory-deprivation helmet to immerse themselves in a stream of auditory and visual stimuli, such as ancient Rome, a human cell, or the bottom of the ocean.

Augmented reality (AR) ditches the bulky gear and uses a tablet or smartphone to layer digital information on the real world, such as catching Pokémon in the park or redecorating your home with virtual furniture.

Mixed reality (MR) combines the two, providing a sensory-deprivation helmet that then—and here's the trick—digitally recreates the surrounding world to mix it with digital layers of information. Think of it as AR on steroids.

XR points to all three and says, with grinning enthusiasm, "Yes, yes, all of that!" and "also any computer or wearable tech that comes in the future." In the end, XR tries to capture that we are in a state of constant change but fails to provide us with a tool for navigating this dynamic state of affairs. If I cannot make sense of them, how can I think critically about how to apply them within a museum?

Out of necessity, I landed on one approach that took me pretty far toward bringing order to the rapid changes I saw around me in digital augmentations. I created a simple matrix across two dimensions.

The first dimension describes the social. I ask: Is the experience intended primarily for private or social use? If the experience is private, then it goes on the "me" side; if the device is social, then it goes on the "we" side.

The second dimension describes the spatial. I ask: Is the experience intended to enhance the user's experience of their surroundings or transport them somewhere else? If the experience is for local use, then it goes on the "here" side; if the experience transports the user, then it goes on the "there" side.

Me versus we. Here versus there. It is short and rhymes, which makes it easy to remember. And it was even easier to apply.

I can take a tool like AR and ask, "Where does it belong?" An AR experience can be experienced on one's own or with others, but is usually about augmenting the space around me. Me/Here and We/Here. If I put on a private VR headset and play a game set in a fantasy world, that clearly falls in Me/There. And so forth.

This then helps me to filter out what does not belong within a museum. Most private experiences are best suited for home use, not the social experience most seek at a museum. And while something like an IMAX film or space show can provide a great We/There experience, transporting a family to the depths of the oceans or the farthest reaches of a universe, most collections-based museums want visitors to connect with the halls and their content. This helped me to focus on digital experiences that enhance an individual's ability to connect with the people and places around them: We/Here.

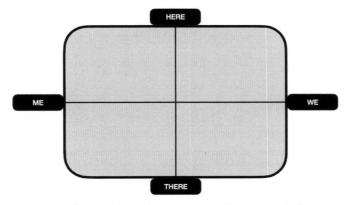

Figure 5.1. The social/spatial extended reality matrix. *Author*

When I first created the matrix, I often struggled to parse these terms being used to describe emerging media. Take Google Cardboard. This simple folded box, created in 2014 by the Google Cultural Institute (which worked with museums to digitize and post their collections online), was built as a virtual reality platform. Its tipping point arrived on November 8, 2015, when the *New York Times* included a branded Google Cardboard with all home newspaper deliveries (I recall receiving mine); *The Guardian* in England did the same a month later. Before these events, Cardboard was a curiosity, an intriguing low-tech, DIY plaything; afterward, everyone was talking about how low-cost "360 VR" could be moved into museums.

I was not convinced, however, that it was useful to call them "VR" devices. While Google Cardboard created ways to bring in the social (launching *Expeditions* to support teachers to share their screen across multiple student devices for a virtual field trip), most examples I saw could more accurately be described as 360 videos. True VR would allow for the social, like playing catch with a friend, while 360 videos were more personal and introspective, like reading a newspaper article. Talking about both VR and 360 video as if they had the same affordances, as I often experienced at museum conferences, was confusing at best and possibly harmful to the development of the space.

To make some sense of it all, I began investigating within the limited space of "360 VR," to understand how it was being applied in museums, what distinguished it from VR, and suggest what we might be doing back at the American Museum of Natural History (AMNH).

I was amazed at the wide range of applications I discovered.

At the Shedd Aquarium in Chicago, visitors waiting in line to buy entrance tickets used VR headsets to watch 360 videos. The videos, produced by teens on a work-study program, took visitors into their underwater exhibits to prompt discussions. I noted that "VR" was the tool but the product was a "360 video." This was a Me/There device used to support a We/Here experience.

Across the street from the Shedd, the Field Museum provided visitors with 360 videos that combined footage of scientists in the field with behind the scenes of their collection spaces. The resulting story arcs were designed to offer visitors a chance to walk alongside scientists as they engaged in a process of exploration and discovery. Since this was about both scientists in the field and their onsite collections, I would label this Me/Here and Me/There.

In New York City, families at the Children's Museum of Manhattan got to dance! Combining both original and licensed 360 videos, the mini-half-domed Dance Portal introduced children and families to the delights of dance in a 180-degree experience. No private viewers for these folks. This was a We/There design.

In California at the Monterey Bay Aquarium, visiting school groups created "360-degree tours" by viewing and combining 360-degree images of exhibits and narrating them, to be watched after returning from their field trip. This struck me as a Me/Here experience.

Finally, visitors in Pittsburgh at the Carnegie Museum of Art were offered something completely different: an interactive experience that remixed time-lapse imagery taken from outside the museum by a 360-degree camera. A visitor would stand in a semicircle of screens which they "played" by physically rotating their bodies left and right, having an experience visible to all around. I would label this a We/Here experience. Then again, if we consider time a dimension of space, and the video displaying moments from the past, would this be We/There?

All five struck me as great examples of digital engagement in museums. However, if I just listed what they were used for—dance, or marine life, or scientists in the field—or their intended audience—visitors on a ticket line, school groups, or visitors in an exhibit—it might seem unlikely that the same set of tools were used to support such a diverse set of activities.

This led me to conclude that 360 VR is a Swiss army knife. It was being used for so many different things: to show visitors the work of scientists, to let students in a school see inside an aquarium, to create tours of a museum trip, to engage visitors waiting to buy tickets, to teach families about dance, to create an interactive video-based data visualization, and the list goes on.

While these digital engagements differed in content, they shared something in common: they used immersive video to let viewers see and pretend to travel to something that would otherwise be inaccessible: behind the scenes (in the field, in the collections), within the exhibits, to dance studios. When I spoke with the designers behind each of these experiences, I often heard the word "connect," as they were using 360 video to connect people with their museum, with the work of scientists, and with the natural world around them.

I also noticed that while there was a plethora of content to license, most of the institutions were making their own original content. Some used expensive or custom-made tools, but others were using inexpensive tools and putting them in the hands of youth.

So what did I take away that could be applied to AMNH? Any topic of interest to the Museum could be addressed within 360 video: marine life, cultural stories, paleontologists in the field, and more. And we could use those videos to connect our visitors with the Halls, their content, and the research behind them. There was a world of rich content out there we could make available but, if we wanted to make our own, the equipment needed was cheap enough to allow for rapid prototyping.

I just needed an excuse to get started. (Be careful what you wish for.)

After three years at the Museum there was a reorganization within the Education Department. The strategic plan I had developed for infusing digital learning in our afterschool programming had taken hold. Staff were now supported to innovate and engage young people through digital learning across their offerings. Where else could I have impact within the Education Department, bringing my expertise in prototyping and evaluating digital engagement?

It turns out my new homebase would be within the Science Bulletins group. For over fifteen years, this creative and talented team brought the work of scientists into the permanent exhibit Halls through videos. For example, in the Hall of Ocean Life, if there was a video about a marine biologist playing on the big screen, Science Bulletins created it. Vivian Trakinski, the Director of Science Visualization, led the group with a down-to-earth and no-nonsense attitude. Her teams always delivered top-quality media, on time and on budget, melding the awe of science with the magic of great storytelling.

Over time, the nature of video had changed within museums. YouTube had transformed access to science-based videos, changing who was watching and where. Science Bulletins would need to evolve, taking everything it knew about bringing scientists and their work to visitors but in ways that moved beyond just video. The collections of scientists were increasingly digital, whether computed tomography scans of a shark specimen or astronomical observations of Mars. And passive video viewing was being challenged by the interactive tools carried in by visitors.

As I joined the team, it was renamed the Science Visualization Group. We focused on the challenge of learning best practices for bringing digital specimens from AMNH scientists into the Halls through interactive, emerging media platforms. And rather than innovate through outsourced work and external partnership, our intentional constraint was to build our own internal capacity by producing everything in-house. We were essentially tasked with performing experience design to engage visitors in our dozens of permanent Halls with modern science practices, through the addition of digital layers of interpretation.

Most projects triangulated opportunities by working with one of the Museum's over two hundred scientists to turn their digital specimens (computed tomography scans, genomic data, astronomical observations) into a digital asset we could then port into a variety of digital tools to be tested with the public (Google's Tango, Hololens, the Vive, and Merge Holocube, among others).

While I had often drawn from my Six Tools for Digital Design when developing scores of new youth programs, these design practices were often in the background. My primary goals most often revolved around youth-learning objectives. Now, in the SciViz Group, this would be inverted. Sometimes we would involve a youth program, but the foreground would be the deployment of a user-centered design process to publicly prototype new ideas and then evaluate the data we collected through observing and interviewing visitors.

One of the first sets of XR projects with which I was involved began with exploring 360 video. Our guiding questions were basic and fundamental, highlighting how new all of this was within institutions like ours. They were organized into three buckets.

The first bucket of questions pertained to the *logistics* required for the Museum to offer visitors a 360 video experience. For example:

- *Will visitors sit or stand to watch the film? If sitting, on what?*
- *How will we keep the equipment charged?*
- *What visitor onboarding was required to support a positive user experience?*

The second bucket of questions pertained to the *functional* aspects of visitors experiencing 360 video within the Museum. For example:

- *Do visitors feel comfortable wearing the headset?*
- *Do visitors experience good audio given the surrounding sound in the Hall?*
- *How does a viewer's social group interact with the viewer when they are immersed in a 360 video?*

The third bucket of questions pertained to the *aesthetic* experience of users. For example:

- *Do visitors watch the whole film?*
- *Would they recommend it to a friend?*
- *Did they feel they learned something in a way that was unique to the medium?*

To begin answering these questions about the potential of XR to enhance the museum visitor experience, we turned to the history of Cuban dance.

Designing 360 Videos

Emerging media was nothing new in the Margaret Mead Film Festival. While traditionally a festival highlighting documentaries from around the world (and named in honor of the anthropologist who worked at the Museum for over fifty years), it often explored other mediums—like videogames and social media—to understand how documentary efforts have evolved over the years. Beginning in 2016, the Mead Festival began to incorporate VR and 360 videos.

The new Virtual Reality Lounge encouraged attendees and, in fact, any visitor to the Museum, to drop by and "take cutting-edge virtual reality for a test drive [to] see how this new technology is transforming filmmaking." Participants put on headgear (a Samsung Gear) and headsets to watch a movie that filled their field of view. Seated on a revolving chair in the Hall of Northwest Coast Indians, they could turn their head in any direction, and look up and down, to view the film. In the first year, visitors could experience the lives of nomadic cultures around the world or dive into the history of Cuban dance.

For two days at the Festival, we observed both visitors in the Lounge and the Festival volunteers running it. We ran interviews and did a follow-up survey with the volunteers.

Logistically, we knew we faced a large learning curve, but we still had a way to go before we could regularly consider bringing experiences like this into our Halls. The Lounge was staffed over the Festival by fifty-seven volunteers; most we spoke with wished they had more training. One volunteer described her experience as "a snowball method of untrained people training untrained people."

Functionally, there were also constant technical difficulties: batteries ran low, devices overheated, image quality fell short of expectations, and two users complained of nausea.

So far *not* so good . . .

Figure 5.2. The Virtual Reality Lounge at Mead Festival in the Hall of Northwest Coast Indians. *Author*

Aesthetically, however, the visitor experience survived both of these logistical and functional challenges. One hundred percent of the visitors interviewed said they would recommend the experience to a friend *and* wished the Museum would offer more 360 films. Nearly all described the experience with words and phrases like "immersive," "it felt real," or "I was there," attesting to their level of deep engagement.

We learned that sometimes all can be forgiven when the digital experience delivers the magic.

We also learned something crucial: do not ask people taking care of visitors to also evaluate their experience. The volunteers were great, for sure. They worked hard to help visitors understand how the gear worked, made sure they were comfortable on their revolving stools, fixed their audio problems, swapped out overheating phones, and more. However, when they also had to administer a survey instrument, and things got hectic (as they always do), the first thing that got cut was the evaluation. We realized we needed to develop a specialized and dedicated group of evaluation volunteers. This would free volunteers from the encumbrance of servicing visitors while allowing them to develop expertise over time in observing and surveying.

The Museum already had an impressive group of over a thousand volunteers. They excelled at delivering free tours to visitors, assisting at public events like the Mead Festival, and chit-chatting about Museum gossip over lunch in the staff cafeteria. As far I knew, there had never before been a group of volunteers dedicated to evaluation and research. It was an intriguing idea. I collaborated with the Tour Guides and Explainers group to put out the word: the Museum was looking for a new type of volunteer.

Meanwhile, we learned something important from the next Mead Festival. The first year we used 360 documentaries created by others. In the second year, two staff members collaborated to produce a new film called *Wapi Utamaduni?* (*Where is the Culture?*). "In this immersive 360-degree short," the promotional material advertised, "WaMeru tribe elders and youth share stories, along with the process of creating a local tribal museum in Tanzania that preserves and features their long-neglected history."

One of those two staff members was part of the SciViz group, so of course as the supportive colleagues we were, we all made sure to watch it (with many helping out in the development of the film). This involvement with the Festival just emphasized that, well, as this SciViz crew were the ones already making films for the Halls, shouldn't we also be making 360 videos?

The answer, of course, was yes. But that just made way for the real question: what should they be about? Before long we decided the films should focus on behind the scenes at the Museum, specifically giving visitors a glimpse of AMNH scientists at work—in the field, in the collections rooms, and in the labs. The films could help viewers place in context the specimens encountered within the Halls. Perhaps videos could be viewed via headsets or small flat screens at designated locations in the Museum, or even on visitors' own phones. We felt we just needed to find the right story.

We could have just picked something related to dinosaurs. Everyone loves dinosaurs. At least, the vast majority do, as evidenced by the daily bottleneck by the *T. rex*, which I often struggled to navigate when late to a meeting. Yet as the Museum is full of many other stories, related to so many other areas of science, we decided to first do some research. Using free 360-degree photo apps on our phones, we toured and documented the places in the Museum visitors never see and most likely were unaware even existed. Imagine the stories those could tell!

We traveled to the Herpetology Department and photographed their collection of turtles, their modern labs, and desks festooned with formaldehyde jars packed with eerily transparent purple specimens.

We explored the Sackler Institute for Comparative Genomics, a research facility housing three modern molecular laboratories doing genetics research, where we photographed machines with names like the CL-1000 Ultraviolet Crosslinker and the Fisher Vortex Genie 2.

We visited the bug colony—that's what it says on the door—in the Osteology Preparation Laboratory, housing three colonies (a century old) of dermestid beetles who toil away cleaning soft tissue from new specimens, day and night, for weeks, and then die, unthanked, unmourned, leaving little behind but poop, the next generation of workers, and remarkably clean bones for scientists to study.

Figure 5.3. The bug colony in the Osteology Preparation Laboratory. *Author*

We took 360 photos of the whale bone collection, the skin room, and, yes, the "big bone" room containing some of the larger of the dinosaur fossils (which shares a wall with visitors unaware of the wonders just feet away as they eat lunch in the main cafeteria).

At each location we sought a vantage point with interesting things to look at, in all directions (including up and down). The narrator would need a pathway for moving throughout the scene that would force the viewer to turn their head in order to keep them in sight. And when it came to specimens, the bigger the better. We recorded the natural soundscape of the room and also took detailed photos.

Rather than digitize our research, we created a physical photo album to present findings from our location scouting. It included handwritten notes related to logistical matters—where it was located, its level of lighting, potential challenges for capturing sound—and all of our photos (attached with double-sided tape). The idea was not to deliver a standard report with a list of recommendations. Rather, it was designed to be a book for inspiration, to be flipped through to reveal unexpected ideas.

In the end, we agreed the topic that would be most compelling and right for the first prototype was . . . dinosaurs. Which was fine! Really, it was. The other stories were not going anywhere anytime soon. When taking a risk with a new medium why not hedge your bets with an already popular subject? Save your innovation for the digital engagement. And, in fact, when Mead Festival attendees were asked what topics we should next tackle in a 360 video, dinosaurs were at the top of the list.

The Paleontology Department—its labs, its collection spaces—are some of the most secure places on the campus. This project could not proceed without the permission and full support of both Mark Norell, Chair of the Paleontology Division, and Ruth O'Leary, Director of Collections, Archives and Preparation.

Together, the SciViz group collaborated on an approach for me to send a request by email. I thanked them for providing access to the Big Bones room as part of our location scouting and confirmed it would be ideal for a 360 VR video, along with the paleo prep lab (where fossils first return from the field in a protective jacket that can takes months to remove). We anticipated a day of shooting across the spaces and wondered, perhaps, might this request seem reasonable?

Ruth's answer, in short, was a polite, "No, thank you," which did not come as a complete surprise; Ruth is often required to play gatekeeper to the resources of the department, and we viewed her response as more of a first beat in a multistepped negotiation.

We had been asking to go into Paleontology's preparations room, where dinosaurs arrived from the research field packed in what is called a plaster jacket, a sort of papier-mâché package that can take months for a preparer to meticulously remove, exposing the fossil within. There was a shipment coming from Mongolia, which we thought would be great to film, the story tracing its arrival into the Museum, its time in the prep lab, and its new home in the collections.

Yet ideas which fit so lovely in one's mind are often not matched by the constraints of reality. Ruth detailed for us those many constraints.

She said they could not predict when the fossil would arrive, and it would be stored initially in a place not fit to be on camera.

The prep lab itself was undergoing renovations, so even if the fossil had arrived our film shoot could delay their work.

We had asked for a day in the Big Bone Room, but that would require a staff member to supervise, and no one had the time available.

Ruth, however, did not actually say no. It was more of a "No, but . . ." She had a great suggestion, one that would free up her staff while giving us access to both the Big Bone Room and a dinosaur expert: recruit a student. AMNH has a graduate program, the Richard Gilder Graduate School, which offers doctorates in Comparative Biology. One of the doctoral candidates, Daniel Barta, was studying dinosaur growth and development under Mark Norell.

We asked Mark for an introduction and Danny was happy to lend a hand. At the same time, Mark offered to let us film him, as well, in his office. Bonus!

It was all coming together. Not the way we planned, but that was fine. Our initial story idea (follow the bone) was easy to let go. What was important was collaborating with our colleagues to figure out what story they thought we could tell, given their availability and the science they wanted to share.

We were still missing a piece. We now had a visit to Mark's office and a trip to the Big Bone Room. We still needed something that tied it all together. We needed a tour guide.

The over one hundred volunteer guides are a dynamic crew who create their own tours of the Museum and offer them for free. They collaborate with the same office we worked with to develop the new team of volunteer evaluators. One of my favorite tour guides was Andrew Epstein, a retired air traffic controller whose remarkable knowledge and dry wit engaged visitors around the world as he took them through the Halls.

We pitched a story in which Andrew is giving a tour in the Hall of Saurischian Dinosaurs. After taking questions from visitors, he suggests they go behind the scenes to learn the answers. First, they go to the Big Bone Room, where Danny Barta explains the dinosaur fossils that surround him. Next, they go to the office of Mark Norell who tours them around his workspace. Then, finally, they return to where they began, in the Hall of Saurischian Dinosaurs, where Andrew concludes the tour.

Andrew responded as he always did to any request for help from the Museum, with a generous and immediate "of course."

We created a storyboard, scheduled the shoot, and got to work filming.

To shoot Andrew's segment we grabbed some friends around the Museum before the front doors opened to the public and pretended to be on a tour, circling Andrew underneath the skull of the *T. rex*. We found a great location for the cameras—which film all around in 360 degrees—with a marvelous view for the future audience, with dinosaurs all around, above, and below. We pestered Andrew with questions, like where scientists find dinosaurs and if we humans could be somehow related. Cobbled together as we were, few might peg us as a group of visitors, and we certainly didn't sound like one. That was all right. We just needed a quick and dirty shot to create a prototype we could test. If I had to shoo away an unsuspecting security guard who tried to walk through in the middle of the shoot, we could live with that. We needed to work fast, and that meant cutting some corners. As long as what we produced was strong in the right places, to allow us to test the experience with future visitors, we would be fine.

In the video Andrew suggests we go behind the scenes to find some answers to our questions, which concludes the opening scene. We then filmed Andrew's concluding scene, which I will describe shortly.

It is always a thrill to enter the Big Bone Room, with a *T. rex* skull greeting you right as you enter. The room itself is rather sterile—a long, gray-floored, white-walled room full of non-descript cabinets

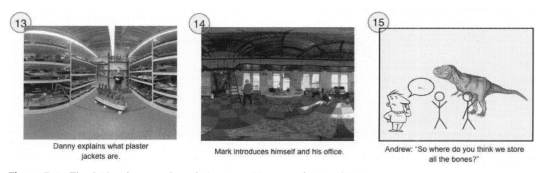

Danny explains what plaster jackets are.

Mark introduces himself and his office.

Andrew: "So where do you think we store all the bones?"

Figure 5.4. The 360 video storyboard. *American Museum of Natural History*

and floor-to-ceiling shelving. What makes it remarkable, however, is what fills those cabinets and open shelves—some of the largest dinosaur bones in the Museum's collection.

Danny stood positioned at the end of one of the hallways, the camera providing a vantage point that allowed the viewer to look around at the surrounding shelves and up and down at the levels of fossils they contained. During the shoot, Jason Morfoot (Senior Producer and Video Editor) and I crouched on the ground behind some cabinets, out of view of the cameras (six Go Pros on a stick) but with a line of sight over some fossils to observe Danny and the action. Danny explained that the enormous *Diplodocus* vertebrae between him and the camera is the same type of backbone we can feel if we run our hands at the base of our neck. He walked around the space and even climbed a ladder to the highest level, all motions designed to get the future viewer to turn their head (and give us something for evaluators to measure as a sign of engagement).

The next scene takes us to the office of Mark Norell. There are hundreds of offices in the Museum, but few are arguably as magnificent and full of wonder as this one. Children's books could be written about this space. Films could be made here (which, in fact, we were). It's truly a magical place.

The first thing that stands out is the shape. The southeast corner of the Museum is called the Astor Turret. The public can experience its rounded shape on the fourth floor, where party promoters describe it as offering "one of the best views in Manhattan, overlooking Central Park and the city skyline." Mark's office sits at the top of the Turret, offering even better views. The room itself is two stories high, with a thin metal balcony circling the second floor, overlooking the black and white checkered floor which Mark had covered with beautiful Persian rugs. More rugs hang as well from the ceiling, which Jason and I perched behind, on the catwalk overhead, as it was the only place we could find to stay in the room to direct the action but out of view of the all-seeing eyes of the cameras.

With the cameras in the middle of the room, the viewer would be able to look all around while Mark, attuned to the medium, could start in one section and then, over the course of one minute, circle the entire space (again, providing our evaluators something to observe as visitors slowly rotated to keep the speaker in view). Jason turned the cameras on, gave the signal, and Mark was off and running or, rather, walking as he guided the viewer on a tour of the final element that makes the room so remarkable: its collection of dinosaur bones. For example, Mark walks up to one of his cabinets, takes out a bone of a tyrannosaurid theropod newly discovered in Mongolia, and walks it over to the cameras for a close-up.

The final scene takes us back to the Hall of Saurischian Dinosaurs, with Andrew in front of the *T. rex* and the rest of us still pretending to be curious visitors. Andrew reviews what we've learned so far. Where can dinosaurs be found in the world? Mongolia. What do we share with dinosaurs? Backbones. And with that, Andrew concludes the tour.

Edited all together, it ran for seven minutes. This was a controversial decision, given that earlier studies had shown our visitors barely lasted past two minutes when watching standard videos projected in exhibit Halls. It was crucial we understand how long visitors might want to be immersed in the world of a 360 video.

We also wanted to learn if it made a difference if there was a meaningful relationship between the subject of the video and the location in the Hall where they watched it. In other words, if the video was about our *T. rex* did it matter if you watched it seated in front of that *T. rex*, or would it be just as engaging seated beneath the blue whale, or next to an asteroid?

We put the video on YouTube, accessed it for streaming on a Samsung phone, and put the phone in a Merge VR Goggle, which is like Google Cardboard but made of a foam-like material. Merge was easy to clean between visitors, and it seemed sturdy enough for frequent usage and the occasional drop to the floor. Would the technical set-up function properly? Would visitors be forgiving of the tech learning curve to engage with the content?

We put these questions to the test through a series of day-time public prototyping sessions. Over six weeks we ran six public sessions totaling twelve hours, iterating the goals and evaluation instruments between each session. We interviewed 101 visitors at three different locations, all on the fourth floor.

One location was the Astor Turret, two floors beneath Mark Norell's office, so visitors could be in a space featuring the same round shape they would soon encounter within the video. The second was next to the towering titanosaur by the new Big Bone Room exhibit, which serendipitously featured the very *Diplodocus* vertebrae Danny displays in the video. The third was across the Museum on the raised viewing platform directly across from the *T. rex*. In summary, the first location put the visitor in a related space, the second by a related specimen, and the third in a location that bookended the video.

After setting up stools in each location, we invited visitors to "go behind the scenes with Museum paleontologists." Before each session we reviewed our equipment checklist:

VR headsets—one per smartphone (purple Merge headsets)
Headphones—one per smartphone (over the ear preferable)
Smartphones—fully charged preferably (Samsung S5 used 80 percent of battery in three hours of use)
Swivel stool—one per smartphone, for visitors to sit on when using the headset
Wipes/cleaning cloth—for wiping the part of the headset that touches visitors' faces in between each use
Optical cleaning cloth—for cleaning the glass lenses

We treated our first session as a tech demo, showing an early version of just Mark Norell taking a tour around his office. Every visitor enjoyed what one described as "feeling in the video." The length (2.5 minutes) was never a problem. We were surprised to see, time and again, how the viewer's group tried to turn what was essentially a private viewing into a social experience. Parents, for example, often chatted with their child to ask what they were looking at, took photos, or physically interacted with them (such as pretending to be a dinosaur biting their hand).

However, we quickly ran into technical issues. For example, the audio headset wire was often pulled out. Even worse, the lack of experience with the medium for most visitors became a barrier. We required a method for users to start the video. Our solution, of which we were quite proud, was programming the experience to begin when the visitor held their gaze for a few seconds over a start button. That seemed intuitive to us, but it turned out to be confusing to most visitors. (Thank you, pilot testing!) Until we found a better solution, we ended up having to hit the play button for each visitor and hand them the device.

In the second session, we now utilized all three locations on the fourth floor. We also used all three videos: Mark Norell's office (ninety seconds), the Big Bone Room (three minutes), and a compilation of both videos with Andrew's fictional tour (seven minutes). Our biggest finding was that visitors, even little kids, had little difficulty sitting down and staying engaged for seven minutes. This was clearly something very different from watching a video on a big screen. And whichever video they watched, and no matter which location they were in, they found the 360 video engaging. But were they learning anything? We would have to explore that in the future.

Visitors continued to push for the social—asking questions of their immersed friend or family member, or poking them just for fun. And finally, something new: most visitors not only turned their head to follow the action in the video, they often raised their hands and reached out to interact with it. What were they trying to touch? In post-viewing interviews they told us they had wanted to zoom in on a particular bone or tap (somehow) to get more information about a specific bone. While they expect a video on an exhibit wall to be a passive viewing experience, when it came to 360 video, however, there was often an expectation of interactivity. What were we to do with that? Design around it, or meet it?

We designed the third session to explore some of these questions: was the content engaging and educational outside the wow factor of the new technology? And, if they could interact with the videos, what did they want to do? To get some answers we removed the Merge Goggle entirely. No more private, immersive experience. Instead, a visitor would hold up a Samsung phone that could be viewed within a group setting and moved around to take in the full scene, like a flashlight illuminating a cave. Now it was a social experience. Sometimes we offered headsets; other times the audio was just played aloud from the device so all could hear.

The learning outcomes were mixed. Some people took away information about the bones, such as "The femur is the longest bone" or that there are still dinosaurs out there to discover. Others frankly ignored the narration, paying more attention to the architecture and saying things like "Sorry, I was too busy looking around." Others came away with incorrect information. "I learned archaeology," shared one person (note: the videos were *not* about archaeology).

Most of the visitors, however (thirteen of seventeen), knew just what they wanted from the potential of interactivity: to zoom in and get closer to objects in the videos.

For the fourth session, we were one of a number of activities at the Museum's Family Game Night, a late fall, after-hours event for members to come play science-themed games and activities around the exhibits. Again, we found the full seven minutes not to be a barrier to engagement. Upon arrival, visitors were told they could wait online or log into a website to reserve a space and be notified when it was time to return. This was a new experiment for us. Would people be willing to return to a station? At one point, the waiting list ran fifty-seven people deep. Even when told the wait could be around forty-five minutes, families still put their names down. Only a quarter eventually returned, but this was a powerful new tool we looked forward to exploring. How could this support and potentially transform a visitor's experience, helping them to be more engaged and relaxed during their visit?

In the final two sessions, we compared the social 360 head-to-head with the immersive 360, forcing visitors to use both. We split the Big Bone video in half, alternating beginning on one device and concluding on the other. We switched the starting and ending device each time to make sure there was no bias in people preferring a format just because it was the first or last they used. It turned out visitors generally preferred whichever format they were using when the video concluded. This suggested it did not matter which of the two formats were made available, as visitors found both social and immersive 360 engaging. This told us that, at the end of the day, we were freed in a sense from the user's needs. In deciding which direction we should take—social or immersive—we could let the needs of the Museum determine the final experience design.

After all of this work, visitors showed a healthy appetite for watching 360 videos, whether immersive or social, and even a seven-minute video held their attention. All of the locations were equally effective in engaging visitors. And by and large the technology worked and visitors quickly adapted to the new medium. In the end, we strengthened our techniques and learned that we had a lot of freedom, rather than constraints, in the design of any future 360 videos.

With our initial guiding questions for 360 videos sufficiently addressed, it was time for a recommendation document to the Museum.

First, we validated our abilities to produce in-house and then offer in the Halls a behind-the-scenes 360 video experience, giving visitors a glimpse of AMNH scientists at work while placing Hall specimens in context.

Second, the videos met visitor needs. People of all ages and backgrounds found the experience compelling and were excited to explore content related to their location within the Museum.

Third, when immersed in the virtual environments, visitors did not always hear or pay attention to what was said by the tour guide or scientists in the video. This was a good reminder of the eternal challenge of keeping content simple and easily digestible. And that sometimes, as Marshall McLuhan so wisely phrased it, the medium is the message.

Fourth, as the headgear required considerable facilitation (to set up the movie, to get the visitor into the headset, to adjust the audio), we would need to continue developing methods for reducing the number of staff we needed to effectively support it.

Fifth, visitors will watch videos considerably longer than those traditionally found in the Halls, but are satisfied with shorter videos as well.

Sixth, the VR headset is more immersive, but for those who wanted to keep connected with their social group the flat screen was preferable. Both directions were ripe for further exploration.

Finally, viewers wanted not just immersive but interactive experiences. When engaged in the immersive experience, they leaned forward, scooted their stool around, or reached out with their hands in what seemed like an attempt to see better or touch the items being shown. When in the social experience, many visitors were seen tapping or pinching the screen or moving it toward or away from themselves to zoom in (which actually had little effect).

We eventually added some interactivity to the current movie, using the "gaze as click" feature to pause the video and project a 360 model of a rotating dinosaur bone. The more we added interactivity to the 360 movie, however, the more we were pushing against the affordances of the medium. The 360 movies are best for immersion through passive viewing, using the language of film to project a setting and tell a story. The more that narrative is told through interactives, the more you are leaving the world of 360 video and entering the world of VR, and its siblings: AR and MR. That would lead us to invite visitors not just to view something in 360 degrees but to explore a full range of motion with tools for manipulating their environment and the objects within it.

That led to a wholly different set of activities: A:B testing immersive oceans.

A:B TESTING IMMERSIVE OCEANS

My favorite Halls are often designed to be their own immersive experiences. The Hall of Gems and Minerals can feel like spelunking through a dark cave. The Planetarium can send you orbiting the sun like an asteroid. The Hall of Ocean Life invites you to swim underwater with the immense blue whale bobbing above.

Beneath that blue whale, we took our next steps into the world of XR. The opportunity was an invitation to run a station for Public Programs' Celebrating Cephalopods, an event that would eventually see nearly five thousand visitors. Cephalopods include octopus, squid, nautilus, and more. We had already created an MR shark, taking a computed tomography scan of a specimen and animating it when visually placed above the model hanging over the entrance to the Hall of Ocean Life. Might we have any virtual cephalopods we could use to engage visitors?

Well, we did not, but we knew where we might find some. At the time, a commercial VR experience, *theBlu: Whale Encounter*, was popping up as an add-on at museums like the Natural History Museum of Los Angeles. Using the consumer-grade HTC Vive, visitors were paying extra to experience a two-minute undersea encounter with a virtual whale. In fact, we had recently tried it out with our own gear on random visitors on the giant screen beneath our blue whale, just to see if it would work. It worked.

A whale, however, is no cephalopod. *theBlu: Luminous Abyss*—a different immersive experience from the same company producing the whale experience—concludes with a squid encounter. We reached out via email to Wevr, the producers of *theBlu*, and got their permission to use it, for free, within our event.

This squid, however, would not be alone. It turned out we were in conversations with another squid-engaged VR production. After some web research I had come across *Ocean Rift*, which bills itself as "the world's first VR aquatic safari park." I emailed Chris Headleand, Managing Director of Picselica VR, and asked permission to use it for educational purposes. It turned out, to our surprise and delight, that Chris was Director of Teaching and Learning for the School of Computer Science at the University of Lincoln (in Great Britain). They normally turned down requests like ours, but realized the data we would collect might be perfect for a paper they were working on about using VR visualizations for ed-

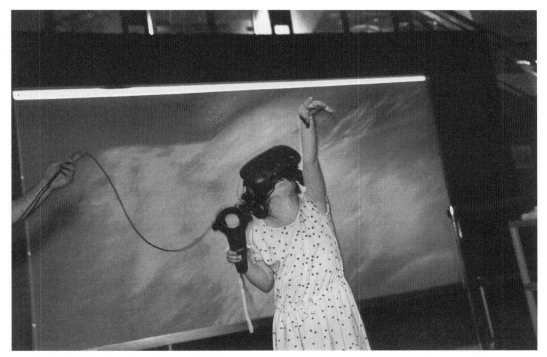

Figure 5.5. Virtual reality whale watching in the Hall of Ocean Life. *American Museum of Natural History*

ucational purposes. "If you are going to use *Ocean Rift*, then this could work out as a really interesting case study," he replied, then asked, "Would you be interested in working with us in this area?"

Now we had the permission we needed to use commercial products for free educational purposes. Public Programs had asked if we had any virtual cephalopods we could use to engage visitors. Yes. And in fact, we now had two.

When the Sunday arrived for the event, we set up in our corner of the room for an anticipated non-stop, five-hour flood of people. This was no longer a simple set of revolving chairs. We needed space for visitors to walk around, swing their arms, and otherwise act in wholly unexpected ways. We worked with the Museum staff in Operations to hang material to mark out the space for each user and to keep others away and safe. As the visitor would be tethered, with a wire connecting their headgear to a computer, a volunteer would need to be dedicated at all times to following the visitor around and keep them from getting tangled or falling. Another volunteer would run the evaluation. This meant each station required two volunteers. A fifth volunteer was assigned to manage the crowds, using a web-based notification tool to sign them up, provide a wait time, send a notification when their turn was approaching, and check them in when they returned.

When a visitor's turn arrived, they had little awareness that we were deciding which of the two VR experiences they would now undergo. We aimed to split visitors equally between the two titles, for the purposes of evaluation and to ensure we maximized the capacity of the stations.

Those in *theBlu* experienced a spooky scene, standing in near darkness at the bottom of the ocean in the midst of a bleached whale skeleton. The VR controller acted as a flashlight, illuminating various sea creatures as it passed them over. An anglerfish with its luminescent lure appeared, slowly circling the outer edges of the visitor's "stage," acting like the timer on a clock, ticking off each subsequent narrative beat. Scuttling crabs arrived, capturing light from the visitor then trailing back off into the dark. Glowing fish swam by, then jellyfish slowly appeared, which wiggled if prodded by the controller,

Designing Extended Reality 127

Figure 5.6. The set-up for the A:B testing of virtual reality ocean encounters. *American Museum of Natural History*

first one, then a handful, then enough to bathe the surrounding whale skeleton in light. It could be quite relaxing. Suddenly, the space would grow dark again, as all the luminescent creatures fled. What was scaring them? Tentacles would appear, the giant squid pinning the visitor with one giant, luminous eye, and then just as quickly speed off. Roll credits.

theBlu provided visitors with a sense of agency: the flashlight could light up anything in the scene, the visitor could walk around the area. However, this agency was somewhat illusory: the effect of the flashlight was limited, the area one could see was vastly larger than the area within which one could walk. The control remained in the hands of the designers, taking the visitor through a narrative which, while devoid of spoken words, had a script as tight as any movie. Scene 1: cue anglerfish. Scene 2: activate crabs. So on until final scene: release the kraken! This is known as being "on-rails," as in a user can only go where rails have been laid down, like a rollercoaster or a Disney ride. The magic here is that the rails were invisible to the user, and all they experienced was freedom and the delight of discovery. While visitors might have felt they were having their own, unique experience, pretty much each one saw the same thing.

Visitors assigned to *Ocean Rift* had a very different experience. The environment was fairly similar: visitors began on the ocean floor and using the VR controllers as propellers they could explore the environment, filled with undersea flora and fauna. And yes, if they were lucky, have an encounter with a squid. Visitors could interact with some of the animals, many which come attached with their own museum-style signage and educational voice narration. The wonder of *Ocean Rift* is that this gorgeous undersea world is procedurally generated. That means the moment a visitor begins exploring the world around them it is created on the fly, and it is different every time. Their VR experience was truly unique. They were not on a rail. There was no narrative. The visitors were free to do what they wanted. If they came seeking a dramatic arc, they needed to build it themselves. *Ocean Rift* only ends when the player decides it is time . . . or when a museum volunteer signaled the same through a tap on the shoulder.

That is at the crux of what we wanted to explore between these two VR oceans, in an A:B format: did museum visitors prefer a ride on-rails, experiencing a carefully designed narrative experience, or did they want the freedom to explore the world around them and carry the weight of creating their own story?

This question was supplemented by a handful of others baked into the day's evaluation:

- Can visitors integrate a timed, scheduled VR experience into their visit?
- Can the Museum meet demands for an immersive, interactive VR experience at a day-long family program?
- Did visitors find the VR experience engaging, educational, awe-inspiring, and/or social?

Visitors did indeed integrate a timed, scheduled VR experience into their visit. Replacing the phys-ical wait line with a registration system was essential; 60 percent of registered groups did something else at the event or in the Museum, then returned to participate in the VR experience, having waited on average fifty minutes. We had presumed the length of the wait would determine who returned, with longer waits predicting a higher rate of failed returns. It turned out length of wait had no impact. What did have impact was the size of the group and the time of day. The smaller the group, and the earlier in the day, the more likely a group was to return. In fact, no group over three people returned, and only two of the last ten groups to register returned.

With the VR station operating at full capacity nearly the whole time, it is fair to say the Museum did not meet the demand for an immersive, interactive VR experience. If we were to continue to offer XR experiences, we would need to figure out ways to increase the throughput to engage more people or risk disappointing visitors.

The majority of visitors told us they found the VR experience engaging (94 percent), educational (56 percent), and social (56 percent). However, to our disappointment, only 38 percent found their VR experience to be awe inspiring.

Finally, did visitors prefer their VR on-rails or within an open sandbox environment?

At first the data was clear-cut: visitors privileged user autonomy over a narrative structure. A total of 68 percent of interviewed visitors (thirty-two of forty-seven visitors) said they would have preferred more of a freeform, playground design over the addition of a more narrative structure. "I would rather just explore," shared one visitor. Yet many appreciated the guidance and structure that narrative ele-ments could provide. "I was disoriented without narrative," said one *Ocean Rift* user.

At the same time, we were aware that we were asking visitors to evaluate their experience based on a literacy they might not possess. Rather than assume, we put that literacy to the test. Before we asked their VR preferences, we first asked them to categorize their experience as either "more of a guided, dramatic narrative, with a beginning, middle and end" or "a freeform open playground." Three-quarters of *theBlu*'s users labeled it incorrectly, as a freeform playground, which told us as much about their VR literacy as it did about the ability of *theBlu*'s designers to trick their users into perceiving a greater sense of autonomy than the VR actually afforded. So perhaps the lesson was that people preferred VR on-rails as long as it provided the right balance of real and perceived autonomy.

OUTCOMES

After these experiments we stopped producing new 360 video content for in-Hall visitors; efforts for new interactive content largely went toward XR. However, we had validated that visitors enjoyed 360 videos, even if the content was not produced by or located at AMNH. And this created opportunities, for both Exhibitions and Public Programs.

Unseen Oceans was a special exhibit that focused on how twenty-first-century technologies like robotic and satellite monitoring were "revealing the unseen habitats of the oceans' most mysterious animals and mapping remote, inhospitable areas in unprecedented detail." One room was dedicated to a near-360 movie projected on the surrounding walls. Visitors sat in the middle as they watched giants of the deep (whale, squids, etc.) swim around them. Could this movie, *Swimming with Giants*, be taken from the wall and put into a personal 360 video experience, to promote the exhibit?

The answer was yes. What was less clear was how. If we offered it within the Hall of Ocean Life, would it tease visitors to check out the paid exhibit or make them satisfied enough to skip it altogether? What if we gave out *Unseen Oceans*–branded cardboard viewers when tickets were purchased, turning the video into an added feature to be experienced at home, and provide a link to watch it on YouTube? Over time, the Museum did all three.

At first, cardboard viewers were distributed to visitors. The landing page for this experience invited visitors to "dive into this video to virtually explore the world under the water and meet some of the ocean's biggest creatures." Instructions were still required—to get them to Youtube and to then "click the VR icon that can be seen at the bottom of the video"—as many were (and perhaps still are) not yet familiar with using YouTube to turn a two-dimensional movie into a 360 experience.

After a few months, however, once the initial excitement of the exhibit opening had dipped down, a new station was set up underneath the blue whale in the Hall of Ocean Life. Run by Public Programs, visitors could take a seat, pick up a viewer, and watch *Swimming with Giants* in 360 video.

Meanwhile, a new special exhibit was under development: *T. rex: The Ultimate Predator*. "Come see the most fearsome carnivore of the Mesozoic," the Museum website promoted upon launch, "and discover other members of the tyrannosaur family." When it premiered the *New York Times* heralded it as a "monster" of an exhibition "combining the latest scientific research into how the creatures developed and lived with startlingly vivid models and whoa!-inducing technology." That "whoa!-inducing technology" included the Museum's first effort at producing original VR content for use in an exhibit: *T. rex Skeleton Crew*.

For over a year we had been visiting public VR engagements around New York City: a VR arcade in the lobby of a movie theater chain, the VR stations at the Brooklyn Academy of Music's Teknopolis, a commercial venue on 34th Street billed as "The Largest Virtual Reality Playground in North America," Philadelphia's Franklin Museum's museum-wide VR deployment, and even a Connecticut mall's VR arcade. I was on a logistics tour: How many users could be supported at a time? How many staff were required, and in what roles? Which VR equipment did they use? How did they clean the devices between users? How much did they charge, and what registration systems did they deploy?

At the same time, we explored the overlooked places in the Museum, valuable public real estate that was underutilized by the public that might be transformed into a VR theater. It could become a site for us to publicly prototype emerging media. On the first floor, a glass-enclosed cafe had sat unused for years, with no plans to re-open. On the fourth floor the "Meryl Streep" theater largely sat empty, featuring the actress speaking in an eerie monotone over an endlessly looping video explaining the scientific significance of the layout of the surrounding dinosaur exhibit. We developed budgets for staffing an ongoing VR experience, explored construction needed to transform one of the spaces (providing me with one of my treasured memories of the Museum, the opportunity to climb on top of the fourth-floor theater), and sketched out different architectural designs for supporting multiple VR stations.

When development began on *The Ultimate Predator*, we were in negotiation with the Taiwanese technology manufacturer, HTC, to develop original content for their new device, the Vive. Could we develop a new VR experience embedded within the new exhibit? Before long, efforts to build a VR theater were put on hold and the research was used to inform the logistics of offering a unique experience to visitors within a paid special exhibit.

Nick Bartzokas, who produced *Skeleton Crew* within SciViz, ensured the virtual *T. rex* was created to match scientific references and scans. "It went through rigorous expert review and adjustment," he told me, "to match the current understandings of *T. rex* morphology, motion, and behavior." When it launched it supported up to three visitors at a time who, with the help of Museum staff, donned HTC Vive headsets and traveled to the past. The experience tasked visitors, as described by the *New York Times*, "with reconstructing a *T. rex* skeleton." The reporter concluded with a delightful warning: "You'll then cower in terror as it comes to life."[1]

In the video by the Museum promoting the experience, Nick says, "You feel like you're in the Cretaceous period, face to face with the *T. rex*, and there's just no replacing that level of immersion." Nick is joined by Vivian Trakinski, the leader of our SciViz group, who talks about how *Skeleton Crew* marked a transition for our work. "We've been experimenting with VR for a couple of years now," she says. "We saw [*Skeleton Crew*] as a real opportunity to move from prototyping and experimentation into full implementation."

Visitors loved it, and it was a popular feature until it, and everything around it, and in the city, and in the world, closed, in March of 2020, due to COVID-19. By then, however, it was clear that while one day the exhibit would travel, the VR would likely stay behind. It was just too labor intensive, requiring as many people to run as it could support.

Still, the future has yet to be written. Maybe there just wasn't the real estate within a traveling exhibit to allow the VR to scale. Maybe, one day, it too will get to travel to other museums, on its own, offering other institutions the opportunity as we once had with *Swimming with Giants*, *theBlu*, and *Ocean Rift*, to explore and experiment with the power and potential of XR.

Meanwhile, when the exhibit first launched, Vivian said in the promotion video, "This VR experience brings the goals of science visualization to life as no other platform could." What those goals are, and what exactly is a science visualization, will be the topic of our next and final case study.

Comparison: Shedd Aquarium (Chicago, Illinois)

The Shedd Aquarium is on a peninsula sticking out into Lake Michigan. It shares park space with other institutions like the Adler Planetarium, the Field Museum, and the stadium for the Chicago Bears football team. While aggregating cultural institutions into one location helps to attract visitors—the Aquarium sees upward of two million a year—it can be difficult for many local residents to make the trip to the remote location. That is why Miranda Kerr, the Shedd's Manager of Digital Learning, turned to 360 videos. If she could not get the teens of Chicago to the Aquarium, maybe she could use this new technology to bring the Aquarium to the teens.

"Part of my job is to follow what's new in the museum technology space and any digital tools that are trending in other spheres," Miranda told me, "then consider implications for the work we do." That work they do is respond to trends in programming and audience needs with digital learning experiences, often through piloting and evidence-based decision making. Miranda purchased their first equipment in the summer of 2016: a 360 camera, a set of five unlocked phones, and VR headsets. Their aim was to pilot both the creation and viewing of 360 video with learners.

The first pilot ran in their Park Voyagers program, which brings educational programming to facilities often in underserved communities. In collaboration with ten other Chicago museums, the program provides free afterschool activities for children and their families. "The 360 video and headsets were the technology we needed," Miranda realized, "to answer the question, 'How can we bring the experience of viewing Shedd Aquarium's exhibits and animals to children offsite?'"

They began by recording 360-degree videos within three of their exhibits that would connect to the habitats they would teach about in the program: coral reefs, the Amazon, and the Great Lakes. "Because we have fishes and other animals that are swimming around," Miranda explained, "a simple photo doesn't capture this in the same way." When the pilot was introduced within the Park Voyagers program, the families who viewed the videos loved the experience. "Some even said they felt like they were in the water with the animals."

What Miranda and her team appreciated most was the volume of questions they received after each viewing. After watching the Great Lakes video, which featured close-ups of their sturgeon exhibit, children would ask, with excitement, "What is that? Is that a monster?" and "Do you have any more videos?" After watching the 360 video about the Shedd's Wild Reef exhibit, the children asked questions about the animals they had just watched swim by. After discussing the 360 videos, the participants created their own coral-themed stop-motion animations.

More pilots followed. Miranda wanted to see how 360 video might capture their educational programs in a new way, taking the camera on a snorkel dive during a marine biology program and on a nature hike during a summer camp. They even took the cameras underwater, right into the live exhibits. To achieve that, they acquired in 2017 an underwater 360 camera. Before the Aquarium opened (to keep visitors out of the shots), they explored a number of creative techniques, including having SCUBA divers and snorkelers hold the camera on a selfie stick, setting up a tripod inside one of their exhibits, and using zip ties to attach it to an underwater robot.

They eventually supported youth in their Teen Work-Study program to make their own 360 videos underwater (to share with guests waiting in line to buy tickets), captured 360 underwater video at an underwater robotics competition, and eventually posted these videos for anyone to view on the Shedd's YouTube channel.

"My big question," Miranda says, "is how can 360 video take our learners to new places and enhance experiences?" When asked if she had any initial findings, she said her learning staff had captured positive comments from the teens creating 360 videos. "Teens gained skills on the applications of VR," she was told.

"I was scared of technology," one teen had shared, "terrified of technology . . . until now."

TIPS AND STRATEGIES

1. User Research

   Think: *How do you learn what visitors want from a medium with which they have little to no experience?*
   Do: *Perform both user research and subject or content research. Figure out the right balance between how to apply the results from each.*

2. Rapid prototypes

   Think: *If you had access to a museum's assets, what might you have prototyped in order to validate interest in 360 movies?*
   Do: *We remixed the assets created for the prototype in different ways. For example, we showed the Big Bone Room video on its own, as part of a longer narrative, and even cut it in half (forcing viewers to experience the full story across two different mediums). Develop interesting questions that can only be answered by remixing your prototype in different ways.*

3.   Public piloting

Think: How is piloting with general visitors walking past exhibits during regular business hours different from piloting with members at a special, after-hours event? How might one account for those differences in the design of a public piloting session, whether to minimize their impact or to leverage them?

Do: Sometimes it feels like we have to run our own pilots; no one knows [fill-in-the-blank] better than ourselves and we want to directly experience how end users react. And sometimes, with limited resources, we have no other choice. But training others to collect data that is valid, reliable, and clearly communicates key findings is essential. Train one or more people to use instruments you develop to run a pilot and then have them share results with you; consider how you might iterate the evaluation instruments and the training for deploying them. If you don't have the resources to engage others, swap with someone else who is looking to do the same thing!

4.   Iterative design

Think: How is iterating a digital experience designed around evaluation objectives different from iterating around other objectives, like, say, learning, engagement, or fiscal objectives?

Do: We designed the first 360 video prototypes to be no more interactive than turning one's head. Then we learned visitors wanted to touch . . . something. Challenge yourself to think outside the box. Take one of your designs and list at least one thing it assumes users want to do with it. Then come up with three to five unexpected and outrageous things people might end up wanting to do with it. Pick one and describe how you might iterate the design to address that desire. Will it meet that desire? Suppress it? Redirect it? Transform it?

5.   Youth collaboration

Think: We learned what we thought we needed to know by the end of this round of piloting. What should we take from that regarding this book's strong emphasis on including youth as co-designers of digital experiences?

Do: Ask young people what apps or sites they are using to consume and/or produce video content. Have them show it to you. Learn what roles they occupy when engaged with video—are they being a consumer looking to relax, a student trying to learn something, an artist seeking inspiration?

6.   Team up!

Think: What were the risks and/or costs involved with partnering with such an in-demand resource as paleontology? What might have been gained or lost by working with a different department?

Do: Strategize how to get help or support from someone you think would never have the time to do so. Then go for it!

7.   Comparative project

Think: While the Shedd's 360 videos were often designed to bring those outside the building into Aquarium-based public environments, the AMNH videos were designed to bring people within the building to private spaces within the campus. What else can you notice is different between the two projects? What else was similar?

NOTE

1.   Jason Farago, "T. Rex Like You Haven't Seen Him: With Feathers," *New York Times*, March 7, 2019.

About Time

I'm standing outside the youngest of the Museum's four cardinal entrances. The first (building 1) opened to the public nearly a century and a half ago, facing south. In the 1930s, new buildings were added east (building 12) and north (building 18). The west arrived only in 2000, through the glass-cubed Weston Pavilion, which stands as a mere echo of the Rose Center located down the hall.

Compared to the others, the western passage feels like an afterthought, like an unplanned-for child born years after its siblings.

Outside the entrance sits a silver time capsule shaped like a giant wonton, designed (or so a plaque reads) to conceal for a thousand years treasures that offer "insight into daily life today": a hair sample from Dolly the sheep, condoms from Zimbabwe, a unicorn Beanie Baby.

What insight might we glean from a Beanie Baby? Does anyone even remember them? Then again, who will remember *Pokémon Go*, whose players currently swarm the capsule as they toss virtual Pokéballs at virtual creatures and spin the capsule to increase their inventory of healing potions and weapons. Not the actual time capsule, of course, but the virtual one included alongside millions of other important locations augmented into the game's Pokéstops worldwide.

Players swipe as one to enact their collective fantasy, the time capsule at their center, the Museum surrounding them. Meanwhile (after collecting my own Pokéballs) I use my imagination to reach for a different shared vision: the building that will soon begin construction, replacing all of this with the grand west-facing entrance the Museum has always deserved.

Desks around the campus share a passion for archival photos of the early Museum, like the crisp black and white of building 1 towering strong like a lone ear in a razed field of corn. Other offices, meanwhile, display not photos documenting the past but old illustrations of imagined futures. The most common depicts the Museum with a church-like tower in the center of a grid of encircling passages, like a rotating space station generating artificial gravity. This vision, unfulfilled, left us instead with something more akin to a labyrinth with halls—dedicated to gems and minerals, to the people of the Pacific, to the Incas—that halt visitors with dead ends that force them to turn back and retrace their steps.

But no more. In a few years, the new building will stitch together all these loose ends into one continuous circle. It will fill up this outdoor space, welcoming visitors into a five-story cavern with new exhibits, classrooms, research labs, or simply providing passageway from one corner of the campus to another. It will try to push into the past the idea of a museum as a cabinet of curiosity, promoting in its place a twenty-first-century vision of a museum as the interplay of science disciplines, as sites of both lifelong learning and innovation.

I look up into the open sky and imagine myself surrounded instead by an exciting new building to explore, with public spaces to delight my family and private ones to explore at work. I look down at the capsule. Where will it go? Somewhere else, I suspect. Just not here.

Once moved it will remain at this spot, in both our expectations and in digital records like *Pokémon Go*, whose players will continue to seek it out, expecting a time capsule but only uncovering its virtual ghost. I wonder who will be first, our visitors or the game, to assimilate the Museum's new map.

In either case, when the circle's complete, it will be about time.

6

Designing Science Visualizations

IN SUMMARY | tl;dr

Subject: This chapter focuses on using the Six Tools of Digital Design for developing science visualizations.

Case study: The case studies in this chapter focus on the evolution of *Galactic Golf*, an astro-visualization that addressed the topics of mass and gravity through a round of mixed reality Martian golf; an interactive science visualization that visitors could hold in their hands based on bat skull computed tomography scans; and Finding Flamingos, a youth program focused on how Conservation Biologists protect endangered flamingos through geographic information system mapping and predictions software. All of these projects were designed to answer questions about the potential of science visualizations to enhance the museum visitor experience.

User research: A small army of graduate student interns armed with both video and still cameras, and a host of evaluation instruments, were simultaneously deployed through four floors of the Rose Center for Earth and Space. Tasked with capturing a snapshot in time—two hours in the life of the Rose Center and its visitors—they took photos, interviewed visitors, captured snippets of overhead conversations, and more. This final snapshot, prepared in an oversized book, focused on neither the visitors nor the Rose Center but, rather, the relationship between the two, identifying key touchpoints.

Rapid prototyping: We created a rapid prototype combining computed tomography scans with a six-sided cube covered in augmented reality targets. Since, at the time, projecting an augmented object onto a three-dimensional target was a new medium, we needed to learn its affordances so we could leverage them in our design.

Public piloting: Public piloting was crucial for evaluating the efficacy of *Galactic Golf* and the augmented bat skulls, as well as the experience we designed around the products. For example, at one point the user observations for the bat experience suggested that while earlier it had proven quite popular it was now no longer of interest to visitors. Interest was being measured, in part, by how often and how long visitors were holding the skulls. Upon further research we learned the visitors were in competition with those facilitating the experience, as they too could not resist the appeal of this new instructional aid. Once facilitators were instructed to let visitors go first, measurements of high interest returned.

Iterative design: *Galactic Golf* began with an interest in exploring gravity on the moon, shifted to gravity on Mars, and then expanded to include gravity on celestial bodies through the galaxy. The augmented bat skulls were iterated in many directions at once, exploring how visitors interacted with them on mobile phones, tablets, a tabletop, and as three-dimensional printed skulls. We also iterated the pedagogy around the product, exploring high- and low-touch approaches, and contrasted live facilitation versus self-directed.

Youth collaboration: The youth in Finding Flamingos were not tasked with designing the digital interactive. Rather, they designed how the digital interactive could be used to engage end users, creating a facilitated experience that employed a multitouch table as an educational aid. This was to inform the role youth might play in a proposed SciViz Learning Lab.

Teaming up: Museum scientists were open to collaboration but, at the same time, had to manage competing requests for their limited time. Some of the benefits that persuaded them to collaborate included viewing our request to turn their research into digital interactives as a novel way to approach their research, as a way to bring their research to a public audience, and due to curiosity about how others might transform their work in new and creative ways.

Comparison: The chapter concludes by offering, for comparison, an exploration of the development of the Q?rius learning space at the Smithsonian's National Museum of Natural History in Washington, DC.

CONTEXT AND GUIDING QUESTIONS

When my work responsibilities shifted from afterschool programming into the Science Visualization Group, I had to ask myself one crucial question: What exactly *is* a science visualization?

Vivian Trakinski, our leader as the Director of Science Visualization, gave our newly reformed department a crash course on the topic.

First of all, science data visualization is about turning large data sets into visuals in order to "help us understand the composition, organization, and dynamics of the natural world." These might be in three dimensions—height, width, and depth—or include a fourth dimension as well, of time.

These data sets are generated with cutting-edge tools, like scanning electron microscopes, computed tomography (CT) scanners, telescopes, satellite instruments, and computer models. They each afford us the same power, allowing us to "probe otherwise unreachable dimensions of nature—including scales that are too big and too small to see with the naked eye, or happen over time, scales that are likewise impossible to observe directly (too slow, too fast, or too long ago)." CT scans of a dinosaur fossil, for example, measure energies; their results are based on how long it takes for energy to pass through different materials, revealing the physical make-up of the inner, unseen fossil.

Vivian wanted us to see how SciViz is a rich and varied practice that modern scientists rely on to "address the remaining mysteries of life and just about everything else!" It brings together the fields of both natural and computer science. That is why our team was in such a unique position, given our access to the wide array of data generated across the many fields of science housed within the museum, and powered by our computer science knowledge and artful communication skills. Vivian also explained that our group used the broader term "science visualization"—not the more specific "science data visualization"—to give us more latitude to engage visitors with a broader range of data visualizations, so our team could focus on communicating new research and discoveries.

The science visualizations Vivian wanted us to consider came in a wide array of forms: climate models, astronomical observations, and simulations (that show us how stars are born and die, for instance). They were satellite maps, brain maps, and even "computer models that can help us figure out how extinct animals moved and behaved by basically animating fossil evidence."

These were all crucial guidelines to keep our team aligned with the goals of our new work. When it came time, however, to teach the topic to high school students, we also needed a succinct definition. After a number of courses, we came up with the following: A SciViz results from **data** being processed **digitally** to produce a **visualization** as part of a **scientific inquiry**.

We learned to explain to teens that the four bolded words and phrases are the criteria they should use when deciding what is, and is not, a science visualization.

- **Data:** We could say "big data," but as it is all on a continuum; "big data" is not wrong, but data is all that's required.
- **Digital:** The data being processed is translated in a digital way. Computers are involved. The data may live in a spreadsheet before processing.
- **Visualization:** The digital data is turned into something one can see. However, it need *not* be a digital visualization—it could be a sculpture based on population density data.
- **Scientific inquiry:** All of these points can be done by a marketing company to predict customer behavior or to make dinosaurs in *Jurassic Park*. We are talking about this activity specifically within a scientific context.

We were surprised to learn that many of the youth presumed a SciViz needed to be interactive. However, this is not essential to be a science visualization. Making a visualization interactive is just a design decision, and it can be a fairly useful one. It is how most of the teens in our programs encountered SciViz. At the same time, to make a SciViz interactive, there's a tradeoff: one usually needs to pare down the size of the data set, losing some of the details, in order to make it run smoothly in a real-time environment.

The SciViz group developed dozens of prototypes, most of which traveled to the floor for public piloting. This chapter will select three case studies to understand through the lens of the Six Tools for Digital Design. The first will explore the evolution of an astro-visualization that addressed the topics of mass and gravity through a round of mixed reality Martian golf.

The second will look at how we prototyped interactive science visualizations using CT scans of bat skulls that visitors could hold in their hands.

The third will look at how we prototyped engagement within an envisioned SciViz Lab through a youth program focused on how Conservation Biologists protect endangered flamingos through geographic information systems (GIS) mapping and predictions software.

The following are the guiding questions that drove the evaluations for all three of the case studies:

1. At the American Museum of Natural History (AMNH), what patterns are we seeing in terms of visitors and who participates in emerging media experiences?
2. In what ways does participating in an emerging media experience affect the visitor in terms of
   - dwell time in particular exhibition areas?
   - understanding key phenomena, concepts, or science practices?
   - affective experiences about being at the Museum?
3. Do visitors share/discuss their emerging media experiences (1) during their visit, (2) after their visit, or (3) in social media? What kinds of things do they share?
4. Are there certain AMNH galleries in which emerging media is more successful?
5. What questions do visitors have in conjunction with their emerging media experience?
6. How do visitors describe the relationship between participating in the emerging media experience and their overall experience at AMNH?

Galactic Golf

From the start, I had no doubt our team would be developing science visualizations using astronomical data. The Museum created and managed for over two decades the *Digital Universe Atlas*, a database containing information from dozens of organizations combined into the most complete and accurate three-dimensional atlas of the universe. When you fly past stars in a space show in the Hayden Planetarium you are not viewing an artist's interpretation of space but a pre-recorded science visualization based on the *Atlas*.

So it was not a question of if we might create interactive astroviz prototypes, but what we might make, where we might offer it, and how soon. There was also interest in exploring the next generation of astrodata. NASA had just provided $6.3 million to fund OpenSpace, which would convert "massive amounts of data about celestial objects, phenomena, and space missions into striking visualizations in real time" allowing one to "fly through the universe and observe processes and specific objects from different views."

In regard to where we might stage it, it was easy to presume the Rose Center for Earth and Space, which housed the Hayden Planetarium. But Rose is a big and complex space. So many opportunities! Where to begin?

Rose is an architectural marvel. It is a giant, six-story glass box containing a Death Star of a planetarium, the Hayden Sphere, which magically appears to float in the middle. Visitor engagement can be broken into four sections. At the highest level is the Scale of the Universe, which is a walkway surrounding the Sphere. Using the planetarium as a reference point, a walkway features signs using the idea of the "powers of ten" to display each step in the scale of the universe down to the scale of atoms.

This level also provides the entrance into the bottom of the Hayden Sphere, which contains not the space show but a short movie about the big bang. This film exits out onto the Cosmic Pathway, a spiral which traces the thirteen-billion-year history of the cosmos down across two full loops.

The Pathway deposits its visitors at the Moon station, which is a small exhibit whose highlight is a physical model of the moon that visitors love to touch. This section has a staircase that leads down to the final section: the Hall of the Universe.

Recessed like a sunken lounge, the Hall of the Universe is the most traditional space in Rose, as unusual as it is. Wide panels describe aspects of the universe, like satellites and constellations. A large AstroBulletin screen projects the latest news and science. The famous 15.5-ton Willamette Meteorite, or Tomanowos to the Confederated Tribes of Grand Ronde, rests on pillars that are drilled down to the foundation of Manhattan.

Again, so many opportunities! To collect some empirical evidence about the opportunities within these spaces, we decided to do a study. We tasked ourselves with creating a snapshot in time—two hours in the life of the Rose Center. This snapshot would focus on neither the visitors nor the Rose Center; rather, it would document the relationship between the two, capturing touchpoints in any way we could.

A small army of graduate student interns armed with both video and still cameras, and a host of evaluation instruments, were simultaneously deployed through all four sections. Visitors can enter the Scales of the Universe either from the macro end or the micro end of the narrative, so we set up a team on both sides. They unobtrusively followed and observed visitors, noting what they looked at and touched, writing down snippets of overheard conversation, and interviewed them afterward. Visitors were invited to be photographed at their favorite location while sharing what made that particular selection so special to them.

Two more teams worked the Cosmic Pathway in a similar manner, one pair following visitors down the spiral, the other up. The Moon only required one pair, as it's a small area, but the Hall of the Universe needed a different approach.

Figure 6.1. A pair of visitors' favorite item in the Hall. *Author*

That Hall is a large open space, with various entrances and exits, making it hard to observe all of its traffic. Studying it is like researching a cocktail party. Teams still followed and interviewed visitors, but we needed some technology to literally capture the full picture. We taped GoPro cameras, which provided a fisheye lens view, to the upper balcony, tilted down toward the Hall so we could see all of its activity at once. After the event, the evaluators watched the footage, taking turns tracking different groups of visitors move across the footage. As they used the video to make their observations, they watched in the footage for an evaluator to hold aloft a white sheet with a large visible number, unique for each set of visitors observed and interviewed in person. This allowed the team to connect two different sets of data—one captured in-person and one captured from the recorded footage.

Afterward, we selectively visualized some of the lessons learned in the data. For example, the Ecosystem Sphere, a glass-enclosed, self-sustaining habitat of algae and shrimp, was the number one thing visitors touched and looked at. Yet it was rarely photographed. The top exhibit photographed was the impressive Tomanowos meteorite.

We compiled into one physical book all of these new data visualizations, all of the best photographs (of visitors at their favorite locations, or close-up details of the Hall), and all of the most intriguing overheard comments or quotes from interviews. This snapshot then became a resource we could pick up to contemplate the relationship in the Hall created between the space and its visitors, asking ourselves where we saw opportunities to enhance that relationship with interactive science visualizations.

Over the years we piloted many prototypes using astrodata within the Hall. In one instance we explored how we could create a field of stars, using real data, and let visitors walk among them. Constellations are one way to visualize a collection of stars. Standing on Earth, looking up, the

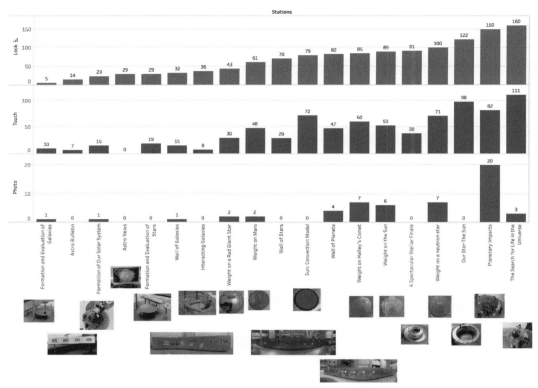

Figure 6.2. A chart of all items photographed, viewed, and/or touched. *American Museum of Natural History*

constellations might appear flat, as if resting on a two-dimensional surface; this is what allows us to look at three stars and say, "Oh, there is Orion's belt!" However, stars do not sit on a flat surface. They sit in a three-dimensional space. Some are closer to or farther from Earth than others; they appear to us as they do because of our perspective. That means if you left Earth on a spaceship and flew far enough to change your view, far outside our solar system, that belt of stars in a straight line might now appear as a triangle.

We explored this one concept through a wide range of science visualizations, digital tools, and iterations. We started with a laptop offering a web-based program (created the year earlier through a Hackathon) that looked at a photo of your face and turned it into a constellation. We created a mixed-reality experience through the Hololens in which the visitor (standing in front of the exhibit illustrating Orion) could walk among a field of stars to observe the connect-the-dot of the constellation transform as one's perspective shifted. We took a version of that Hololens constellation, worked with a youth program to create an escape room, and explored how a private extended-reality experience could generate social engagement. Finally, we moved these explorations to the large AstroBulletin screen, using a Kinect sensor to support gesture-based controls by the visitor. After a number of iterations, this turned into Star Pose, in which a visitor is presented with a series of constellations on the screen that they need to match with their body. Successful matches triggered an animation that revealed the constellation rotating in a three-dimensional space.

Flipping through the snapshot, one thing that jumped out at me was how much people loved standing on the scales on the floor to learn their weight on celestial bodies. Visitors in the photo were always looking down toward their feet, to read their new weight. What might it be like to experience looking back up to see you are actually next to a Moon rover and can explore the lower gravity?

There are five scales scattered around the Rose Center, one of the few holdovers from the original planetarium that the Rose Center replaced when it first opened in 2000. I admire the design of those simple scales. When you see one you feel a pull to stand on it, because you already know how to use a scale. Its scant copy reads "Your weight on the moon" along with a red digital number appearing on a display. And that's it. It's like an intellectual pile of Lego blocks that challenge you to put it all together to make sense of your experience, which most people do standing up straight, head down reading the display. Hmm? The number I see on the display is *not* my weight. What's going on? Comparing the two—what I know with what I see—I realize I weigh less on the moon. That might make me wonder why. Maybe I know that gravity is less on the moon, and maybe I realize that is because the moon has less mass than the earth. Or maybe I don't. But in an instant the scale tossed me a challenge and I can then choose whether to accept it.

It can be quite wonderful watching visitors go through all of these motions, again and again, in just a few seconds, and note how they often bring the people around them into the experience.

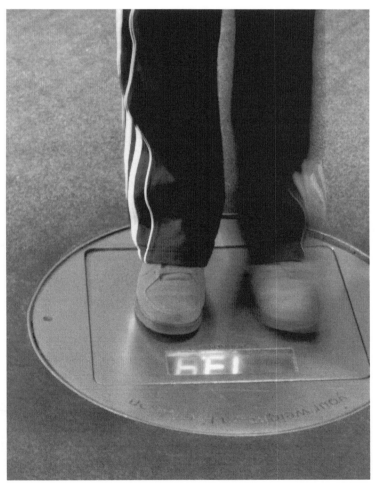

Figure 6.3. "Your Weight on the Moon" scale. *American Museum of Natural History*

So that's where we started, asking ourselves the following: what if you could expand the elegance of the scale through digital tools, allowing the visitor both to observe the lunar surface spread out around them and then explore how gravity differs on the moon? Working with Nathan Leigh, a Postdoctoral Fellow in the Museum's Department of Astrophysics, we explored a number of game options that relied on gravity. A tossed ball? Basketball? Throwing a ball into a bucket? It turned out a nice arc to the ball helps to illustrate some of the gravitational differences, and that led us to golf . . . *Mooniature Golf*!

We had presumed we had access to good lunar surface data—and we did—but positioning at the human scale was a level of resolution we just couldn't acquire. Luckily, the lunar scale was only one of a number of scales sending our visitors around the universe. That's when we learned more about our interplanetary photographer, the Curiosity Rover, and considered instead using the Martian scale. That's how *Mooniature Golf* turned into *Martian Golf*.

We aimed to hew close to the existing Hall experience—you look at the scale and you're invited to make a comparison between what you already know and what it tells you. After a number of over-elaborate concepts, we came up with the idea for a single golf hole, on the Martian surface, next to Curiosity itself.

For the user interface, we went with the Hololens clicker. We wanted something physical that could be swung like a golf club with a simple user interface. So one click and hold to start the swing, and then release the click to end the swing, sending the ball flying. To bring home the educational objective, the ball now flew in two arcs—a smaller blue arc showing how the golf ball would fly under earth gravity, the higher green arc showing how it would fly on Mars. If the visitor failed to get a hole in one, then Nathan, whose voice had been providing narration throughout on the Hololens, provided feedback on whether the next swing should be harder or softer.

Ah, but when the ball landed in the hole, with a satisfying (albeit unscientific) clunk, the Curiosity rover was activated, rolling back and forth, as if joining you in a victory dance.

We then added one final, non-digital element. After finishing the hole, Nathan instructed the player to return to the facilitator and get a score card. The score card, like a sheet used in miniature golf to record swings, is actually for recording your weight on all scales in the Hall, along with two questions that extend this theme about weight and mass: first, was your weight more or less than on Earth, and second, does that mean your new celestial location has more or less mass than Earth?

With the new score card, the experience was now extended to the full range of scales all around the Hall of the Universe. Since the focus was no longer on just Mars, we changed the name to *Galactic Golf*.

The score card was not just part of the visitor experience—it was also an evaluation tool. It allowed us to evaluate whether a facilitated digital experience could motivate visitors to engage in a longer, self-directed, analog experience. At the same time, we used the sheet to evaluate their understanding of the key learning objectives. That made those sheets worth to us their weight in gold. It would break our heart if they filled out their sheet then took them home or tossed them out. We needed a way to motivate visitors to return them, like the deposit on a soda can. Luckily, we could use our small farm of three-dimensional printers to incentivize the return of score cards by offering cute prints of the Gale Crater, the site where Curiosity first landed.

After observing and interviewing around eighty people, here are some of the key lessons we took away from this round of prototyping.

Mars is engaging: The vast majority of visitors (83 percent) offered positive reactions throughout *Galactic Golf* and nearly all made it to the end. The Martian surface was engaging as well: The majority of visitors (67 percent), when interviewed, said they liked looking at the Martian surface; one said "It gives you a real experience of standing there and knowing what it looks like."

The Martian surface was understood to be based on scientific data: Seventy percent of those who had an opinion understood that the virtual Martian landscape came, somehow, from equipment

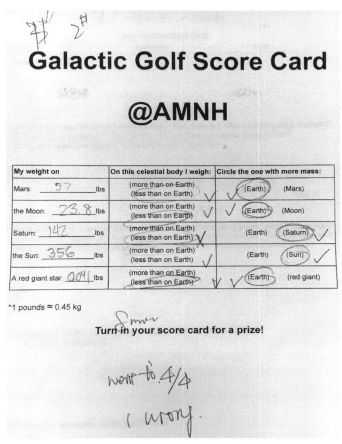

Figure 6.4. An example of a completed Galactic Golf score card.
Author

on Mars (rather than, say, the imagination of an artist). That was a win for extended reality prototypes using astrodata.

The Learning Objectives came through: A majority of visitors (63.3 percent) attributed the difference between the Earth and Martian golf ball arcs to gravity and mass, and a majority (61 percent) said they learned this from *Galactic Golf* itself.

Those with time found the score card engaging: Just over half of those offered the score card accepted the additional challenges (those who did not most often had timed space show tickets) and the vast majority who accepted the challenges returned the score card (89 percent). A total of 71 percent went to all four additional scales while the rest went to all but one scale. The score card asked visitors to decide on each scale whether in comparison they weighed more or less on Earth; this was answered correctly 89 percent of the time. It also asked which of the two celestial bodies had more mass; this was correctly answered 86 percent of the time. In other words, visitors most of the time successfully connected mass with gravity.

Social: While designed to be a single-player experience, 74 percent of visitors interacted with their social group during *Galactic Golf*, most often by describing what they were seeing or being photographed.

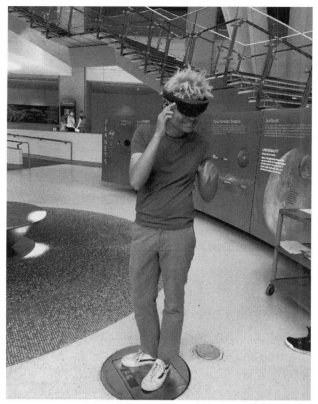

Figure 6.5. A visitor playing *Galactic Golf. Author*

Galactic Golf was an embodied SciViz experience, in which you swung your arm to interact with a Martian-based science visualization. A different series of pilots went in a different direction, prototyping what might happen when the SciViz could be held in the palm of your hand.

Handheld Data

On any given day, I could easily produce a list of awe-inspiring locations for a behind-the-scenes tour of the Museum, such as Paleo's Big Bones room, Exhibition's Fabrication Department, or Osteology's "bug colony" of dermestid beetles. Depending on my mood, destinations might be added or removed. One, however, would be a perennial: the Microscopy and Imaging Facility (MIF).

The MIF shares the same floor with the vast majority of the science departments. I presumed that was intentional, as the MIF is a shared resource supporting all of their work. If you have a specimen in need of a CT scan, the MIF could meet your needs with its impressive million-dollar machine, turning items both big and small into massive quantities of data.

That data usually sits on the MIF computers before being transferred to each department's bespoke solution. Scientists would then study their scans to advance scientific understanding of the natural (sharks, dinosaur fossils) and constructed (pottery shards) worlds.

Occasionally, a scientist might receive a request to access their data. It was usually from a colleague at another institution, looking to pursue their own research, not to educate and entertain the public, which we sought to do. We found most Museum scientists were delighted by our requests, as it was novel and could bring their research to a public audience. They were also curious to see how others might transform their work in new and creative ways.

Over time we collected CT scans from a number of sources: a mako shark, provided by paleontologists John Maisey and John Denton, microfossils (between 0.001 millimeter and one millimeter in size) provided by Fossil Invertebrates Manager Bushra Hussaini, and bat skulls provided by Mammalogy Research Associate Abbie Curtis. We would disarticulate the scans and then reconnect the parts so we could animate them in different ways, making the shark's mouth open and close, or its body swim.

Could their CT scans be integrated into a SciViz project? Would visitors be engaged by interacting with them? Could they be used to highlight the scientific endeavors taking place in the Museum around them? We sought answers to these questions by putting these manipulated CT scans into wearable devices, like a virtual reality insect (a root weevil) on an HTC Vive, and a mixed-reality mako shark skeleton on a Hololens.

Our designs took inspiration from the educational opportunities within each CT scan but also the affordances of our digital tools. A new set of digital affordances unexpectedly arrived when we discovered and welcomed a new type of augmented-reality device into our toolkit: the Holocube.

The Holocube from Merge was designed to work with a mobile phone. With a nice weight in your hand and the slightly squishy feel of a stress ball, the six-sided cube offers a visual cue to the mobile device's camera. Each app decides what to do with that cue. Maybe it interprets the cube as a spinning globe, or a beating heart, or a weapon for defeating an alien invasion. In other words, the Holocube is dumb—just a collection of prettified QR codes—with all the intelligence residing in the app. And that's what made it so compelling—the technology is invisible to the user (like the paper cards in Disney World's *Sorcerers of the Magic Kingdom* or the coin in *MicroRangers*).

We created a rough prototype to explore what this cube might allow us to do with our CT scans. We built an app which offered four experiences. In the first, the cube is surrounded by a column of rock which the user can rotate or turn over as the mako shark ominously circles around it. In this example, the user is not holding the shark but rather using the Holocube as a device to control the shark's movement.

In the second experience, the cube *is* the shark—and the visitor is invited to play with it, as one would with a wooden block. You can turn the shark upside down, move it in the air like a toy to eat your friend, or move it toward the phone's camera to reveal the layers within the CT scan. We also added some touch features—click on the screen (not the cube, which would probably be more intuitive) to watch the jaws open and close.

The third experience came from a youth course on microfossils. The youth had gone into our collections to research some previously unstudied forams (ancient creatures the size of a grain of sand). This is not uncommon, as scientists who return from the field do not always have the resources to study everything accessed into the collections. One of their CT scans was turned into a digital specimen one could hold and, with a click, look inside as it separated into two halves, revealing its beautiful interior chambers.

And the final experience was a bat skull, which one could observe and interact with through physical manipulation.

It took just a few days to code the app but, once it was up and running, we took it out to the Hall of Biodiversity, where we just happened to have the mako shark overhead and a bat on the wall. Located between the two, we set up an iPad on a stand and invited passersby to "hold a shark in their hand."

After months of anxiously handing over devices to children that cost hundreds, if not thousands, of dollars, it was quite a relief to watch them fight over a block of foam. People loved it. When you work with a new piece of technology, you need to spend time and energy learning how to operate it. But everyone knows how to "operate" a block. Its design is an invitation to play, and that's what people did. They picked up the Holocube and marveled at the digital specimens in their hand. And while they played with the specimen or its animations, we offered facilitation that connected the toy in their hand back to the scientist who produced it, the tools they used to create it, and the research questions they used it to explore.

We tried other directions as well—like accessing the front camera, rather than the back, so you could see yourself with the object, as well as making a smaller one-cubic-inch cube (thank you three-dimensional printer!) to see if children preferred the shorter distance between their hand and the iPad's camera. In total we conducted six hours of public evaluation over five sessions (188 people observed; eighty-eight people interviewed).

Overall, we found that while the mobile device's flat screen was less immersive than an extended reality device, the Holocube had many advantages over wearable devices: it required less facilitation, encouraged social interaction, could accommodate a larger flow of users, and was relatively cheap and easy to deploy.

More specifically, handables were compelling and intuitive. I just coined that—a "handable"—but whatever word we might use, visitors loved augmented objects they could hold in their hands. It seems to satisfy a tactile need. And while the novelty of the experience was a draw, it was also easy for users to master and required little or no technical facilitation.

Unstructured exploration was engaging. Users enjoyed the moment of designed discovery—the shark swimming or the microfossil opening up—but were equally engaged, if not more so, when exploring specimens through observation. The scans themselves were fascinating. Some users spent ten minutes or longer exploring their CT scan.

While only one person can hold the cube at a time, multiple people can see the screen, as it was large and mounted in place. The setup seemed to encourage social interaction, with groups huddled around the screen, commenting on the image, and giving instructions to the cube-holder.

We saw that content does not have to be gamified to be playful. Unstructured play, as with the Holocube, can also promote highly engaging social interactions.

Many visitors were eager to learn from facilitators about the scans (e.g., what microfossils are and why scientists study them). The facilitators were coordinated by Nick Martinez and led by Joshua Sosa and Ravi Rampatsingh, Nick's Internship Assistants. As the technology was simple to use when compared with wearable extended reality technology, the Holocube freed the facilitator to focus on content. In fact, the Holocube seemed like it could be a good fit as augmentation on teaching carts (particularly as these carts contain objects so the connection between actual and digital is readily at hand). This began the focus of the next iteration: testing the Holocubes on a teaching cart within a Hall providing related content.

On the third floor, connecting the epic Akeley Hall of African Mammals with the delightful Hall of North American Birds, lays a rather tight and dingy hallway. It is most often used as a thoroughfare for visitors passing between the two Halls. However, if they happen to slow down, by intention or the occasional logjam, they might notice its name: The Hall of New York State Mammals. Among staff, however, it is known as Roadkill Hall since, as the Museum website describes it, "Here one finds the squirrel, chipmunk, woodchuck, porcupine, rabbit, . . . raccoon, mouse, rat, and white-tailed deer." In other words, the animals many New Yorkers encounter dead on the side of the road.

Among this "diversity of local wildlife" are bats. We decided this would be the perfect place to create a Holocube-based prototype to evaluate if this "handable" experience could enhance visits within a Hall whose content mirrored work being performed by scientists behind the scenes.

Collaborating with Mammalogy Research Associate Abbie Curtis, and her adviser Nancy Simmons, we learned that scientists can learn a lot about what bats eat by just looking at their teeth, known as dentition. The teeth of vampire bats, for example, are sharper for puncturing their victims, while fruit eaters require a different shape and placement. This is an easy and pretty cool idea to understand, of interest to all ages, and could be supported by handing visitors a dozen bat skulls (augmented of course, from CT scans) triggered by a Holocube.

Figure 6.6. Augmented reality bat you can hold in your hand. *Author*

Nick Martinez provided volunteers to run the educational component of the cart while my graduate student interns administered the evaluation material. Together, over three months, they interacted with and interviewed 647 visitors. Our goal at first was simply to understand how visitors in a Hall responded to interacting with tangible CT scans. Based on what we learned, we iterated and then evaluated a number of different experiences, such as A:B testing a heavily facilitated experience versus one that was completely self-guided.

Visitors walking through the Hall, for example, might be invited to experience something new: "Would you like to hold a virtual skull?" or "Would you like to try a science experiment?" or "Would you like to try something cool?" The facilitator would then use the Holocube, an iPad, and the content of the Hall to engage the visitor in a series of observation and deduction activities that highlighted bat dentition, diet and evolution content, and the role of CT scans within Museum research.

At one point we removed the Holocube completely, putting the content on an iPad app and on a large interactive multitouch-table display. The screen asked visitors questions and gave different screen responses depending on what the visitor selected. Once we learned that the high rate of foreign visitors (over 50 percent) made an English-only text guide far from practical, we re-focused on learning how to even begin to evaluate visitor interactions with the table. Sometimes we used a light facilitation model—using the table in place of the tangible augmented reality—and sometimes we let visitors interact with the table on their own, coming up with their own ways to make meaning out of the digital skulls.

In addition, a set of evaluators observed an estimated 1,835 visitors as part of a dwell-time study. As visitors entered and exited the Hall, some glanced at the dioramas as they passed, others stopped to explore the dioramas up close, and others engaged with the augmented-reality bat skulls. What difference did the CT bats have on dwell time, if at all?

First, we had to figure out what was going on with the rather unexpected finding that visitors rarely touched the Holocube. In the first ninety-eight sessions, we found that only 15 percent of the visitors controlled the Holocube during their time with the facilitator. While many still held the item at some point to view at least one bat skull, 45 percent never touched it even once. If our entire premise was that visitors would be engaged by holding a CT scan, what was going on? Well, we were forgetting the other part of this equation, the facilitator, who did not want to give up the cube!

After interviewing the facilitators, it became clear they felt they were in competition with the visitors for control of the Holocube. They found it to be an excellent educational tool. Since they were the ones deciding who got access to the Holocube, visitors never stood a chance. By simply changing the design of the facilitation, and requiring facilitators to invite visitors to hold the object, everything changed. That 15 percent rate of visitor control shot up to 92 percent; that 45 percent rate of those who never once touched it plummeted down to 3 percent. Sometimes when designing a digital experience, it can be easy to miss key components within its broader ecosystem. In this case we had not given enough initial attention to the design of the curriculum but, once adjusted, the problem went away.

Next, we learned that we were achieving our educational objectives. A total of 83 percent of visitors, when interviewed after the experience, demonstrated that they understood their activity included CT scans and that scientists used these scans in their research. In addition, 73 percent displayed an understanding of the relationship between diet and dentition. So far so good.

Figure 6.7. Joshua Sosa working with visitors in Hall. *Author*

Finally, it is common sense, but it is good to have the numbers to back it up: the facilitated digital experience generated six times longer dwell time in the Hall than the Hall's exhibits on their own. Visitors walking through averaged a few seconds in the hall, those looking at at least one exhibit averaged just over a minute, and those with the facilitated digital experience almost six minutes.

These findings suggested we might be on to something. We recommended bringing CT scans from Museum scientists to the public through self-facilitated screens and on the *Explorer* app. We recommended locating these activities in high pass-through locations, to get visitors to stop and connect with the space and the objects around them.

At the same time, it was hard to ignore how much the cart facilitators loved them as well. Should the Holocubes be also developed for facilitators to use to engage visitors? We recommended evaluations continue with Nick and his programs, to bring the augmented bat skulls with the detention activity to the Museum Education and Employment Program and Saltz carts.

FINDING FLAMINGOS

Over my six years at the Museum, there was one cool idea that would just not go away, patiently waiting for an opportunity to step into the spotlight: a Learning Lab.

This particular definition of a Learning Lab, if brought to life, would be a radical new space for the Museum. It had been articulated a few years earlier through a partnership between the MacArthur Foundation and the Institute of Museum and Library Services (IMLS). At the time, MacArthur was putting over one hundred million dollars into researching and supporting a new framework for understanding learning in the digital age. Termed Connected Learning, it advocated for opportunities for young people to pursue interests and passions with support from friends and caring adults that create a bridge to future academic or career success. IMLS launched Learning Labs around the country through museums and libraries as physical spaces dedicated to spreading Connected Learning practices.

AMNH already had its Discovery Room and the Sackler Educational Laboratory, where children and teenagers could engage with hands-on learning. Neither, however, was a hang-out space where youth could shape their own activities, nor join ongoing projects, nor collaborate with their peers, nor build relationships with adult mentors, nor formally facilitate learning for others. They were largely for families, visitors, or school groups, and not teen-centered spaces.

It was hoped that an IMLS Learning Lab might come to the Museum. When I first began at the Museum, I helped design plans for the space it might occupy. But it was not to be. Still, the notion lingered. A year might go by without any news and then, suddenly, I would hear a major donor was considering it, documents would be prepared, and we would wait. Then nothing, or a "not just yet" or a simple "no" would end that opportunity.

Eventually, the concept took on a new frame—a Learning Lab focused on science visualizations—that could have a home in the massive new investment in the latest and greatest of additions to the campus: The Gilder Center for Science, Education and Innovation.

Ever since building 1 opened to the public in 1877, the Museum's campus of nearly two dozen interconnected buildings has grown like a set of Legos missing instructions. Much of it makes no sense in hindsight, with dead ends all over the place, adjacent buildings with different floor-to-ceiling heights, and staircases that lead nowhere. The Gilder Center, at nearly a half billion in budget with 230,000 gross square feet, will fill in the largest gap in that Lego set, replacing those dead ends with full loops for visitors across four floors.

When it opens, the Gilder Center will be more than just building 22. Designed to open close to the 150th anniversary of the founding of the Museum, it is an opportunity to reposition AMNH as a natural history museum for the twenty-first century. It frames the Museum as not just an institution for public exhibitions but one driving active scientific research and advancing education across all levels. These activities are not new for the Museum; rather, what would be new would be taking the science and education that so often happens behind the scenes and foregrounding it for the public. That would include, for example, new, state-of-the-art learning spaces for the youth of New York City.

This could also include a cutting-edge experience for youth learners and visitors alike: a new SciViz Lab.

In the earliest stages for the idea, we envisioned a space offering digital and multimedia tools for creating and interacting with science visualizations. It would answer questions like: What are scientific data? How can data be manipulated and interpreted using a variety of visualization techniques? How can visualizations provide insight into the latest scientific discoveries? The data would draw from research that cut across science domains, and often bring them together in a multidisciplinary manner. And it would feature the digital tools of science visualization created and utilized by scientists working in the Museum.

In essence, it would bring together in one place all three aspects of the Center's promise for science, education, and innovation.

That all sounds great on paper, but to realize it presented us with an interesting and unique set of challenges. We had (we thought at the time) three years to develop a lab grounded in Museum science research and practices that also looked different from traditional coursework that existed in our current youth programming.

So which Museum research did we want to draw from? And what would this new type of coursework look like? We needed a series of youth-learning experiences to experiment with, around content, format, and curricular approaches, to give us the ability to hone in on what exactly we wanted to communicate to the youth about science visualization. To solve this, we needed to bring an iterative design practice to the development of a new slate of SciViz youth programming.

First, we created the SciViz Brain Trust, a monthly meeting of skilled scientists and educators across the Museum to join in brainstorming and evaluating ideas for the new space. Second, we held a design charrette that brought these scientists together with Museum educators to explore innovative techniques for building a learning experience around their data.

These techniques needed to address two sets of questions. The first were related to the curriculum. For example, Which content areas are most suitable for teaching SciViz, and which attract youth and motivate them to learn? The second set of questions were related to better understanding the relationship between youth and the planned Lab. For example, To what extent do youth feel that they are engaging in programming that they can't get anywhere else, and what type of feedback can youth provide that can inform the design of the space?

That charrette proved quite generative, producing pedagogical opportunities we would mine for years to come.

A team led by a paleoanthropologist and the head of the Discovery room came up with an intriguing approach to teach how morphology and locomotion can be used to understand and work out evolutionary relationships among extinct organisms. The idea was for visitors to walk across a pressure map that records their footprint and gait to compare against data collected from previous visitors and against a projected Neanderthal's gait. (A version of this was eventually worked into an educational program.)

Another group came up with an idea to teach how scientists investigate form and function in bat skulls and teeth to understand each specimen's relationship to diet, ecology, and evolution. How? Through a user rotating a cube to observe a digitally augmented bat skull through a smartphone or tablet to gather evidence before viewing a "mystery" skull to evaluate. (And, yes, observant reader, this is where the idea for the handheld bats in the previous section first originated.)

A team led by scientists from the Museum's Center for Biodiversity and Conservation (CBC) were enthusiastic about using a multitouch table around which visitors could change variables and parameters to inform predictions about a habitat's biodiversity. They wanted to teach how they use environmental data (climate, soil, water, land cover) to predict the distribution of species within a defined geographic space. It turned out in their work these scientists were using GIS and predictions software to protect endangered flamingos. Once they created a predictive model and visualized it on a map, they compared it against observed data collected from drones in a process known as ground-truthing.

Flamingos? GIS and predictions software? Now this was a concept with legs (or, as it were, wings)! What an amazing opportunity to engage youth around both science content and cutting-edge digital science practice. This all quickly became the core of a new youth program: Finding Flamingos.

The lead educator, Christina Newkirk, and I met scientists from the CBC, Felicity Arengo and Mary Blair, to flesh out the details. Felicity, an Associate Director of the Center with decades of field research, shared tales of joining eighty trained volunteers to count flamingo populations high in Argentina's Catamarca Province. Mary, Director of Biodiversity Informatics Research at the Center, was a Conservation Biologist who focused on primates, with research integrating spatial modeling and molecular genetics to understand the evolutionary processes that generate biodiversity.

Finding Flamingos became a five-session, all-day course, to be held over a spring break. Behind the scenes, the CBC would create a digital app to be run on a multitouch table that would simulate their work using GIS data. Mary worked with Felicity to develop the budget for the program and determine how their own team of programmers could be harnessed for this project. The role of the new course would be to train youth to work with the app on the table and design a facilitated learning experience for taking visitors through it.

In other words, we designed Finding Flamingos to prototype a process for combining scientists, educators, and youth into a team tasked with producing youth-led digital learning experiences in the future SciViz Lab.

When it came time to recruit for the program, we had to decide the best way to frame the opportunity. Sure, we were focused on developing lessons to inform the SciViz Lab, but we presumed the teens would not care about that. However, which would they be more interested in: the field of science (conservation biology), the tools of science visualization (GIS, predictive mapping, etc.), or the subject (flamingos)? The title of the program—Finding Flamingos—suggests how we resolved this question, but look further into the course description to note how we found balance between the three directions:

> High in the mountains of Chile, flamingos have settled into some of the harshest marshlands in the world. Despite surviving the perils of altitude, flamingos are now at risk of extinction in the 21st century. How are Museum scientists using big data and geographic information systems (GIS) to protect flamingos? With the help of science visualizations, particularly mapping and predictions software, Conservation Biologists are hard at work saving the remaining populations of these unique birds. In this one-week Spring Break class, you will work side-by-side with museum scientists to learn about conservation biology research, work with interactive science visualizations, then design an experience with these digital tools to educate others.

Over the five days, the youth went behind the scenes into the Ornithology collections to learn how specimen-tagged GIS data is used for biology research, they traveled to the Bronx Zoo to take field notes on flamingos, and they visited Museum exhibits to identify the educational roles played by science visualizations. They learned how to identify the range and habitats of South American flamingos, describe current threats to their populations, and explain conservation biology in the context of flamingo conservation. Finally, they learned coding, how to communicate the role of GIS in modern conservation biology research, and how CBC's new tabletop interactive simulated their research.

While Christina delivered the program, I worked with a team of graduate school interns to evaluate it. I will be the first to admit we may have gone a bit overboard in the methods we deployed to collect data on the efficacy of the program. As we were intentionally piloting how we might evaluate courses designed to support the new Lab, we wanted to try a wide variety of approaches so we could iterate the most effective combination of techniques.

At least one observer was present in the course for the entire run of the program, sitting in the back of the room taking active field notes, looking for data that might provide insight into any of the identified evaluation questions. Once the course concluded, we interviewed the course designers, instructors, and scientists. A teen pre- and post-survey was conducted using Qualtrics at the start of the first day and at the end of the last. Finally, we introduced a digital backchannel into a youth program for the first time, using Slack, encouraging youth to drive their own course-related conversations and respond to daily prompts (like something they learned they might share with another when returning home that day).

On the fourth day of the five-day program, we dove deeper into science visualizations as a form of communication and introduced them to CBC's new multitouch-table interactive. The youth learned how they could choose variables to model the flamingos' geographic distribution. A map of their model would appear. Touching different parts of the map would zoom in to a photograph of the actual habitat (ground-truthing), revealing whether the animal in question was actually there and, more importantly, if the habitat prediction was accurate. When no flamingo was found, they were introduced to threats to biodiversity in the area (such as deforestation, hunting, mining, climate change). They practiced using and presenting the interactive. As one teen wrote in Slack, they decided their goal was to "teach others the flamingo interactive [so they could] correlate flamingo regional populations to the various variables such as precipitation and temperature." The core ideas they aimed to communicate were "Flamingo tracking and SciViz." They got it.

And then they did it. On the fifth day, we brought in staff so they could practice and iterate their presentations and ended the program with a "friend and family" visit (including some funders) so they could run their activity "for real."

Figure 6.8. The friend and family visit. *Author*

As the evaluation was extensive, so were the findings. The following are a few highlights.

We asked: How are youth best supported in learning with tools of science visualization? We learned that initial inclination in the description of the program was correct: lead with content (flamingos) and science subject (conservation biology) before getting to the SciViz (GIS, predictive mapping). This order established the context for understanding why a science investigation could benefit from the tools of science visualization. If the order was reversed, SciViz became a solution to a problem not yet defined, an abstraction without any real-world application.

We asked: Are youth motivated to engage in science research and communication with SciViz tools? All youth in the program were asked in their course application about their motivations to join the program; only 20 percent mentioned GIS or science visualizations in their application. In the post-survey, when asked if the course made them more interested in a variety of topics, 67 percent said "most probably" or "definitely" about GIS and 80 percent said the same about "other forms of science visualizations." Our takeaway: while the majority of teens are not thinking about SciViz, when introduced to the topic in ways we intended to offer through the new Learning Lab, the majority left with a new interest.

Finally, we asked: Can youth communicate about the tools of science visualization? Yes indeed! We were quite pleased by how well they could describe the importance of SciViz in their formal presentations. The idea of training teens to be docents in a new SciViz Learning Lab seemed within reach.

We learned much more—about how to work with scientists to create new digital-learning experiences, about how to frame existing Hall and collections content through a SciViz lens, and more.

At the end of the course, it felt like our planning for the Learning Lab was effectively building upon our various efforts prototyping SciViz around the Museum and focusing those efforts on a clear path into the future.

OUTCOMES

The combined results of the evaluations of our SciViz piloting, which included the three case studies, were delivering clear answers to our guiding questions.

- All visitors, across all ages, were enjoying these new digital experiences. They overwhelmingly reported they would recommend what they experienced to friends and wanted to have more experiences like this in the Museum.
- Interacting with emerging media properties was increasing visitor understanding of science content and stimulating them to want to learn more.
- Even when they were designed to be personal or private experiences, the activities were highly social. Even when secondary screens were not available, visitors found ways to talk to or perform for their family or friends.
- Most visitors expected to encounter interactive emerging media opportunities while in the Museum.
- Finally, we demonstrated that the Museum had the capacity to engage visitors in the permanent halls with interactive science experiences through both original and off-the-shelf emerging media properties.

We used these findings to report our work up the food chain and made recommendations for our next phase of work.

We recommended the creation of a dedicated visitor-facing emerging media space located in a permanent hall that could act as an ongoing source of information for both Gilder and the whole Museum. We recommended the creation of more self-directed digital experiences to be used within permanent Halls to increase dwell time, extend content learning, and deepen the visitor experience.

We recommended expanding visitor access to CT scans through Holocube stations positioned around the Museum, through experiences developed for the *Explorer* app and for the teaching carts, and more.

In short, after two years, dozens of pilots, and thousands of interview and visitor observations, we were recommending the SciViz team pivot from a rapid research and development focus to one geared for production.

A number of these recommendations came to pass. For a time one side of the Hall of Biodiversity was transformed to offer a regular location to bring SciViz digital interactives to the public. Nick's college and high school students continued for years to use the augmented bat skulls on their teaching carts while evaluating the augmented reality versus the multitouch-table versions. Some of those CT scans made their ways onto the *Explorer* app. Star Pose was offered, and continued to be evaluated, on the AstroBulletin screen in the Rose Center for around a year.

At the same time, the process we were using was itself being recognized as an asset to be touted. The following is language I was asked to developed for a National Science Foundation grant for a SciViz initiative:

> In recent years, the Museum has increasingly employed an iterative design process that includes rapid prototyping sessions which conclude with interactions in the exhibit spaces with the general Museum visitors. Feedback from these public sessions are incorporated into the next iteration within a development cycle that supports a human-centric design that addresses their real needs and interests. For example, after a year of developing visitor experiences that engage them with digital data produced by Museum scientists, we learned that visitors love interacting with data visualizations that provide for direct interactions, that the same data visualization can be ported to different digital tools, and about the importance of involving Museum scientists, educators and youth learners during the development process.

This succinctly captured the Six Tools for Digital Design in one paragraph. It's all in there: user research, rapid prototyping, public piloting, iterative design, youth collaboration, and teaming up.

Unfortunately, I am not in a position to share much of what happened next. Soon after the teens presented the multitouch-table interactive within Finding Flamingos, I announced to my colleagues that, within two months, I would be leaving the Museum.

Comparison: National Museum of Natural History (Washington, DC)

During the period I was working on the development of the SciViz Lab for the American Museum for Natural History, Rebecca Bray was the Chief of Experience Design at the Smithsonian's National Museum of Natural History in Washington, DC. To learn more, I reached out to learn how they developed and ran their innovative Q?rius (pronounced "curious") space.

Designed mainly for ten- to eighteen-year-olds and their loved ones, Q?rius opened in 2013 as an interactive and educational lab with microscopes, touch screens, interactive activities, and a "collection zone" housing over six thousand different specimens and artifacts that visitors can handle. "The space itself is really very flexible," Rebecca told me. "Everything there is on wheels, except for a large collection space, and even in there everything is very modular and flexible."

It was designed to be a space for visitors to do hands-on interactive work around the specific kinds of natural history science explored by researchers. At the same time, it is also a space for their education team to experiment with new ways of interacting with the public.

"We think of it as our learning lab as well," she shared. "We do a lot of experimenting and testing of new ideas in there."

Like all youth-centered spaces for learning, they had to negotiate the right balance between screens and objects. The outside exhibit design company they were working with recommended leaning heavily on screens. "You should have a lot of technology," they were told, "because teens love technology." When Rebecca's team did some studies, they learned something else. "People really value their encounters with the authentic objects of the museum," she told me. "So we said, 'Let's actually de-emphasize the screens in the space and have the focus be on doing things with the objects.'"

When they opened, they still offered screens, not as a destination but as a tool to get visitors to the objects. They provided videos on touch screens of scientists in the field combined with click-through instructions regarding how to interact with the objects in the room. "After having it in the space, we pretty quickly realized that it wasn't working," Rebecca said. "People couldn't do both." Visitors did not want to both interact with the screen and with the objects. "It was just too much."

In response they stripped away even more screens from the space and used paper guides to focus the activities on the objects themselves. Some screens remained, however, providing more information about objects, but their use was separate from the activities, as an augmentation, and not essential to the object-oriented experience. "That was an important learning," she reflected, "but it's still an ongoing question about this balance between screens and non-screen experiences."

Rebecca and her team also took into consideration how screens supported or hindered social interactions. They had to be big enough for everyone to see and to be able to fit around. "At some point in the design process we thought about having everybody carrying around an iPad that would be like their personal digital Field Book as they go around the space collecting objects." The lack of social interaction moved them back to computers with a public screen, but the idea of the Field Book remained. Each child creates an account and then adds objects to their collection as they move through the room. "We knew we didn't have enough money to do it perfectly," Rebecca told me, "but we still decided we had enough that we could pilot something and be an enjoyable experience." They found that visitors enjoyed curating their digital collections in their web-based Field Book, often revisiting them once they returned home.

Youth play an official role, continuously providing feedback on Q?rius. "We have over a hundred teen volunteers, and some of those have been leveled up to be captains." These volunteers help the Museum develop activities and programs while providing feedback on how visitors use the space.

New activities are created through an iterative design process. A design team of educators work with scientists to create rapid prototypes and take them out into their Halls for testing and observations. "We have developed some assessment instruments that we use to test things and to see, really to understand, how visitors are interacting with it and how to move along a spectrum of understanding." A new activity has to be tested at least ten times to generate enough data so they can first understand how people are interacting with it and then use that data to refine the design.

In fact, creating a culture of rapid prototyping and testing is something Rebecca brought not just to Q?rius but to the Museum. "It's a difficult thing," she admitted. "It takes a lot of time and you really need to train your staff to know how to do it." But she felt strongly that it is important to test everything they do in a deep way and not rely on feedback from visitors through surface-level questions, like asking whether they liked the title of a new activity.

As much as she is succeeding in creating a space for engaging the public in an iterative design process, it can sometimes feel they are never doing enough. "When we were in the conceptualization stage, I wish that we had actually been able to do more," she told me, "to really spend some time actually making the stuff that we thought was going to be in the space and getting it in front of visitors and being really reflective and really thoughtful about how they were responding to it."

TIPS AND STRATEGIES

1. User research

   Think: Most SciViz requires a level of literacy to properly interpret. Consider what literacies are required to decode the written or visual language in your design and how you might perform user research to better understand the current level of user expertise.
   Do: Get to know a location better. Build an agile team. Decide on your measurement tools. Pick a date and time. Document the relationship between that location and its occupants. Curate the produced assets in a delightful manner.

2. Rapid prototypes

   Think: As with the creation of the Finding Flamingos *program, sometimes the most significant thing being prototyped is the process itself. If you wanted to iterate your design practices, what could you prototype to explore a new way of working?*
   Do: Create a rapid prototype for a design that leverages assets unique to a particular location.

3. Public piloting

   Think: Galactic Golf's *score card combined a physical component with a digital interactive to create a more holistic experience. Brainstorm what physical elements could have enhanced the augmented reality bat skulls or the* Finding Flamingos *tabletop experience.*
   Do: Like the score card, create an instrument that is so integral to the experience that users never realize they are being evaluated.

4. Iterative design

   Think: All three case studies were part of a much broader initiative to iterate the design of digital engagements with SciViz. How does it change the iterative design process when lessons learned are applied across projects?
   Do: Rather than iterate a design within a prototype, iterate it across two or more separate prototypes. That is, take the learnings from the first iteration and rather than apply it to the same project apply it toward a different one.

5. Youth collaboration

   Think: What do youth contribute as the forward-facing representatives of a digital experience?
   Do: Design something in collaboration with youth in which they mediate the experience between visitors and the digital interactive.

6. Team up!

    Think: *As we teamed with scientists to leverage their existing assets, whose work could you leverage in a way that also helps them meet their needs?*
    Do: *Partner with someone who needs you as much as you need them, in a mutual exchange of resources (no one is paying the other), each bringing something different to the partnership.*

7. Comparative project

    Think: *Regarding the Six Tools for Digital Design, what does the development of* Q?rius *have in common with the development of the SciViz Lab at AMNH? How does it differ?*

A Gem of a Hall

I nestle onto a cozy ledge in a dark corner of the gold room in the Hall of Gems and Minerals. The screen behind me is white, blank, and has been for some time. The fuzzy fabric I once rolled around on as a little boy is peeling off the walls, held up in places by tape.

Outside the theater, I hear the voices of the pre-recorded narrators piped in from overhead speakers, guiding no one past their cases of magnificent samples, arranged in a circle, endlessly looping from one station to another, imparting wisdom. I wonder how many more cycles they have left before they are permanently silenced in a few hours, when the Hall is closed for demolition.

I imagine much of the collections behind glass, or within arm's reach, will return like old friends when the Hall reopens, with a new design, in just a few years' time. But the inviting playfulness of the mysterious cavern that has dutifully housed them these past four decades will be lost forever.

The space is a wondrous mix of light and dark, of raised platforms and sunken dens, creating rich sight lines and multiple pathways, perfect for a young explorer.

This was my first favorite Hall in the Museum, as a rambunctious seven-year-old, exploring the cave-like room with my sister, running up and down the curved ramps past topaz and tourmaline, resting on the petrified wood before brushing the purple amethysts in their geode bed, stomping up and down the carpeted curved benches cum staircases, and slipping down the giant jade slide.

It can feel like a betrayal, when a museum hall closes. That is quite an uncommon occurrence, but when it does, what happens to all the memories once stored there, of childhood visits, of first dates, of times we eventually brought children of our own?

When I leave, I do not walk. I run, down the curved ramp, arms pumping in imitation of the oblivious children around me, lost in their own play, the light from the petrified wood flashing by as I speed out toward the exit.

7

Exit the Museum

When I announced I was leaving the Museum, I simply told people it was time for me to move on. We had institutionalized many of the new practices I was brought in to advance—hurrah!—and I was ready for a new adventure. Short and sweet.

I am not sure, however, if I was able to pull it off. Misleading people is not my strong card.

When I was informed I was being let go, I was not surprised but disappointed. The time for advancing my flavor of disruptive innovations had shifted. We agreed I would stick to the story—that it was my decision—and in return I could finish out the remainder of the fiscal year. I was relieved to have the opportunity to complete each of my ongoing projects, so it felt like a fair compromise, if not a reluctant one.

Given I still had over two months, I had time to say my proper farewells. I made a list of the people I was closest to in the Museum, people I worked with, ate lunch with, held meetings with. I listed people without whom none of the digital projects in this book could have gotten off the ground. I listed people who did me favors, people who were generous in spirit, time, and resources, people who were just such a delight to be around and made me aspire to be my best.

As the list grew, from ten colleagues, to thirty, to over seventy, I was amazed. It was the ultimate embodiment of the sixth tool for digital design: teaming up. It truly took a village.

I decided to connect with each person, one on one, with a personalized message. In addition, inside the envelope I prepared to leave on their desk, along with my note of appreciation, I included a postcard. For years I had collected from eBay old postcards of the Museum, often displaying them like their own exhibit by my desk. Many included their original mail date, their stamp, and the missive penned between a traveler to New York City and a loved one back home, situating my contemporary correspondence in a chain going back over a century.

Yet I knew that would not be enough. I wanted to also invite each person to participate in a designed experience, something social, unexpected, mysterious, and full of wonder. In other words, I wanted them to have a collective experience to feel all the ways I feel about the Museum.

Pasted on the back of each postcard was a block of text, *in medias res*. Often it would begin and end with an ellipsis. The source of the text was obscure and unfamiliar. Along with the text were two clues for unraveling it. The first was an annotation that positioned it in a series, such as seven of eleven. The second clue, at the bottom, were two arrows, one pointed right and one pointed left, each with its own name. These names of colleagues were designed to be familiar to the recipient of the card, two people they already knew at the Museum.

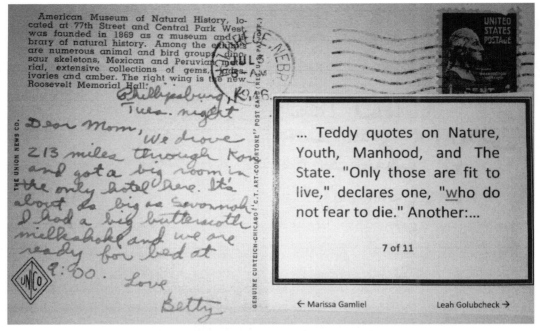

Figure 7.1. A farewell postcard with a hidden message. *Author*

When my colleagues received their cards and tried to put them in order, they soon learned that there were multiple chains of cards, each building a different story. They could not attach any #7 card to any #8. They had to find their two assigned partners if they wanted to complete their unique chain.

A few people noticed something else on the postcards. Some of the story segments had a letter or two printed not in black but red, and it was underlined. Clearly there was something else going on. Someone decided to crowdsource the challenge through a collaborative Google Doc. They modified a Dan Brown book cover and named it *The Barry Code.*

Everyone they could find with a postcard was invited to add their sentence fragment. As they came together like jigsaw puzzles, stories emerged about the Museum. These were original short tales I had written as I walked around the Museum trying to capture its magic in terse prose (the Interstitials, in fact, found throughout this book). Above each story was a space reserved to combine the red letters in order. Each sentence was different, but the meaning was always the same: Find Tom Baione and say, "Take me to the room with the hidden box."

Tom is the Director of the Department of Library Services. The Museum's library is a marvel. With books going back to the fifteenth century, it is one of the largest natural history libraries in the world. As a research library with a climate-controlled rare book room, numerous special collections, and more, movement beyond the public reading room is tightly restricted. That means most people have never heard of my favorite room nestled away on one of its many secluded floors: the Memorabilia collection.

The Memorabilia room is dedicated to telling through objects the story of the history of the Museum. Ephemera from exhibits, like the original models used to construct the dinosaurs. Audio equipment used to record indigenous tribes in expeditions from a century past. Personal notes and artifacts used by explorers to the North Pole. A true cabinet of wonders.

I asked Tom if he would mind being the focus of the revealed messages. I explained that a handful of groups might come to his office and ask to be taken to a room with a hidden box, with no idea why or what might happen next. Tom would then bring the explorers into the Memorabilia room and, once there, present them with a box containing a prize for each group member to take back to their desk: tiny three-dimensional printed busts of Teddy Roosevelt (often viewed as the patron saint of the Museum, for better and for worse) and ones of myself as well. I was thrilled when Tom agreed to deliver this final piece of the experience.

Of course, by the time the first group reached Tom's desk, I had already left the Museum (and moved on to the Girl Scouts). I never expected to have any line of sight on their activity. This playful experience was my leave behind. That all changed, however, when their collaborative Google Doc was first shared with me. Visiting the Google Doc, I could see which group was closer than others to completing their short stories and how far along they were in breaking the code that led them to Tom.

When I first saw that collaborative document, saw how far they had taken it, how they had used digital tools to collaborate and play with the Museum, I could not have been more pleased.

In retrospect, I felt privileged to have been part of the Museum's next step in digital engagement. Yet without an ongoing commitment to put resources toward digital disruptions, I was concerned they might revert back to old habits and once again fall behind.

This, unfortunately, was a pattern I have since seen across the museum sector: while only a few years have transpired between the writing of this book and the events within it, almost all of the people introduced in these pages, both within and from outside the Museum, now work in other sectors. I have seen some of our best minds move on to public television, to universities, to health care organizations—all institutions committed to helping people and bettering society. Just not museums.

There was a period when digital learning and digital engagement became all the rage, perhaps out of a concern that programs and practices were growingly quickly out of sync with the lives of members and visitors. For a time, the voices of luddites were drowned out by those calling for progress, who sought new ways to leverage the power of digital tools to mediate informal learning.

Then, slowly, the trend began to slip back into an old groove. As many digital innovators began to leave or were pushed out of museums, their new positions were often left unfilled. While I was proud to step into the shoes of the Museum's first "Associate Director for Digital Learning," I am also sad that it appears I will also be its last. It turned out that many new positions like my own were not destined to become integrated into the museum of the twenty-first century. Instead, museums are setting themselves up for another cycle of falling behind and desperately fighting to catch back up.

It feels almost callous to draw upon this to make my point, but it would be irresponsible not to: the COVID-19 pandemic was a litmus test that offered museums the opportunity to demonstrate how many already lived in the future and how many were stuck in the past, how many had diversified offerings and how many privileged the in-person experience to the exclusion of the digital and the remote.

Nine months into the nationwide shutdown, I had an interesting conversation with a staff member of Outschool, an informal online learning platform that connects parents and their children with online learning opportunities with live instructors. Earlier in the year they had experienced an explosion of activity. In February of that year, the month before schools went online around the country, they had around 150,000 registered families. Now, in the fall, they have over 1,500,000. They saw similar growth in the number of participating teachers (from one thousand to fifteen thousand) and live online courses (from ten thousand to one hundred thousand).

I asked, "So what did it feel like within the company, when things shifted?"

She responded, "It felt like we moved ten years into the future."

I had been hearing similar feedback from others who had been prepared for remote learning, but these responses never struck the right chord with me. I suggested an alternative view. I reminded her that, in fact, their services did not change in any significant way between February and March of 2020, that line in the US calendar between pre-pandemic and what was to come. They had already been offering that "future" before the pandemic hit. The effect of the pandemic, I suggested, was not to send society into the future. Rather, it was to slingshot reluctant people holding onto the past into the present.

Museums are custodians of our civic and cultural treasures, but that does not mean their practices need to be stuck ten years in the past. Rather, to maintain meaning for society they need to do better at living in the present.

This book opens with a quote from writer and futurist Alvin Toffler. He wrote in his bestseller *Future Shock* that "change is the process by which the future invades our lives."[1] Toffler is playing a linguistic trick here, inverting the standard flow of time. All around us, the future is invading the past. We'll only see it, however, we can only be prepared for it, if we know how to look for it.

Toffler tells us to look for it in the changes. If the future is different from the present, then at some point something has to change. Once, everyone was tied by a cord to a telephone. Today everyone walks around with their own mobile device. Once, computers were enormous devices managed by institutions for a select few. Today we rely on them to manage most aspects of our daily lives. What did it look like when those changes first became manifest?

When I say museums are at risk of being stuck in the past, I am referring to the dangers of not institutionalizing positions which are rewarded for their ability to recognize the invading future and prepare to meet it.

In retrospect, the opening quote from Toffler would have paired well with a second from Alan Kay, educator and computer pioneer. Kay once said, "The best way to predict the future is to invent it."[2] While Toffler is a Paul Revere crying out from his horse, "The future is coming! The future is coming!" Kay is telling us that we have some agency over what arrives. Beyond simply responding to an invading future, we can be the driver of that change.

Lonnie Bunch, Secretary of the Smithsonian Institution, has modeled what it looks like for museums to invent that future. Speaking at a MuseWeb conference in 2021, a year after his sector was devastated by pandemic-driven closings, he challenged us all to consider a question he had posed to staff across the Smithsonian: "What are technology's unique qualities and how do we ensure we are not just using it for what it could have done ten years ago?"[3]

Asking the question, however, is not enough. He recognized he needed to operationalize their response. He created what he called "a new normal" group, tasked with recommending how the Smithsonian could emerge from the pandemic "more nimble, changed, and accelerate the use of digital."

Bunch concluded that "the way forward is to help the public embrace ambiguity, to be comfortable with flexibility and nuance."

I would argue that if they want to be equipped to shape the future and play a meaningful role within it, museums need to do the same.

NOTES

1. Alvin Toffler, *Future Shock* (United Kingdom: Random House, 1990), 1.
2. "We Cannot Predict the Future, But We Can Invent It," Quote Investigator, accessed November 23, 2021, https://quoteinvestigator.com/2012/09/27/invent-the-future.
3. Barry Joseph (@MMMooshme), Twitter, April 7, 20121, https://twitter.com/mmmooshme/status /1379840452644462592.

Appendix

The following is a list of some of the best resources I have found to support the practices described in this book. While reading them I often found myself wondering, "Yes, but what does this actually look like in practice? Do people really do all of these things?" I wanted to see these practices put in context, motivating both my work practices and, for others like me, why I wrote this book.

CARDS

For some reason, designers love to teach through decks of cards. My three favorites are:

- Stanford d.school's *The Design Thinking Bootleg* (originally known as *The Bootcamp Bootleg*). It is digitally available for free. Search for it online.
- IDEO.org's *Design Kit Travel Pack*, which they currently sell on Amazon.
- LUMA Institute's *Innovating for People: Human-Centered Design Planning Cards*. Also available on Amazon.

DESIGN

- *Understanding Comics*, by Scott McCloud
- *UX Strategy*, by Jaime Levy
- *How to Make Sense of Any Mess*, by Abby Covert
- *Articulating Design Decisions*, by Tom Greever

I love all of the books by Rosenfeld Media. Check out their latest after reading the following:

- *The User's Journey: Storymapping Products That People Love*, by Donna Lichaw
- *Design for Kids: Digital Products for Playing and Learning*, by Debra Levin Gelman
- *Service Design: From Insight to Implementation*, by Andy Polaine, Lavrans Lovlie, and Ben Reason

Same with A Book Apart. Check out their latest after reading the following:

- *Design Is a Job*, by Mike Monteiro
- *Designing for Emotion*, by Aarron Walter

- *Creative Chaos*, by Drew Davison and colleagues
- *The Persona Lifecycle*, by John Pruitt and Tamara Adlin
- *Hooked*, by Nir Eyal

GAME DESIGN

- *The Well Played Game*, by Bernie De Koven
- *Rules of Play: Game Design Fundamentals*, by Katie Salen and Eric Zimmerman
- *The Art of Game Design: A Book of Lense*s, by Jesse Schell (which also has its own deck of cards)

EVALUATION AND ASSESSMENT

- *Practical Evaluation Guide: Tools for Museums and Other Informal Educational Settings*, by Judy Diamond

DISRUPTIVE INNOVATION

- *Disrupting Class*, by Clay Christensen
- *Switch*, by Chip and Dan Health

LEARNING

- *A New Culture of Learning*, by Douglas Thomas and John Seely Brown
- *Smarter Than You Think: How Technology Is Changing Our Minds for the Better*, Clive Thompson
- *The Anti-Education Era*, by James Paul Gee
- *What Video Games Have to Teach Us About Games and Learning*, by James Paul Gee
- *Rethinking Education in the Age of Technology*, by Allan Collins and Richard Halverson
- *The Ecology of Games: Connecting Youth, Games, and Learning*, edited by Katie Salen

DIGITAL CULTURE

- *Hanging Out, Messing Around, Geeking Out*, by Miti Ito and colleagues
- *Being Digital*, by Nicholas Negroponte
- *Indistractable*, by Nir Eyal

Index

About the Author

Barry Joseph, based in New York City, has more than twenty-five years of expertise in digital engagement in the non-profit sector, applying digital media to successfully advance missions and reach social and business objectives. Over eighteen of those years were spent working with museums, such as the Field Museum, the Museum of the Moving Image, the Noguchi Museum, and the US Holocaust Memorial Museum. Most notably, Joseph spent six years at the American Museum of Natural History developing and overseeing a digital learning strategy for the Education Department and leading evaluation and assessment within an internal group prototyping in-hall digital engagement with visitors. In addition, as Vice President of Digital Experience, Joseph was business lead for the Girl Scouts of the United States's collaboration with the Smithsonian Science Education Center, which successfully prototyped how a new mobile app could bring learning content into the homes of girls around the country. This book joins his first, about seltzer, and his second, a pandemic memoir about adapting traditions during a time of change. Visit barryjosephconsulting.com or Joseph's blog at mooshme.org to learn more.